"Charlotte Dennett—one of the gutsiest women in America—has written an energized, no-holds-barred account of her efforts to hold our leaders criminally accountable for shredding the Constitution. This is a woman who is not scared to call illegality by its true name and who believes in the rule of law the way the Founders intended. The 'accountability' movement deserves broad attention and deep support from across the political spectrum and this book is an unmissable part of its story."

—NAOMI WOLF, bestselling author of
The End of America and *Give Me Liberty*

"What our political culture is missing most is exactly what Charlotte Dennett has provided here: a credible, inspiring blueprint for restoring accountability to our political system. Even for those who believe that something has gone terribly awry, this book makes the definitive case of urgency as to why we must no longer permit lawbreaking and deep corruption from our leaders."

—GLENN GREENWALD, former Constitutional
lawyer and Salon columnist

"George Bush took America to war in Iraq on a lie, causing incalculable death, horror, and suffering. In this very important and consequential book, Charlotte Dennett, a true American patriot who has been on the front lines of trying to bring Bush to justice, informs all who care deeply about this country what has to be done so that it never happens again."

—VINCENT BUGLIOSI, attorney and bestselling author of
The Prosecution of George W. Bush for Murder and *Helter Skelter*

"Dennett's book describes, from the inside, the birth of a movement to hold top U.S. officials to the rule of law. The eventual success of that movement will be furthered by the success of this remarkable book. Dennett has done us a great service, first by her work and now by her chronicling of it."

—DAVID SWANSON, cofounder of AfterDowningStreet.org
and author of *Daybreak: Undoing the Imperial Presidency
and Forming a More Perfect Union*

THE PEOPLE
v.
BUSH

Accountability Now!

Charlotte Dennett

THE PEOPLE
v.
BUSH

One Lawyer's Campaign to Bring the President

to Justice and the National Grassroots Movement

She Encounters Along the Way

CHARLOTTE DENNETT

CHELSEA GREEN PUBLISHING
WHITE RIVER JUNCTION, VERMONT

To Jerry—and to freedom seekers everywhere.

Project Manager: Patricia Stone
Developmental Editor: Joni Praded
Copy Editor: Bill Bokermann
Proofreader: Eric Raetz
Indexer: Peggy Holloway
Designer: Peter Holm, Sterling Hill Productions

Front cover photo: WASHINGTON—JANUARY 11: Police prepare to arrest an activist dressed in a
orange jump suit in front of the U.S. Supreme Court, January 11, 2007, in Washington, D.C.

Printed in the United States of America
First printing January, 2010
10 9 8 7 6 5 4 3 2 1   10 11 12 13

Our Commitment to Green Publishing

Chelsea Green sees publishing as a tool for cultural change and ecological stewardship. We strive to
align our book manufacturing practices with our editorial mission and to reduce the impact of our
business enterprise in the environment. We print our books and catalogs on chlorine-free recycled
paper, using vegetable-based inks whenever possible. This book may cost slightly more because
we use recycled paper, and we hope you'll agree that it's worth it. Chelsea Green is a member
of the Green Press Initiative (www.greenpressinitiative.org), a nonprofit coalition of publishers,
manufacturers, and authors working to protect the world's endangered forests and conserve natural
resources. *The People v. Bush* was printed on Natures Natural, a 30-percent postconsumer recycled
paper supplied by Thomson-Shore.

Library of Congress Cataloging-in-Publication Data
Dennett, Charlotte.
  The People v. Bush : one lawyer's campaign to bring the president to justice and the national
grassroots movement she encountered along the way / Charlotte Dennett.
     p. cm.
  Includes bibliographical references and index.
  ISBN 978-1-60358-209-4
  1. Dennett, Charlotte. 2. Lawyers--Vermont--Biography. 3. Pacifists--Vermont--Biography.
4. United States--Politics and government--2001-2009. I. Title.
  KF373.D44A3 2009
  973.931--dc22
                         2009045355

Chelsea Green Publishing Company
Post Office Box 428
White River Junction, VT 05001
(802) 295-6300
www.chelseagreen.com

CONTENTS

Preface | vii

1 | *Everyone Cheered. Then What?* | 1

2 | *Invincible Vince* | 17

3 | *The Brave Little State of Vermont* | 41

4 | *The Little Campaign That Could* | 57

5 | *What Does It Take to Prosecute the Powerful?* | 80

6 | *Leahy's Truth Commission and the Jersey Girls* | 100

7 | *Lawyer Hoax: The Stealing of America, and the People Who Fought Back* | 127

8 | *Sovereign Impunity* | 151

9 | *Making Sense of It All: What's Really Going On?* | 186

10 | *More Tales from the Front Lines and Lessons for the Future* | 204

Acknowledgments | 239

Appendix: Resources for the Accountability Movement | 242

Endnotes | 252

About the Author | 273

Index | 274

Many Americans consider it common knowledge that we have just lived through eight years of a rogue presidency. The question is: Have we set the stage for another rogue presidency in the future? Many believe the answer is yes, and as you will read in *The People v. Bush*, one way to prevent that is by prosecuting high-level officials for crimes committed in office.

This book is a cry for justice and accountability. Many Americans, pressed by hard times, are forgetting that the epidemic of lawlessness during the Bush era was a major cause of their misery. The Republican right wing is inflaming discontent. Dark times could happen again, and they could be worse.

Corporate America has corrupted both major parties and all three branches of government, starting with the executive branch. President Bush lied so that he could send troops to fight his oil war in Iraq. He had people tortured and defiled the Constitution in order to boost his power while suppressing dissent at home.

Is this the kind of president we want for our children and grandchildren?

There are those who believe we live in a plutocracy, that it feeds on empire, and that it will take a gargantuan effort to change our country's political direction. I'm up for that effort. So are a growing number of others that you will read about in the pages ahead.

As I write this, we are at an odd juncture, with President Obama not even a year into his first term and many in the nation watching to see just how far the demands of empire may sway his judgments. Emerging from a war we can't justify, another one that's escalating, and a crippling economic crash, Americans might easily find themselves feeling cynical.

My goal in writing this book is to help those craving justice choose action over cynicism. If you feel powerless to make that choice, then consider these many things we already have going for us.

1. *A growing human-rights movement.* Spurred by two foreign wars and

appalled by torture, this movement's most active members are human-rights lawyers, peace activists, civil libertarians, and people of faith.

Reverend William Wipfler, formerly head of the Human Rights Office of the National Counsel of Churches, is one. He sent an eight-page letter to Attorney General Eric Holder (reproduced on PeoplevBush.com) decrying previous inaction in the face of known U.S. war crimes. "I have interviewed and counseled the victims of the most heinous abuse imaginable, and then have had to leave them, wondering if they could ever heal their spirit," he writes.

"For that reason, and for them, I insist that there must be accountability, and that accountability must respond to the highest standards of accepted domestic and international rule of law and not solely to political expediency." I can just hear House Speaker Nancy ("impeachment is off the table") Pelosi say, "Ouch!"

2. *Evolving international law.* It's easier now to prosecute offenders because international law has evolved. In 1998, Chilean dictator Augusto Pinochet was arrested in England for murdering, torturing, and "disappearing" political opponents in Chile between 1973 and 1990.

Also in 1998, the International Criminal Court (ICC) was created. The ICC tries the most serious of crimes, including genocide and war crimes. Previous U.S. administrations have refused to be a signatory to the ICC, an issue that is likely to come before the Obama administration for rectification.

Two Spanish judges are currently conducting criminal investigations into alleged war crimes by Bush et al. against Spanish detainees in Guantánamo. The ICC, meanwhile, has begun an investigation of possible war crimes by U.S. forces committed in Afghanistan in 2001.

Gail Davidson, a Canadian lawyer who heads the worldwide Lawyers against the War (LAW), has twice tried to bring Bush to justice. In both cases, she relied on Canadian and international laws that prohibit war crimes, but no judge or prosecutor would enforce them.

When I asked Davidson why she persevered, she replied: "When Bush began bombing Afghanistan in 2001, the memory of that famous photo of a little girl running and burning from aerial bombing in Vietnam came to mind. I thought of my own grandchild running and burning and not having anyone say, 'You can't do that. This war is illegal.' "

She also likes citing Gandhi: "First they ignore you, then they laugh at you, then they fight you, then you win."

3. *Time.* Movements take shape and gain focus with time—and we have time on our side. Already, as I write this, calls for prosecuting high government officials have gone mainstream. U.S. Attorney General Eric Holder has appointed a special prosecutor to look into alleged crimes committed by the CIA. In Britain, the Chilcot Inquiry is holding hearings on alleged government fraud and illegal collusion with the United States leading up to the Iraq war. As time goes on, more action will unfold. But it will take steady prodding from citizens willing to make accountability a priority.

Aside from these concrete signs of progress, we also have some deep historical influences to guide a movement focused on restoring accountability and maintaining civil societies. For me, those influences are embodied in the form of Lady Justice, one of the oldest symbols in human history. Dating back to Ancient Greece, the birthplace of democracy, Lady Justice adorns the world's courtrooms, often clothed in flowing robes and always holding aloft the scales of justice, equally balanced. Often, too, she is blindfolded to make a simple point: True justice must be blind to rank, power, or privilege. We are all equal under the law.

I first encountered Lady Justice in the foyer of a federal courthouse in Manhattan. Aloof from X-ray machines and armed guards, she seemed to fling herself out at me like a giant Nike, the goddess of victory and triumph. Her arms outstretched holding perfectly balanced scales, her head held high, her eyes blindfolded, this huge, white-cloaked apparition made me stop and stare.

Today, she remains a powerful reminder that we cannot tolerate the rich and the powerful living above the law.

As Americans, we also have our revolutionary forbears to inspire us. Pamphleteer Tom Paine cried out in 1776, "O Ye that love mankind! Ye that dares oppose not only the tyranny but the tyrant, stand forth!" In 1863, Abraham Lincoln gave a stirring reminder at his Gettysburg Address that our democracy must never be allowed to die, just as those who died in the civil war must never be allowed to die in vain. He made a promise: "That this nation, under God, shall have a new birth of freedom—and that government of the people, by the people, for the people, shall not perish from the earth."

Today, with our first African American president, those words have a new resonance. We can still hope, but we must strengthen our resolve to act.

Cambridge, Vermont
December, 2009

CHAPTER ONE

Everyone Cheered. Then What?

Everyone cheered. That's what Bob Kiss remembers most about inauguration day 2009, when he stood in a crowd beneath the helicopter usually known as Marine One and watched it lift off, carrying George W. Bush away from the White House—for the last time—and heading for Texas. For Kiss, the Progressive mayor of Burlington, Vermont, the moment was sheer bliss. Listening to him recall it days later I was reminded of how I felt while watching the same event on TV: "Sayonara, Mr. President!" I blurted out, leaping from my living room couch. "See you in court!"

Did I really say that? The president, "in court"? For a split second, I was startled by my own words. *There you go again,* I thought to myself. What next?

Like Kiss, I am a Progressive—in a state known for its progressive ways and tenacious political behavior. We are a small state that takes on big issues. And sometimes we surprise ourselves in the process.

The last time I surprised myself was on September 18, 2008, before a roomful of snapping cameras and TV lights in downtown Burlington. On that day, I announced both my candidacy for attorney general in Vermont and my pledge, if elected, to prosecute George W. Bush for murder—in Vermont.

It was a scary and exhilarating moment. Scary because I had never run for political office before, let alone for the highest law-enforcement position in the state. Even scarier because I had decided to include in my platform the prosecution of the former president of the United States for the ultimate crime, a crime that could actually put him behind bars. But it was also exhilarating because sitting next to me was one of the best legal minds in the country: Vincent Bugliosi, the former prosecutor from Los Angeles made famous for his successful prosecution of the Manson family for the seven Tate-LaBianca murders. People also knew of him as the coauthor of *Helter*

Skelter, the biggest-selling true-crime book in publishing history. I had come to know him by reading his latest book, *The Prosecution of George W. Bush for Murder.*

Even as a relative newcomer to electoral politics, and even as a Vermonter who knew there was widespread antipathy in my state toward George W. Bush, I figured this particular campaign issue was going to be a hard sell. But with Vince Bugliosi at my side, helping me grapple with some huge legal issues (I don't think anyone had ever previously suggested prosecuting the president of the United States for murder), I felt confident enough to give it a try. And I'm glad I did it, because it became a transformational experience, not only for me, but for the extraordinary handful of individuals who bravely came to Vermont to join me and a small circle of friends in this campaign.

We are now all members of the accountability movement, a growing nationwide phenomenon that takes as its basic underlying premise the belief that no one, not even the president of the United States, is above the law.

From the very beginning, our campaign took on a life of its own. People appeared out of nowhere to join it. Others I never dreamed of meeting came to support me. The press came calling. All of a sudden, I was leading The Little Campaign That Could.

It all began in late August, 2008, when the Progressive Party leadership, knowing that I was a lawyer, asked me to be their candidate for state attorney general. The party, which is arguably the most viable third party in the United States,[1] had successfully elected six members to the Vermont legislature. But in order to maintain its major-party status in Vermont, it needed at least one of its candidates to gain over 5 percent of the vote in a *statewide* race. Although we had only two months before election day, five of us agreed to run for top slots—lieutenant governor, secretary of state, treasurer, auditor, and attorney general. We all agreed to be write-in candidates during the September 11 primary, and it was left to us as to whether we wanted to "stand" or actually "run" for the position after the primary. After all, it was already pretty late in the game, with the November 4 election only two months away.

I was busy at the time, with many things on my plate, so I only tentatively agreed to run. Still, I started to bone up on the position of attorney general, realizing that the incumbent, a Democrat, headed up a public agency that is actually the largest law firm in the state, with a staff of eighty lawyers in both its criminal and civil divisions. In short, to be an effective candidate, I realized I would have to speak intelligently—and with a vision—on many of the major issues confronting Vermonters, including the environment, consumer fraud, employment discrimination, and, of course, serious criminal behavior, including sex crimes—at the time a hot issue in Vermont because a young woman had been brutally murdered by her uncle, a known sex offender.

Then, a week later, a friend put Bugliosi's *The Prosecution of George W. Bush for Murder* in my hands, knowing that it would appeal to me both as a lawyer and as a former journalist in the Middle East. Bugliosi wanted someone to prosecute Bush for sending American soldiers to Iraq under false pretenses. The deaths of four thousand American soldiers and hundreds of thousands of innocent Iraqi civilians weighed heavily on him. Prosecuting the president should be done, he argued, not just to bring about justice, but also as an act of deterrence, so that future presidents would think twice about committing heinous crimes while in office.

As I began to read the book, one passage particularly struck me. One way to bring Bush to justice, Bugliosi wrote, was to have a state attorney general prosecute the former president—should one wish to take up the cause. There were many things that had led me to consider running for Vermont's top law seat, but this was the clincher.

Before I knew it, the legendary Vincent Bugliosi was flying east for a conference on prosecuting war criminals, and on September 12 I was meeting him for the first time. By September 15, I agreed to take up the prosecution issue, but only if he would agree to be my legal counsel during the campaign, and my special prosecutor should I win. There were two reasons to appoint a special prosecutor: in cases where there was a possible conflict of interest, or (as applied to my situation) if the attorney general simply needed another lawyer to do the case. The attorney general position is largely administrative, so asking for help was not unusual. In my case, I needed assurances from Bugliosi that he would lead the criminal investigation of George Bush's war-related crimes, bring the indictment, and conduct the prosecution, should I be elected attorney general. He agreed, and by September 18 my race was official.

My debut: A heart-stopping press conference

I began my press conference with a simple announcement:

> Good morning, ladies and gentlemen. My name is Charlotte
> Dennett, and I'm running for attorney general on the Progressive
> Party ticket. I have with me a special guest, legendary prosecutor
> Vincent Bugliosi, who has flown here to show his support for my
> endeavor. I will appoint him as my special prosecutor if elected, and
> we shall seek an indictment of George W. Bush in Vermont after he
> leaves office.

We both knew that the odds were against us. It would have been hard
enough to prosecute George W. Bush in an American courtroom for authorizing torture at Guantánamo and Abu Ghraib, or allowing unlawful wiretapping. But here we were, announcing that we were going to prosecute
George W. Bush for *murder*, for the deaths of Vermont soldiers who had been
led into the war in Iraq based on deliberate lies. We pressed our case, knowing there would be objections: Bush had never (some would say, never dared)
set foot in Vermont; as commander in chief, he had the consent of Congress
to send the troops off to war; he personally didn't intend to kill these brave
Vermonters.

We were prepared for all these reasons and more. Bugliosi, both at my
press conference and in numerous interviews, had made it very clear that he
would never, "never in a million years," propose the prosecution of George
W. Bush for murder if he hadn't assembled the best evidence and sound legal
grounds to convict him. But we soon discovered that our biggest hurdle was
to convince Vermonters that George W. Bush should be viewed just like the
rest of us citizens once he left office—in other words, that he would lose his
immunity to prosecution for crimes he committed while in office.

Vermonters, indeed all Americans, were comfortable with the notion that
a sitting president could be subjected to impeachment for violating the rule
of law. But the mere thought that a president-turned-private-citizen could be
subjected to the rule of law through criminal proceedings was a novel idea.
Eventually, however, that idea would also enter the public discourse, shep-

herded in by the degree of premeditated lawlessness during eight years of the Bush administration, beginning with months of planning—long before 9/11—to get us involved in a war on false pretenses.

It seemed that never before had a sitting president showed such pervasive contempt for the separation of powers embedded in the Constitution. When I took my place behind a microphone at the September 18 press conference, I was confident that the majority of Vermonters believed as I did, that George W. Bush had come perilously close to destroying the one thing all Americans, regardless of political persuasion, hold dear: our democracy.

"We are living in a culture of lawlessness and fear," I said, as I tried to ignore the glare of the cameras. "Lawlessness by the very powerful; fear because the powerless don't know what to do about it. As a result, we no longer have accountability in this nation. I believe someone has to stand up and say, 'Enough is enough. The crimes of the Bush administration must not go unpunished.'"

I motioned toward Bugliosi sitting next to me. He was looking deadly serious, his chin cupped in his hand, his face registering no emotion other than grave concern. "I can think of no better person to serve as special prosecutor," I said, noting his record of 105 out of 106 successful felony jury convictions and 21 murder convictions without a loss. "And I can think of no better state to do this—a state that has the highest per-capita loss of soldiers in the war in Iraq, a state where 36 towns voted during their town meetings to impeach President Bush." Vermonters felt frustrated, I added, that impeachment efforts went nowhere. "Now there is another avenue for us."

Then I turned the microphone over to Bugliosi, a man I had met only a couple of weeks earlier but who, in that brief time span, had convinced me that every word he uttered came from a deep well of conviction—a profound love of country and an equally profound sense of outrage and injustice over what had occurred over the last eight years under the Bush administration.

"No man, not *even* the president of the United States, is above the law," he began, his voice emphatic and clear. It was a statement he would make over and over again, knowing that the American people had trouble wrapping their heads around this seemingly paradoxical concept of a vulnerable commander in chief. But what he said next shocked me for its boldness.

"Yet, for whatever reason, this bedrock of American legal principles, which is so essential to American democracy and to who we are as a people, has been ignored by this nation's establishment." He paused, then went on. "An establishment that has in effect decided that George W. Bush should not be held accountable for his monumental crime of taking this nation to war in Iraq under false pretenses."

What? I knew Bugliosi was not one for mincing words. In his earlier book, *The Betrayal of America*, he had called the conservative justices on the U.S. Supreme Court the "Felonious Five" for effectively stealing the 2000 elections and appointing George W. Bush president. And even though I have a soft spot in my heart for anyone who "irritates the establishment," here he was firing a direct salvo, at the opening of my campaign, at those unseen "powers that be" in a way rarely heard in American civil discourse.

"But even the very powerful," he added, his voice rising in emotion, "cannot abort the wheels of justice." If they could, "the America of our Founding Fathers would cease to be and we would be a totalitarian state."

That's all it took: one simple sentence that really defined the situation we were in then, and are in now. The Associated Press, to my surprise, actually repeated Bugliosi's criticism of the nation's establishment. I couldn't help but picture in my mind's eye some unknown "establishment figures" in a huddle over how to respond to my candidacy. And when I say establishment, I mean Democrats as well as Republicans. After all, the incumbent attorney general in Vermont was a Democrat.

Reverberations

The Associated Press's John Curran called the White House press office for a comment and was referred to the Republican National Committee (RNC) spokesman, Blair Latoff, who promptly denounced my campaign. "It's extremely disappointing that a candidate for state attorney general is more concerned with radical left-wing provocation than upholding the law of Vermont," Latoff sneered. "These incendiary suggestions may score points among the most fringe elements of American society, but can't be settling for anyone looking for an attorney general."[2]

His reply got picked up by *The Wall Street Journal*'s legal blog, generating a firestorm of reaction. Comments ranged from whether other wars had been fought on false pretenses, to what impact my actions would have on the body politic, to whether I was a traitor—or, at the very least, out of my mind.

But the story also generated an online debate over the war. And not all the comments from this presumably conservative *Wall Street Journal* blog were pro-Bush. "Nothing will bring back the thousands of young Americans who have died in an unjust war," wrote one reader. "Why is it hateful to demand justice for the unjustified deaths of (at least) tens of thousands of people?" asked another. Still more voices chimed in—not just on the war in Iraq, but on despotic governments in general and even past presidents who had, in their view, acted above the law by bombing Cambodia, or even launching the Civil War.

"Let's not forget to condemn another Republican president, Lincoln, for waging the bloodiest war in American history to increase federal power, fully aware that his actions were contrary to the Constitution," wrote a reader who claimed that Lincoln's stated goal of ending slavery was really mass deception— much like the search for weapons of mass destruction was in Iraq.

Clearly, my pledge to prosecute Bush had struck a nerve. Legal debates followed, with many readers voicing their anger over the fact that Bush and others in his administration had committed war crimes. At the heart of the comments was an overwhelming sentiment that the president had lied to make way for a preemptive attack on Iraq, and in the process violated the Geneva Conventions and the U.S. Constitution. "I'm as conservative as you can get," said one reader. "That doesn't mean I have to let criminals walk."

Political predictions, too, abounded. Was Bugliosi's idea of prosecuting the president for murder in an American courtroom too far-fetched, or could it really happen? What kind of precedent would this set? Would future presidents use better judgment entering war? Or would they avoid wars that might be necessary for fear of prosecution? Were we focusing on the past at the expense of the future?

Needless to say, there were comments that questioned my sanity. But the comment I liked the most was this: "If and when Charlotte Dennett becomes the Vermont attorney general, the American people should be glad and look forward to her having the integrity and guts to prosecute Bush for murder."

The array of emotions was quite astounding—reflecting, I think, the sheer novelty of what we were trying to do. The debate went on for four days, while Bugliosi and I worked, via phone, on a response to the Republican National Committee. Vince had returned to the West Coast after the press conference, and since he didn't use a computer, I would fax him a draft, he would go over it, and fax it back. We discovered we worked well under pressure, fired up as we were over slurs from the Republican National Committee. On September 24, I posted a response to Latoff on *The Wall Street Journal* blog, one combining Bugliosi's razor-sharp dissection of a poor argument with my efforts to redefine the word "fringe elements." Here's an excerpt:

> A *New York Times*/CBS poll taken as early as January, 2005, showed that the majority of Americans believed that George Bush had "intentionally misled" this nation into war. In Latoff's mind, is the majority of the American public a "fringe element"? Or is it the prosecution of Bush for his monumental crime that Latoff feels would appeal only to the "fringe element"? If so, is it Latoff's position that George Bush is above the law? It is my sense that the RNC and the President are the fringe elements, far removed from reality and disconnected from the horrors of this cataclysmic war. They don't have to fear that a loved one's shattered body will return to this country in an aluminum box, following four thousand other brave young soldiers into a cold grave.
>
> As the election draws near, the RNC and the Bush Administration will undoubtedly step up their attacks on Mr. Bugliosi and me. But if they do so, they risk further alienating the very people they seek to win over—the majority of Americans.[3]

To my surprise, the RNC never uttered another word about my race. Meanwhile Vermont's incumbent attorney general, William Sorrell, whom I was running against, reacted dismissively to my pledge to prosecute Bush in Vermont. It might make "good political sound bites," he told the Vermont Press Bureau, perhaps not realizing how "good" Vermonters might feel about bringing Bush to justice. But he was certain there wasn't a local state prosecutor who had the authority to do what I was calling for. Prosecute the president in Vermont? Ridiculous! Vermont didn't have the jurisdiction, since the killings took place in Iraq. And the only place that *did* have jurisdiction was overseas, at the International Criminal Court (ICC), located in The Hague, the Netherlands. That was the only place, he insisted, where Bush could be prosecuted for war crimes.

Vince and I had to laugh at his statement. We never said we were planning to prosecute Bush for war crimes. Our charge was murder and conspiracy to commit murder. So he got his crimes mixed up. Even if prosecutors had wanted to prosecute Bush for war crimes, they couldn't have done it at the International Criminal Court at The Hague, because the United States is not a signatory to the 2002 treaty creating the ICC, and hence the ICC would have no jurisdiction. So here was the incumbent attorney general of Vermont, the top law-enforcement officer in the state, getting his law all wrong—including his claim that Vermont had no jurisdiction to prosecute Bush.

On the contrary, Vermont *did* have jurisdiction under the "effects doctrine," which provides that even if the crime was committed outside of a state (i.e., the killing of American soldiers in Iraq), if the crime had a harmful effect on the citizens within the state (which the killing of Vermont soldiers surely did have), Vermont would have jurisdiction.

We did our best to expose his errors, but after our initial press conference, the press seemed to lose interest. Meanwhile, whenever the press *did* quote Sorrell, they simply accepted his legal misrepresentations as fact. If the attorney general of Vermont said the prosecution of Bush couldn't be done in Vermont, then he must be right. Right? Thanks to the press's lack of familiarity with the law, Sorrell succeeded in setting up a straw dog that was easy to knock down. Making our quest look impossible, he also made it look ridiculous. The sound-bite war was Sorrell's to win, and he did it easily.

In the end, I lost the election, coming in a distant third, as a Progressive, in a four-way race. There were actually many reasons for my loss: The Obama surge caused a lot of voters to vote a straight Democratic Party ticket, which included on the ballot an eleven-year incumbent as attorney general; savvy Republicans voted for the incumbent Democrat to lessen our challenge to Bush, their party leader; repeated losses on Wall Street seriously began just when I entered the race in mid-September only one and a half months before the election, causing voters to fret about spending money on seemingly "extraneous" issues; a dearth of news about the war in Iraq in the months leading up to the election; too much focus on a single issue; lack of media attention after the initial press conference; lack of name recognition; and not enough money to reach voters in the short time period left.

Reflections

The first part of this book goes into greater depth about my campaign, not only because I think others can learn from it, but because I, too, needed to come to terms with the results. Had I overestimated Vermonters' dissatisfaction with George W. Bush and his war? Polls showed some 60 percent disapproved of Bush's war in Iraq, and Vermont returned the highest percentage of Obama votes (next to his original home state of Hawaii) in the nation. Shortly after the election, I stopped in at a little mom-and-pop video store in the northern rural town of Hardwick to ask for directions. Owner Alan Gagnon, middle-aged, wearing a plaid flannel shirt and looking appropriately grizzled with long, shaggy, gray hair, looked up and recognized me. "Hey, we voted for you!" he said. "We heard about your race from the blog, 'What's a Citizen to Do?' We played a video of you over and over in our store. There was a real buzz out there." If only we had known earlier. How many other Vermonters would have reacted the same way?

But there was another demographic factor at play here, one that came as a surprise and relates to the second half of my book dealing with the national accountability movement. By far the greatest response I got to my campaign came from beyond Vermont's borders, from around the country. Emails, letters, and donations—from California, Oregon, Washington State, New Mexico, Arizona, Tennessee, Colorado, Missouri, South Dakota, Alaska, Wisconsin, Illinois, Indiana, Idaho, Iowa, Georgia, Virginia, North Carolina, Oklahoma, Minnesota, and Ohio—and that's not counting most of the East Coast. We even got letters of support from around the world—from Canada, Spain, Israel, Bermuda, England, and Italy—all pouring into my cramped little campaign office in Burlington, Vermont, cheering me on. "Thank you for your courage," they said. "You are a true American patriot." I was genuinely moved. And amazed. To be called an American patriot was truly an honor. To discover a huge hidden movement of like-minded patriots was thrilling.

Indeed, by my reckoning, the hundreds of people who wrote me and donated some $30,000 during my short campaign (mostly through small donations of $50 and less) were not fringe elements. They had heard and watched Vincent Bugliosi, in lectures and on radio and TV, explain how and why Bush could be prosecuted for murder. They had heard him say that he couldn't do it himself, since he was no longer working for the district attorney's office. And they had heard him talk about how a "courageous, patriotic lawyer from Vermont" had stepped up to the plate. His standing-room-only and nationwide audiences responded enthusiastically when he put out his "tin cup" and asked for money to support my campaign. They wanted accountability—before, during, and after the November 2008 elections. The thought of George Bush returning to Texas to live a normal life without any consequences for his acts deeply troubled them and, I believe, most Americans.

The New York Times columnist Bob Herbert struck a chord when he wrote, on December 29, 2008, "I don't think he [Bush] should be allowed to slip quietly out of town. There should be a huge hue and cry . . . over the damage he's done to this country." Thousands of readers replied, most in agreement. A few days later, some four and a half million Americans voted on the official Obama Web site for their top recommended priority, and "appointing a special prosecutor for Bush and [Vice President Dick] Cheney" topped the list.

It should be pointed out here that the vast majority of respondents probably had in mind the prosecution of Bush and Cheney for crimes like torture and domestic eavesdropping, not for the crime of murder and conspiracy to commit murder, which (Bugliosi's best-selling book notwithstanding) had received far less media attention. Nonetheless, the overwhelming pro-prosecution response on Obama's Web site put the president-elect and his fellow Democratic Party leaders somewhat in a bind. Throughout the campaign, Obama had been calling for bipartisanship, for peace, harmony, and unity. He wasn't about to change his message once he got elected. On January 12, he told ABC, on the question of appointing a special prosecutor, "We are still evaluating. . . . We're going to be looking at past practices and I don't believe anyone is above the law. On the other hand, I also have a belief we need to look forward, as opposed to looking backwards. . . . My orientation is going to be moving forward."

These words would be revisited again and again in the coming months by journalists, bloggers, lawyers, and activists.

What's going on here? Confusion after the inauguration

Did Obama really believe what he said about moving forward and not looking backward? Or was he just buying time until he could get bipartisan support for his stimulus plan to rescue a shattered economy? He was saying, "Let's look to the future," but his party's activists, comprised of hundreds of thousands of progressive Democrats already disappointed over the failure of their party to impeach President Bush, were saying something else: *"Do something!"*

They looked to their leaders for guidance, but they got confusion instead. Or so it seemed. Even I, who had spent an intense two months talking to voters about the worst of Bush's lies and deceptions, felt as much in the dark as anyone else. What did the Democratic leaders and Obama want? What were they going to do? Two years earlier, when their House majority leader, Nancy Pelosi, declared that "Impeachment is off the table," she and others explained that the Democrats didn't have the votes. They also had "much more important things to do" and didn't need the distractions of an impeachment proceeding while they focused on winning the White House. Funny, but now they had the votes. Yet they still seemed to be waffling, using the failing economy as their latest rationale for inaction on impeachment.

Moving forward without holding Bush accountable certainly was not what the pro-accountability people wanted to hear. They wanted something more definitive, especially since Cheney had already admitted to—almost bragged about—authorizing torture during a postelection interview with ABC. Bush did likewise—on the very same day that Obama hedged his bets about pursuing prosecution when he took office.

What, many of us were wondering, is going on?

It didn't matter if you were a lawyer or an average citizen, it seemed like something was going on behind the scenes. And most assuredly it was, with Republican lawyers working out their defense strategies and Democratic lawyers keeping their options open. Because, let's face it, never in American history had such blatant illegality occurred—and been *documented*. This was uncharted territory. Everyone's sensors were out there, and amid all the speculation there was also the looming question of what would happen on January 20, 2009, when Bush left office. Whom would he pardon? Vice

President Cheney? Former Defense Secretary Donald Rumsfeld? Secretary of State Condoleezza Rice? *Himself?*

There was something surrealistically awkward about those final moments when the newly inaugurated president and his first lady bid farewell to George and Laura Bush on the White House lawn. Obama, only hours earlier, had seared Bush in his speech. "As for our common defense, we reject as false the choice between our safety and our ideals. Those ideals still light the world, and we will not give them up for expediency's sake." Bush had put on a brave face throughout the inaugural address. Yet when the first couples said goodbye on the White House lawn, they exchanged hugs and smiles as if nothing serious had happened, as if the transfer of power from one of the most corrupt and lawless presidents in American history to one of the most liberal members of the Senate was all very natural, as if this was a signal to the world that peace, love, and harmony would now be the order of the day. No bad feelings, Mr. President. *God bless and have a nice flight home.*

It wasn't until this most momentous of sunny days faded into darkness that I realized that January 20 had come and gone and there had not been a word about pardons. *Bush didn't pardon any of his senior officials.*

Why not? Over the next couple of weeks, I asked around. People had theories, but no one really knew. Perhaps pardoning his partners in crime would just confirm, in the public's mind, that crimes had been committed. (In fact, pardons can be given even when no crimes have yet been proven— preemptively getting someone off the hook and sparing everyone the ugliness of a trial.) Perhaps Bush's lawyers were wary of stirring up unnecessary controversy, which would only further reinforce Bush's legacy as the "worst president in U.S. history" on the eve of his leaving office. And then there was this haunting thought: Bush's lawyers were supremely confident of their legal strategies and truly believed that Bush and his cohorts would live out their last days untouched by criminal prosecutions. In other words, they would continue to live and function above the law.

Only in August, 2009, would *Time* magazine break the story of the last-minute, behind-the-scenes maneuverings between Bush and Cheney over whether to pardon Cheney's closest aide, I. Lewis (Scooter) Libby, for obstruction of justice. The article revealed a great deal about Bush's second term, the president's efforts to undo some of the damage of his first term, the people he relied on to undo the damage (not the least of whom was the experienced counselor to former presidents, lawyer Fred Fielding), the reason why Cheney had fought so hard for Libby's pardon, and why Bush rejected his pleas.

It all comes down to this, and it comes straight from Libby's prosecutor, Patrick Fitzgerald, in the closing argument of Libby's trial: "There is a dark cloud over the vice president." It was most likely Cheney who had his aide leak the name of a covert CIA officer, Valerie Plame, to the press, in apparent retaliation against her husband and former diplomat, Joseph Wilson, for writing in *The New York Times* that he had evidence that the Bush administration had misled us into war in Iraq.

Which means it all comes down to the war in Iraq. Cheney has vigorously insisted that it was the right war, that it was a necessary war, that it had to be fought to keep America safe. And in his zeal to defend the war, he apparently let his own aide, Scooter Libby, take the fall. He may feel bad about that, but he may feel even worse when the spotlight begins to shine on him and his role in advising Bush to take some of the actions he did before and during the war. Is Cheney more worried about being prosecuted than he is letting on? And is Bush, the ultimate "decider," also worried?

Judging by the article in *Time,* they should be:

> The fight over the pardon was also a prelude to the difficult questions about justice and national security inherited by the Obama Administration: How closely should the nation examine the actions of government officials who took steps—legal or possibly illegal—to defend the nation's security during the war on terrorism? The Libby investigation, which began nearly six years ago, went to the heart of whether the Bush administration misled the public in making its case to invade Iraq. But other Bush-era policies are still coming under legal scrutiny. Who, for example, should be held accountable in one of the darkest corners of the war on terrorism—the interrogators who may have tortured detainees? Or the men who conceived and crafted the policies that led to those secret sessions in the first place? How far back—and how high up the chain of command—should these inquiries go?[4]

Bush would have a role in the commutation of Libby's jail sentence, but he also noted (with Fred Fielding's assistance) his respect for the jury's guilty verdict and acknowledged that Libby's professional reputation would suffer as a result of his felony conviction. According to *Time*, it all came down to whether Libby had lied to prosecutors and lied to the jury. Bush decided to set a moral tone, one that will forever hang over his head: "Our entire system of justice relies on people telling the truth," he wrote. "If a person does not tell the truth, particularly if he serves in government and holds the public trust, he must be held accountable."

Commented *Time*: "Bush's allies would say later that the language was intended to send an unmistakable message, internally as well as externally: No one is above the law." That's quite a remarkable assertion, seeing as how the buck stops with the president, whose lies cost the deaths of over four thousand of his own countrymen.

While the title of this book is *The People v. Bush*, and references throughout are often made to Bush as the defendant, the list of co-conspirators and, hence, co-defendants, is likely to be quite long, including but not limited to his vice president, two secretaries of state (Colin Powell and Condoleeza Rice), the secretary of defense, and the top lawyers of the Justice Department, including attorneys general (John Ashcroft and Alberto Gonzales). Indeed, one of Spain's most heralded judges is pursuing an indictment against these top officials under the doctrine of universal jurisdiction and will continue to do so unless someone in the United States pursues a criminal investigation that goes to the top of the chain of command.

In the following pages, you will discover, as I did, that nothing is certain about how far *this* country will go to hold the Bush administration to account, because we've never been in this situation before. Certainly, when I embarked on my campaign, I had no way of knowing that a movement for accountability would make the prosecution of Bush-administration officials the top issue on President Obama's Web site when he came into office. Or that his new attorney general, Eric Holder, would eventually yield to intense pressure from the human-rights community by appointing a special prosecutor to investigate the CIA's "enhanced interrogation techniques." Or that the CIA's torture had been approved by the highest levels of the Bush administration, rationalized by top Justice Department lawyers, and applied to high-level detainees in a desperate attempt to get false confessions and false pretexts for the war in Iraq.

As I embarked on my journey down the "prosecution road" after the election, I was unsure, as were most Americans, of what role Congress would play. And what was my own Vermont Senator Patrick Leahy's idea of a "middle way"—an independent truth commission designed to get at the facts and then make recommendations? Why did Leahy's idea fail by the spring of 2009? Would the people on the top get off, regardless of which methods were used to bring some accountability to eight years of lawlessness?

The parrying among lawyers, each trying to establish the legal turf on which a real battle for accountability might take place, is a necessary and, I would argue, fascinating part of this story, because it tells a lot about how power is wielded and abused in the nation's capital. Fascinating, too, is the vast network of people across the country and the world actively seeking justice. Not driven solely by rage over Bush's reckless disregard for human life. Not driven by revenge. But driven instead by a desire to uphold the mandates of our Constitution, and to preserve democracy by allowing no one—not even our president or the people in his cabinet—to act above the law.

One man in particular helped elevate this movement for accountability onto a new stage, from impeachment to prosecution. That man was Vincent Bugliosi. He took a huge risk, both personally and to his own professional legacy, by writing a book that asked the nation to prosecute a president for murder. But will such coverage pay off?

CHAPTER TWO

Invincible Vince

During my campaign, people invariably asked how I came to team up with Vincent Bugliosi. "It happened very quickly," I would answer in the briefest possible manner. "First, I read his book. Then I met him a couple of weeks later in Massachusetts at a conference on prosecuting war criminals. And before you know it, he was flying to Vermont and helping me kick off my campaign."

Looking back on it now, I think we made a great team. I say that with a smile, not out of boastfulness. He was a self-described "trial lawyer who also happened to be a writer." I was a writer who happened to be a lawyer. How we met, formed an alliance, and became friends is a story worth telling. It's not often that a lawyer gets to team up with one of the most formidable prosecutors in the country to take on one of the most lawless governments in American history. If Vincent Bugliosi was off his rocker, or if I had been a lawyer with no ethics bent entirely on grabbing good political sound bites (as my opponent tried to make me out to be), this would not be a story worth telling.

The simple fact is, when Vincent Bugliosi wrote a book about how to prosecute a former president, he wrote it as a call to action. Because he was no longer a prosecutor, he needed a sitting district attorney or attorney general practicing law to help carry out his plan, turning a plan on paper into a plan of action.

I'm sure I was not the kind of lawyer he had anticipated would come forward. Long before becoming a lawyer, I had been writing on (and aching over) the struggle of indigenous peoples against foreign oil companies in Latin America and the Middle East. Then, in 1997, I became a licensed attorney in Vermont specializing in civil litigation. Whatever criminal work I had done was on the defense side of things. Instead of taking the typical law-school route, I mentored in a law firm for four years and "read for the law" the Abraham Lincoln way before qualifying, under Vermont law, to take the state and federal bar exams. In 2008, not long after Bugliosi's book came out, I was neither a district attorney nor an attorney general. I was simply a candidate for attorney general, agreeing to run on a third-party ticket for the Progressive Party.

On reflection (along the lines of "Why me?"), I've concluded it was probably my deep, personal connection to the Middle East that propelled me forward and had me calling Vincent Bugliosi on the phone, asking him if he had found a prosecutor yet to take up his challenge. In a way, it was like going back to my roots, having been conceived in a Bedouin cave in Jordan and born in an American hospital in Beirut. I was the daughter of an American school teacher and a diplomat/master spy. The unexpected death of my father when I was six weeks old sent my family back to the States, but I returned to Beirut with my mother to attend high school in 1963. After college, I returned to Beirut again, to take up assignments between 1973 and 1975 as a roving correspondent for various Beirut-based English-language publications that had me traveling all over the Middle East.

So, I was an American whose early life had been shaped by events in the Middle East and whose early career was spent trying to unravel some of the political realities of U.S.–Middle East relations. This background probably pushed me out onto a limb, however subconsciously, when in 2008 at age 61 I found myself running for office on a very controversial subject, one that had me seeking justice for those who'd been harmed—both Americans and Iraqis—by the brutality of Bush's murderous and ill-conceived war in Iraq. I was beyond my comfort zone, but I felt I was doing the right thing.

The catalyst

As I touched on in the previous chapter, this strange and unexpected journey into the political unknown began when a close friend called me one morning in late August, 2008, and, in an excited whisper, asked if I had heard about a book called *The Prosecution of George W. Bush for Murder*. That friend was Robin Lloyd, a filmmaker and peace activist whom I had first met some twenty-five years earlier leading a demonstration in her home-town of Burlington, Vermont. She was protesting human-rights abuses in El Salvador. My husband, Jerry Colby, and I had recently moved to Vermont to quietly finish up our book on Latin America: *Thy Will Be Done. The Conquest of the Amazon: Nelson Rockefeller and Evangelism in the Age of Oil.*

So we naturally crossed paths with Robin. Then in her midfifties, she was a slim, energetic dynamo who did everything in her power to make this a better world, whether championing women's rights, protesting nuclear power, or carrying on her father's tradition of publishing *Toward Freedom,* a progressive magazine featuring oft-censored news from the Third World. Robin's great-grandfather was none other than Henry Demarest Lloyd, the "father of investigative journalism," whose signature work, *Wealth Against Commonwealth,* was the first exposé ever written on the Standard Oil fortune of John D. Rockefeller, Sr. It never ceased to amaze me that Jerry and I, also Rockefeller biographers, would chance upon and then befriend Robin in a small city in northern Vermont.

When Robin told me about Bugliosi's book, I had already heard about it through word of mouth on the Internet, that marvelous "people's alterna-tive" to the mainstream corporate media and its political news gatekeepers. It had already become a *New York Times* best seller, and I was eager to read it. Robin offered to lend me her copy, and the following day she put it in my hands. She didn't let on that she had an ulterior motive.

Robin knew that I had decided to run for attorney general on the Progressive Party ticket. I was unsure of how I would approach the race when she gave me the book and suggested that I read over the section about what citizens could do in their separate states. A week later, that book liter-ally changed my life.

I had thrown it into the backseat of my car before heading south to New York City to visit my husband, who worked during the week in Manhattan as president of the National Writers Union. One of those many mornings when I had to sit in my car in the West Village waiting for alternative-side-of-the-street parking to kick in, I began thumbing through the book.

Even in liberal, freewheeling Manhattan, opening that book was like tast-ing forbidden fruit. I recall slinking deep into my seat, pressing the front cover against my lap to conceal the title, then opening the book to the first chapter. Much later, I would learn from Bugliosi that his own wife had counseled against his using the word "murder" in the title—that it would scare people off. "But what was I to do?" he said to me. "Just put the word 'prosecution' in the title? Prosecution for what? Bird watching? If I didn't put the word 'murder' in the title, everyone would find out anyway after reading the book." That was Honest Vince talking. To him, the most important thing was his credibility. He wasn't going to try to slip anything past us. He would suffer for his provocative title in the short run, but probably in the long run his book would stand the test of time for the citizens' political movement it helped generate.

The first page began with a direct challenge: "The book you are about to read deals with what I believe to be the most serious crime ever committed in American history—the president of this nation, George W. Bush, knowingly and deliberately taking this country to war in Iraq under false pretenses, a war that condemned over one hundred thousand human beings, including four thousand young American soldiers, to horrible, violent deaths."

Now that was a pretty dramatic and challenging statement, and it gave me pause. Together with my husband, I had spent eighteen years documenting the deaths in the 1960s and '70s of one hundred thousand Amazonian Indians by methods borrowed from, and often endorsed by, our own government.[5] These two genocides—one committed against the Amazonian Indians in the twentieth century shockingly with U.S. complicity and the earlier one committed against North American Indians in what Helen Hunt Jackson called "a century of dishonor"—struck me as unrivaled in the annals of serious crimes in American history.[6] With one caveat: The killings had occurred over extended periods of time rather than being compressed into eight years under one president.

Then there was that icon of horror known as World War I. President Woodrow Wilson had made a campaign promise to keep America out of that war, then broke his promise upon reelection and sent about two million Americans to war, some one hundred thousand of whom died in combat or from disease. Whether or not there were provocations that eventually got us into that war, like the controversial sinking of the munitions-laden *Lusitania* in 1915, the fact remains that Wilson actually anguished over what he did. So much so that after the war he ignored doctors' advice and toured the country warning Americans that the ideals they had fought for (among them "making the world safe for democracy") had been betrayed. His pleas for "self-determination of peoples" and a world free from secret diplomacy and war had gone unheeded abroad as victorious European nations prepared to divvy up the spoils of war among themselves. These spoils included the oil regions of the Middle East, where they imposed colonial-style protectorates that would inflame local sentiments and become a major cause of the Middle East conflict right up to the present day. At home, Wilson's calls for a League of Nations met with similar derision. He was on a whistle-stop tour of the West when he collapsed with a stroke, never to fully recover his senses or his presidency.

George W. Bush, on the other hand, has shown absolutely no remorse about the bloody and unnecessary invasion and occupation of Iraq. The degree of premeditation he employed to get us into the war—including getting phony legal justifications—makes this an exceptionally bad crime committed by an exceptionally bad American president.[7]

Getting into the evidence

Bugliosi clearly knew that his readers would be skeptical about his proposition that Bush was guilty of murder. "I am fully aware that the charge I have made is an extremely serious one," he writes. "That inevitable shock is a burden I know I have to overcome." Most people, he acknowledges, "see what they expect to see, what they want to see, what they've been told to see, what conventional wisdom tells them to see, not what is right in front of them in its pristine condition."[8]

On the other hand, Bugliosi admits to having a talent for seeing things as they are. To illustrate his point, he gives an anecdote about how the world has come to perceive Iraq's Saddam Hussein, thanks to misleading news reportage.

One day in 2005, he begins, as Saddam Hussein's trial was about to begin after his capture, "I called my wife over to the breakfast table where I was reading the paper and said to her, 'You are *not* going to believe what I'm going to read to you. It is nothing short of unbelievable.'"

His disbelief was focused on the opening day of the trial, when any good prosecutor would have started his opening statements on a strong note. Instead, "the prosecutor was starting out on no note at all. In fact, he was starting out with no crime at all."

According to *The New York Times,* he continued, the crime allegedly committed by Hussein was in fact actually conceded to by Hussein's prosecutor as a response to an assassination attempt on Hussein. Some twelve to fifteen shots had been fired on Saddam Hussein's motorcade on July 8, 1982. Nearly two years later, Hussein authorized the prosecution of 148 men on the charge of conspiracy to murder. Eventually, 102 of the 148 men were convicted and executed for trying to assassinate the Iraqi dictator. (Forty-six had died in the infamous Abu Ghraib prison, but a man whose brothers had been executed later admitted that other members of his family had been interrogated and released.)

The point is, and here is Bugliosi at his most incredulous: "Hussein was convicted and put to death for executing those who were members of a conspiracy to murder him!! (He was not convicted of any other crime he is believed to have committed.) *To repeat, Hussein was killed for killing those who had first tried to kill him."* [9]

And yet, Bugliosi continued, *The New York Times* said Saddam Hussein deserved to die for his "horrendous crimes," the *Los Angeles Times* said Hussein was executed "for one of the massacres" of his people—"a crime against humanity"—and reporter Christopher Hitchens opined that "Hussein was convicted of massacring the inhabitants of a Shiite village, Dujail, in 1982." (Dujail, Bugliosi points out, was in 1982 a town of some seventy-eight thousand.)

All of this brought back to me allegations of media deception beginning in 1975 when I had been one of the first American journalists (along with a reporter from *Time* magazine) to visit Iraq after the Baath Party regime reopened its borders to Western journalists. Iraq had previously kept them out because, our Iraqi government hosts claimed, the West's press reportage on the Iraqis' alleged mistreatment of the Kurds had been false. Over and over again, Iraqi government officials and Kurds allied with the Baath government told us that charges of Iraqis gassing the Kurds were lies. (At the time, the Iraqi government was fighting a Kurdish insurgency armed and financed by the Shah of Iran, Israel, and the CIA near Iraq's mountainous border with Iran. It was a prolonged war of attrition, and its purpose, our Iraqi hosts told us, was to bog down the Iraqi army on its eastern frontiers and undermine the Baath regime.) To this day, I can neither prove nor disprove the allegations about Iraq's gassing of the Kurds in the early 1970s, when Saddam Hussein did not personally rule Iraq as dictator, but was a vice president in charge of overseeing Kurdish autonomy. There were two sides to this story, and the Iraqi side seldom got told. (*Time* never reported their findings; I reported mine in *The Daily Star* of Lebanon.)

Now, some thirty years and a million deaths[10] later, I was clearly encountering lies. This time they weren't allegations of lies. They were real, proven lies, and they had been told by our president so that young soldiers would go to war thinking they were fighting a man linked to al-Qaeda and the 9/11 attack.

Bugliosi's first three chapters lined up the evidence of Bush's lies, dwelling in particular on how Bush had insisted (falsely, it turns out) in October, 2002—on the eve of a congressional vote that would give the green light to the invasion of Iraq—that Saddam Hussein was an imminent threat to the security of our country. In fact, only days earlier Bush's own intelligence agencies had told him just the opposite.

Some of Bugliosi's evidence I already knew, but a lot of it was quite new. The question was, as Bugliosi wrote, *"What should we, as a nation, do about it? As of the publication date of this* [Bugliosi's] *book, apparently nothing."*

Bugliosi was going right for the journalists' conscience. It was all well and good for journalists to document the evidence of Bush's crimes, and for the public to read about them. But then everyone seemed to just walk away, letting the facts fall where they may and forgetting about them. This was not good for American journalism or for constitutional, and therefore accountable, rule by the people, or for democracy in America.

Now he had me. Journalists could write. But prosecutors could act. They could enforce the law. They could even, Bugliosi argued, put the president behind bars once he left office.

I was now an hour into the book, inevitably drawn to his section on "The Legal Framework for the Prosecution." Here was Bugliosi-the-lawyer at his best. Like any good practitioner, he anticipated every possible objection that the other side might use against him. And he knew he would have some very powerful adversaries: not just lawyers, but irate Republicans and squeamish Democrats who would try their utmost to deep-six his case.

It took him eighty-seven pages of text and forty-four pages of endnotes to do it. It seemed to me he covered all the territory needed to mount a good case.

He started with the big questions. How could Bush be prosecuted and convicted of murder when he didn't personally kill anyone? Where was the necessary *mens rea*, the "intent to kill," for a murder conviction? After all, as commander in chief, Bush had the authority to send troops off to war. And then, the big jurisdictional question: How could he be prosecuted in the United States when the killings took place in Iraq?

With the kind of devastating precision that Bugliosi is known for, he marshaled a series of legal arguments that I, as a civil attorney, had never heard of, like "the vicarious liability rule of third-party innocent agents" and "the effects doctrine on jurisdiction." At first glance, Bugliosi's legal weapons gave the impression that, if nothing else, this wiry seventy-four-year-old former prosecutor would put up a good fight if he ever confronted George W. Bush or Richard Cheney or Condoleezza Rice in an American courtroom.

But really now, what were his chances of getting that far? Pretty slim, I thought. Worth the fight? Who knows when, how, or where it would end up? Everyone else was complaining about Bush. No one was *doing* anything about it.

It was at that moment, in the middle of that muse, when I stumbled on the sentence of all sentences in his book, the sentence that would rocket me onto a whole new trajectory. "Any state attorney general in the fifty states (or any district attorney in any county of any state) could bring a murder charge against Bush for any soldiers from that state or county who lost their lives fighting Bush's war," wrote Bugliosi.

I stopped reading and stared out the window, ruminating over what I had just read. "Any attorney general." I pondered that for a moment. What sitting attorney general was going to risk his or her job, career, reputation, and who knows what else, to prosecute George W. Bush for murder?

But wait a minute. What if someone running for attorney general took up the challenge?

"Any state." Any state? Oh my God, what about Vermont? The state where thirty-six towns voted on town-meeting day in 2007 to impeach Bush. The state whose southern town of Brattleboro had made world news by resolving to arrest Bush if he stepped foot in Vermont. The state that had almost succeeded in getting its legislature to pass an impeachment resolution.

And, sadly, the state that had suffered the highest per-capita loss of soldiers.

But wait. For all of Bugliosi's legal sophistications, one would have to consider the court of public opinion. Bush had never set foot in Vermont, giving the Green Mountain State the distinction of being the only state in the union never to be blessed with a presidential visit from him.

Could Vermont possibly have jurisdiction to prosecute him? And did he really intend to murder the soldiers when he sent them off to war?

I was asking the same questions everyone asks when first confronted by the seemingly preposterous notion that a president could be prosecuted inside a state for crimes he committed outside a state. I read through those seemingly arcane legal doctrines again and concluded that if anyone knew his stuff, it had to be Vincent Bugliosi.

Surely he would not risk his reputation by making false or wild arguments in a book, let alone a courtroom. Or would he?

Taking stock

I let it all percolate for a few days, telling no one, not even my husband, that I was considering developing a plank in my attorney general race for prosecuting the president for murder. This could, after all, prove to be a very risky venture. Beyond personal safety issues, there was my professional reputation to consider. How would fellow lawyers judge me—and perhaps more important, how would judges judge me?

Already, even without adding the Bush prosecution to my platform, I had to consider how much risk I was willing to take. To begin with, most, but not all, of my lawyer friends were Democrats—just like the incumbent attorney general, William Sorrell. What would they think of my challenging one of their own? Sorrell had been in office for eleven years. His mother, the renowned Esther Sorrell, had helped build the Democratic Party in

Vermont. While Sorrell was not one to make waves as attorney general, he had run what effectively was Vermont's largest law firm with a moderately steady hand. He had also guaranteed large infusions of settlement cash into state coffers as Vermont's share of a large class-action suit against American tobacco companies. Political insiders told me it would be political suicide to challenge him. He was popular among both Democratic and Republican leaders and had run in the past as the candidate for both parties.

Mine would be an uphill race. Still, I wondered what Vermonters outside the state's most populous Chittenden County and outside the "in-crowd" of Democratic Party politics thought of William Sorrell. The Republicans had never mounted a serious candidate against him. Sorrell was a comfortable office holder who might be worthy of a challenge in a not-so-comfortable political year, when, at least nationally, middle-of-the-roaders seeking the safest routes to office were being challenged by mavericks.

Then there was my own Progressive Party to consider. This year it was defending six seats in the Vermont legislature and fielding another eleven candidates. With many fewer resources than the two other major parties, it would probably be stretched thin and could probably offer only nominal assistance. More importantly, it had to consider how a Progressive candidate pledging to prosecute George Bush for murder would play with the public. The party had fought a long struggle to earn the respect of Vermont voters and the media. One slip-up on my part, one tiny suggestion that the Progressive candidate for AG was slightly unhinged for going after the president of the United States, and the party could be delivered a serious setback.

By the last weekend in August, I decided to "go privately public" with my musings. I started, naturally enough, with my most trusted adviser, Jerry.

What would my husband think?

The one thing I valued most about Jerry in nearly thirty years of marriage was his honesty. He was a stand-up guy. "Gerard, we'll always stand by you, no matter what. Just tell the truth," his parents would tell him. It stuck with him, no doubt buttressed by a strict Catholic upbringing whose Sisters of Mercy, Jerry would tell me, "showed no mercy" if you had done something wrong and didn't own up to it. I could count on Jerry to consult his conscience about the right thing to do and to tell me honestly what he thought about my running against Sorrell. And on a plank that would include, but not be limited to, the prosecution of George W. Bush once he was out of the all-powerful White House.

Jerry also had street smarts, which meant I could trust him with my life. Raised in a working-class neighborhood in Queens, New York, Jerry knew how to watch where he was going and how to avoid trouble if trouble beckoned. That was a quality I had come to appreciate when we traveled together for the first time as investigative journalists in Latin America, where military dictators of that time routinely unleashed death squads.

Amazingly, Jerry led us through that six-month investigation unscathed. In the years following that trip, he also showed another quality, an almost bull-dog determination to get the facts when others had long since given up on the story.[11] Now, as president of the National Writers Union, Jerry would not be able to campaign with me as much as both of us would have liked. His job kept him in New York most of the week. He had agreed to be my campaign manager over the phone and on the weekends, but this was just if I were going to run, or perhaps stand, for attorney general. Adding the prosecution of Bush into the picture would, I knew, considerably complicate matters.

"Um, Jerry," I began cautiously, "have you seen this book by Vincent Bugliosi?" I put the book in his hands. "Robin lent it to me. It's quite an indictment of Bush. But there's more to it than that."

"Uh oh," said Jerry. "Does that mean you have an idea?" Jerry knew me well, and when I suggested that something was up, that maybe I had an idea worth considering, he instinctively braced himself. Some of my ideas were, shall we say, unconventional. And judging by the title of Bugliosi's book, he could see an idea coming at him full throttle.

When I told him what I had in mind, he frowned.

"This is not a great time to be doing something like this."

"True."

"You go up against Sorrell on this issue, and you could hurt any likelihood of working with other lawyers in Vermont."

"True."

"You could be taking on a huge risk just when we don't need it."

All true.

"I completely understand where you're coming from, Jerry," I said. "But consider this: If I don't do this, who will? No Republican is going to do it. And probably no Democrat. You and I both know how they wimped out on impeachment. Somebody has to do it. Read the book and you'll see what I mean. Just start with the Introduction and then go to Chapter Three, 'Prologue to the Prosecution.'"

The Introduction, I knew—about the loss of over one hundred thousand individuals in a senseless war—would get to his conscience.

And Chapter Three—about the need to hold criminals responsible for their acts—would get to his indignity over injustice. "As adults," Bugliosi had written, "most of us have learned that there are consequences in life for our misbehavior . . . [and yet] there hasn't even been any investigation of Bush's conduct, nor has one even been seriously proposed."

Finally, I appealed to Jerry's warrior instincts. The battle, if engaged, would have to be done right, with precision and intelligence. "I've read through Bugliosi's legal arguments and I think they're pretty airtight."

He hesitated, then cautiously took the book. "Okay, I'll think about it," he said. "But if you do it, you better get the Progressives' approval. This could affect their candidacies."

Winning over the party

This turned out to be a far easier task than I expected. The very next day, I approached Anthony Pollina, Vermont's best-known Progressive, who had recently decided to run as an Independent for governor.[12] Anthony, Jerry, and I greeted voters together at Anthony's booth at the Champlain Valley Fair. During a break from campaigning, I went up to him and showed him Bugliosi's book. Then, in *soto voce*, I asked him what he thought of the idea of my teaming up with Bugliosi to prosecute Bush in Vermont.

He listened. He looked carefully at the book. Then he said, "I like the idea."

The following day, I had the perfect setting for cornering other leaders of the Progressive Party: on a boat. *The Spirit of Ethan Allen*, a friendly little cruise ship christened in honor of one of Vermont's revolutionary heroes, had just left the docks of Burlington for a birthday-party sail around Lake Champlain for Independent Senator (and progressive) Bernie Sanders. I spotted party chair Martha Abbott standing by the bow of the boat. Martha, a no-nonsense Vermonter and tax consultant who had previously run a strong campaign for state auditor, was the culprit who convinced me to run for attorney general. Still, she had not anticipated my coming up with an issue as controversial as prosecuting Bush.

Fretting over how she would respond (although it didn't hurt to have a party leader like Pollina supporting the idea), I walked up to her and told her about my brief discussion with Pollina. "Oh, I'm not surprised," she said. "Anthony loves that kind of thing. You know, new ideas, new approaches." Her only concern, she said, was that I not focus my campaign entirely on the Bush-prosecution issue, as there were many things the attorney general did and many things that Vermonters needed from that office. I fully agreed.

With heart in throat, I walked up next to Mike Bayer, the party's treasurer and one of its founders. Mike was a hardliner who, like Martha, was disinclined to favor anything that seemed far-out. Once again, to my amazement, he smiled, eyes twinkling, and said, "Go for it."

At this point, with initial indicators pointing up and only two more party leaders to consult (legislators David Zuckerman and Chris Pearson, both of Burlington—who would, in fact, be equally enthusiastic), I figured it was time to get in touch with Bugliosi. But how to find him? Then, quite out of the blue, coincidence arrived in the form of my friend, investigative journalist Kristina Borjesson.

Seeking Bugliosi

An independent filmmaker and refugee from the censor's pen at prime-time television, Borjesson had been working on a documentary when she called in late August. "I need to get away for awhile," she explained. "Would you mind if I came to Vermont and spent a week at your place?"

"Not at all. Come on up. There's plenty of room." Jerry and I lived in a renovated farmhouse in one of the most beautiful mountain valleys in

Vermont, right beneath the majestic man-faced profile of Mt. Mansfield. Borjesson was an attractive, tall blonde who could have lived the easy life in Haiti, where she grew up, and instead chose a career in journalism. And not just any kind of journalism. She was fearless in her pursuit of the truth, no matter how high up she went. She'd been shunned by CBS after she probed too deeply into the cause of the midair explosion of TWA Flight 800 after it took off from JFK Airport back in 1996. I had met her in conjunction with a book she had edited, *Into the Buzzsaw: Leading Journalists Expose the Myth of a Free Press,* which featured (among other hair-raising stories) Jerry's travails in the suppression of his exposé on the powerful duPont family.[13] We became friends—she, the daughter of a military attaché; me, the daughter of a cultural attaché; both of us conceived in Jordan; both of us fascinated and horrified by the world of espionage that our fathers had frequented.

When she arrived at our Vermont farmhouse, we hauled several boxes of files from her car into the guest room. She planned to do a lot of reading, writing, and reediting of a documentary she was working on about the Bush administration's apparent fixation on intervening in Iran. But within the first twenty-four hours of her stay, everything changed, and all her boxes of files sat in the guest room untouched.

She had barely settled in when I broached the subject of Bugliosi's book. I knew she'd be interested in it. It was gutsy, it had new evidence about the deceits that had led us into the Iraq war, and it had a new approach: from a former prosecutor assembling his evidence as if preparing for trial.[14]

"You know," I began, "I'd like to get in touch with Bugliosi to see if he's found anyone to do the prosecution. But I'm having difficulty finding him. Even his own publisher won't respond to my phone calls."

Kristina jumped to her feet. "I know how to find him." I stared at her, disbelievingly. "His publicist is the same as my publicist," she said, and went to her purse and pulled out her address book.

"Her name is Ilene Proctor. She's told me a little about her work on his book."

She called her publicist. "Hi, Ilene? Listen, I've got a good friend here, Charlotte Dennett, who's an investigative journalist, but she's also an attorney. She'd like to talk to Vince Bugliosi about his book. She might want to help. Can you give me his phone number?"

Proctor gave it to her in minutes. "Your friend better call soon," she warned, "because he's leaving his home in L.A. shortly, heading for a speaking engagement in Seattle."

With no notes, no well-thought-through idea of what I was going to say, I dialed the number.

A woman answered. It was his wife, Gail. I explained briefly who I was. Within two minutes, I was speaking to Vincent Bugliosi.

The connection

A pleasant male voice said hello. I introduced myself and explained the purpose of my call. As a candidate for attorney general, I said, I was considering taking up the issue of prosecuting Bush, but I needed to know what he thought of that and if anyone had stepped forward yet.

He seemed interested. Perhaps even relieved to hear a lawyer on the other end of the phone.

His publisher, he explained, had sent the book to all fifty attorneys general in all the states, and only one had responded. Unfortunately, that attorney's state did not give the attorney general jurisdiction to prosecute criminal cases, so the issue of his involvement had become moot.

"It's going to be difficult to find someone with the courage to step forward," he said. Then, as if in an afterthought, he asked:

"Does your state attorney general have jurisdiction over criminal prosecutions?"

"Yes. In fact, I can read it to you straight from the AG's Web site."

> The Attorney General may represent the state in all civil and criminal matters. . . . The Attorney General shall also have the same authority throughout the state as a state's attorney. The Attorney General shall have the general supervision of criminal prosecutions.

That satisfied him.

Ideally, he continued, Bush's prosecution should occur on the federal level, in the District of Columbia, with the U.S. attorney general as prosecutor and the resources of the Department of Justice at his disposal.[15] But he doubted that would happen. Washington seemed paralyzed by fear, and we had all seen the fate of possible impeachment hearings—not that impeachment was necessarily desirable, he added. "Impeachment doesn't bring true justice. Bush would be removed from office, but he'd still be a free man." And Bush, Bugliosi indicated in no uncertain terms, did not deserve freedom considering what he had done.

"I believe I have established a case beyond all reasonable doubt that the president is guilty of first-degree murder," he added emphatically.

"Well, I've read your legal framework," I responded. "I started with your evidence, and that seemed pretty solid. Then I read your legal arguments. You've clearly thought them all through."

"Well, I've had some experience, you know." He cited his twenty-one murder convictions without a single loss. He knew that always impressed people. Americans love a winner.

"So what's been happening with your book?" I asked. The writer in me wanted to know.

"It's been completely blacked out by the mainstream media. The liberals are terrified of the right wing and the left doesn't know how to fight. The right has no fear of the left, but I've been told they fear me."

I asked him to explain. It was, after all, a rather sweeping indictment.

He recounted an experience he had with a radio host in Montreal. The Canadian journalist told him that the American media might cover him if they thought he was "some kind of a nut case"—an oddity, or a crazed crusader worthy of a short human-interest segment. But because he was nationally known as a serious and successful prosecutor, they wouldn't go near him because they wouldn't want to give him a large forum for his views. To me, a writer who had also experienced this kind of suppression, this explanation seemed plausible. Later in my campaign, it was proven true. When anyone attacked me or my campaign, they omitted Bugliosi's name entirely because it lent credibility to my efforts.

Despite the media blackout, however, his book had been a best seller for about seven weeks, thanks to alternative radio and TV and word of mouth. "Of all the books I've written, I've never seen such passion as for this one," said Bugliosi. "People have been giving me standing ovations. The response has been tremendous."

He told a story about a man in Seattle who made a living selling gourmet coffee on the Internet. After the man read the book, he put up an announcement on his Web site: "Instead of buying my coffee, why not buy Bugliosi's book instead?" He even set up his own Web site: www.prosecuteGeorge Bush.com.

Bugliosi told me he knew a bit about Vermont—how the people of Brattleboro had passed a resolution authorizing their town attorneys to bring an indictment against Bush and Cheney for violating the Constitution. The news that Vermonters would arrest Bush if he crossed state lines had spread all over the country. "Of course, that's impossible," Bugliosi said. "The town attorneys don't have the jurisdiction or the authority to do such a thing." He laughed. "But it was the spirit that counted."

Then he told me that he was heading to the East Coast the following week to be a featured speaker at a conference on prosecuting high-level government officials. It was being held, he said, at the Massachusetts School of Law in Andover, Massachusetts.

Andover? I couldn't believe my good luck.

"Oh, that's not far from me," I said. "It's just a four-hour drive. I know because my brother lives in Andover. Maybe we could meet."

I had never heard of the Massachusetts School of Law. And I had grown up in Massachusetts, in a somewhat exclusive little town north of Boston called Winchester. How could this school be prestigious if I had never heard of it? And how and why did this law school have the chutzpah to host a conference on prosecuting Bush and his ilk while they were still in power?

It didn't matter. I'd find out soon enough. Lawyers, Bugliosi told me, were coming from all over the country to be at this symposium. This would give me the opportunity to see what they thought about Bugliosi's theories. And the timing could not have been better. To think I had only just begun to weigh teaming up with this famous prosecutor, and now he was telling me he was flying east in a matter of days.

"I'll be speaking Saturday afternoon, September 13th," he said. "If you come down, we can go out to dinner."

"Fine with me."

"Meanwhile, if you want to check me out more, just go to the Web and you'll find my testimony on July 25th before the House Judiciary Committee.

That's John Conyers' committee. He called it a 'Hearing on Executive Power and Its Constitutional Limitations.' But the subtext was impeachment."

Representative Conyers (D-Mich.), one of the more courageous and outspoken members of Congress and a strong advocate of impeachment, had read Bugliosi's book and invited Bugliosi to speak. "I told him I would be happy to travel east and testify, but not on impeachment. I would only testify on prosecuting George Bush for murder."

Amazingly, Conyers agreed. Bugliosi apparently delivered such an impassioned speech that it got one hundred fifty thousand hits on YouTube. "You might want to check it out before we meet," he said.[16]

Over his decades-long career, Vincent Bugliosi had managed to show many sides of his persona to the public. On the dust jacket of his book, he appears as a handsome, balding man sitting comfortably in a Windsor chair in his living room, dressed in a dark suit but with no tie. His white shirt is open at the neck, his left hand rests comfortably on his knee, and his face is open and intense. His deep-set eyes stare out beneath heavy brows as if to challenge anyone who dares question his integrity. "I have nothing to hide," he seems to be saying. "What about you?"

In his filmed testimony before the House Judiciary Committee, Bugliosi is impeccably dressed in a dark blue suit and elegant, striped silk tie. Sitting before the microphone—his brow furrowed, his face strained from the intensity of the moment—he is now all business, wired up, and ready to squeeze as many words as possible into the short time span allowed. And he's not afraid to say that he's less than happy with the ground rules he's been given.

> Mr. Chairman. I've been told that the rules of this House dictate that although I can quote what President Bush said, I am forbidden from accusing him of any crime or even any dishonorable conduct, only being allowed to use the words "Bush administration" or "administration officials." This will not allow for the best of articulations, but I'll do the best that I can.

His yellow legal pad in front of him, he lays out his case against the Bush administration. He has evidence that proved beyond a reasonable doubt, he says, that the Bush administration had taken the nation to war under false pretenses, and therefore, *"under the law,"* his voice rising, "they are guilty of murder for the deaths of over *four thousand* young American soldiers who have died so far in Iraq fighting their war. And let us not forget," he continued, "the over one hundred thousand *innocent* Iraqi men, women, children, and *babies* who have died horrible, violent deaths because of this war."

The emotional inflection in his voice has everyone electrified. This man knows how to deliver an opening statement.

He lays out his evidence, focusing, because of time constraints, on President Bush's October 7, 2002, televised address to the nation, in which Bush claimed that Saddam Hussein was an imminent threat to the security of this country:

> He was telling millions of unsuspecting Americans the exact opposite of what his own CIA had told administration officials just six days earlier, in a classified report on October 1st, that Saddam Hussein was *not* an imminent threat.
>
> But it gets worse. On October 4th, the Bush administration put out an unclassified summary version of the classified report that they could give to Congress, which they called "the white paper." In this white paper, which I have in front of me, the conclusion of U.S. intelligence that Saddam Hussein was not an imminent threat was *competely deleted*. Every single one of these all-important words was taken out.

Bugliosi pauses for effect, looking at the congressmen, then continues:

> So, Congress and the American people never saw any of this. Since we are talking about a matter of war and peace with the safety and lives of millions of human beings at that time hanging in the balance, and with Congress about to vote in one week on whether it should authorize George Bush to go to war in Iraq, what could possibly be worse, I repeat, what could possibly be worse, and more criminal, than the Bush administration deliberately keeping this all-important conclusion from Congress and the American people?

The terrible reality is that the Bush administration has gotten away with thousands upon thousands of murders, and we, America, the American people, cannot let them do this.

He mentions a previous House Judiciary Committee issuing four articles of impeachment against President Bill Clinton in 1998 for doing something "infinitely less significant" than what the Bush administration did in this case. Bugliosi continues, his voice rising even more:

Indeed, it is a calumny, a slander, of the highest rank to even talk about them in the same breath. If a House Judiciary Committee can recommend that President Clinton be impeached for what he did, all the more so, with all the highly incriminating evidence I set forth in this book, you should not have any difficulty making a criminal referral to the Department of Justice to commence a criminal investigation of the Bush administration to determine whether first-degree murder charges should be brought against certain members of this administration. Whether Republican or Democratic, all Americans should be absolutely outraged over what the Bush administration has done.

Now, his voice shaking, Bugliosi delivers his climax:
"How dare they do what they did! *How dare they!*"
The room erupts in applause. Congressman Conyers pounds down with his gavel. A Republican asks that the room be cleared. The House Judiciary chairman had been generous in his introduction of Bugliosi, even holding up his book before the cameras. But now his Republican colleagues are getting riled. Conyers cautions the room against any further outbursts, then allows Bugliosi to wrap up. Bugliosi remains fired up:

Directly because of this administration's war, right now, as I am talking to you, there are well over one hundred thousand precious human beings in their cold graves. Speaking metaphorically, I want you to hear, as I do, their cries for justice. . . . It would greatly dishonor those in their graves if you were not to refer this case to the Department of Justice. If we want this nation to become the great nation it once was, widely respected around the world, we can hardly do this if we don't take the first step of bringing those responsible for the war in Iraq to justice. Thank you.

I sat back in my chair and took a breath. This man, I thought, knows how to fight!

I looked forward to meeting him.

Face to face: The lawyers convene

It was with mixed feelings that I drove into the parking lot of the hotel in Andover where the lawyers had convened.

I had just come from the annual convention of the Vermont State Labor Council, AFL-CIO, where members would be voting on which candidates to endorse in Vermont's races. At the reception launching the convention, I had tipped off the council's president that I was running for attorney general and might take on some pretty controversial issues. Lindol Atkins, known for his bluntness and raucous humor, looked at me and said, "You've got a lot of balls to take on Billy Sorrell!" He said it with a smile, but I knew then that my chances of getting a labor endorsement were slim.

I'm a member of the council's executive committee and I considered these people my friends, but I knew that the labor movement in Vermont did not make hasty decisions based on friendship. They dealt in the real world of power, of working with elected representatives to get what their constituents needed, and their relations with Attorney General William Sorrell, Lindol advised me, were reasonably good. If I wanted to get their endorsement as a Progressive, I had to show that I had a good chance of winning. I also had to be very up front with them, and that meant no hedging on what my platform would look like.

By the time it was my turn to address the convention the following morning and ask for the delegates' support, I was more than a bit nervous. When I got around to the subject of prosecution, I reminded the audience of the national AFL-CIO convention in Chicago in 2006, when all but one of more than three thousand delegates voted its opposition to the war in Iraq, calling for the return of soldiers "as rapidly as possible."

"Even though the press didn't cover it, this was history-making," I said. "For the first time ever, the American labor movement voted against a war while it was still in progress. And we all know why. Because this war was affecting our families, our sons, and our daughters."

Now, I explained, I was heading down to Andover, Massachusetts, to attend a meeting of lawyers from all over the country. "They will be investigating whether to bring criminal charges against members of the Bush administration for its conduct leading up to and during the war. Depending on what I see and hear, there's a possibility that, if elected, I may get involved in prosecution efforts, including against the president."

They listened quietly and applauded politely when I ended. I later learned from Jerry on my way down to Andover that the delegates endorsed William Sorrell 19 to 9. I had gotten just over 30 percent of the vote. And these were friends.

By the time I left the convention, drove to Massachusetts, and arrived in Andover, it was too late to hear Bugliosi speak. My friend Kristina—the same friend who had come to Vermont to visit and then put me in touch with Bugliosi—had traveled ahead of me and caught the first day's proceedings. She had told him I was coming, and when I arrived, she led me to him. He was in the hotel lobby surrounded by well-wishers and autograph seekers—elegant in his three-piece suit, all businesslike, and yet, a man seemingly without airs. He gave me a big smile when Kristina introduced us, outstretched his hand, then excused himself politely from his fans and immediately led us into the hotel dining room where we found a table for three. He pulled out our chairs before taking his own seat. It was the first sign that we were in the presence of a gentleman.

In the two hours we got acquainted, we talked about our pasts—his as assistant district attorney in Los Angeles, mine as an investigative journalist for thirty years and a personal injury and family lawyer for the past eleven. He talked about his other books, I showed him a copy of *Thy Will Be Done*. We both expressed appreciation for well-documented arguments, as evidenced by our mutual admiration for footnotes, even if they ran on for pages. Our conversation was becoming an intimate meeting of the minds. We seemed to click, almost instantly.

I apologized for missing his speech on Saturday afternoon, explaining that I just couldn't break away from my state labor convention in Vermont to get down to Andover in time. He asked how it went. I told him, rather ruefully, that I got only 30 percent of the vote. "Why that's good!" he said sweetly. "That's a good start." I was surprised by this reaction and inwardly appreciated this support. Here was another good sign—a sign that Vincent Bugliosi was not only a courageous fighter, but also a kind man.

I explained my background in the Middle East and told him that I was working on a book about the origins of U.S. involvement in the Middle East. The book, I added quickly, was based on the experiences of three generations of Dennetts—my grandmother, the missionary to Istanbul; my father, the diplomat and Office of Strategic Services (OSS) spy;[17] and myself, the journalist who was trying to figure out U.S. foreign policy in the Middle East during the last century leading up to my father's mysterious death. My father had warned against U.S. troops ever trying to occupy Middle East countries. "This is another reason why I'm interested in this project," I said.

"All very interesting," he said, "but don't forget, if you are going to prosecute Bush, you have to stay focused on that alone." Here was the disciplined prosecutor talking to me. He knew exactly what it would take to assemble the case. At one point, he told me (as if to reassure me) what Harvard's famous appellate lawyer, Alan Dershowitz, had once said about him. "If you created a hall of fame of prosecutors, Vince would be in the entranceway. There is no prosecutor I'd fear more if I was guilty. He *will* get at the truth." I would later read testimonials from other legal luminaries about his prowess. F. Lee Bailey called him "the quintessential prosecutor." And Robert Tanenbaum, the top homicide prosecutor in the Manhattan DA's office, had said, "There is only one Vincent Bugliosi. He's the best." How could you go wrong working with someone with those credentials?

He seemed unfazed over the fact that I was not a prosecutor. Jerry Brown in California had become attorney general, he said, and "he didn't know a damn thing about criminal law." If I could get myself elected attorney general, he added, he would help me in any way he could, up to and including being appointed my special prosecutor, if that was my wish. "You see, my book is just an academic argument without someone to prosecute. I'm no longer with the DA's office, so I can't do it. That's why I need someone like you, if you get elected."

Even though I had read his book and been struck by its sincerity and his testimony before the House Judiciary Committee, I still could not get over his passion for justice and determination to prosecute Bush. He wanted, at the very least, to put the soon-to-be-former president behind bars for life.

At one point, when Kristina left the table to talk with a journalist, he leaned toward me and said, "You realize that if you get elected we will both have to take security precautions." I nodded. "Believe me," I said, "I've talked it over with my husband. We've thought it all through."

"Well, that's good. I just want you to know what you're in for." I liked his bravery. My husband, himself an investigative journalist of thirty years whose first book was a massive unauthorized biography on the richest family in America, had once told me a Roman adage: "Fortune favors the bold." Well, good fortune, or luck, we'd never counted on. And we'd never made a fortune, that was for sure. One of our literary agents once said, "You'll never make money trying to tell the truth," which was one reason I decided to become a lawyer. But even after getting my license to practice law, it seemed that the pursuit of justice was more important than the pursuit of money, and if that required being bold, so be it. At least now I was ready to be an apprentice to one of the top criminal lawyers in the country.

Two hours with Vincent Bugliosi and I was getting some idea about what this battle would require of me. I could only hope I was up to the task.

CHAPTER THREE

The Brave Little State of Vermont

Meeting Bugliosi the man, not just Bugliosi the prosecutor, was a highlight of the Andover conference and a major factor in my decision to put "prosecute Bush" into my campaign. But it was not the only factor. The following day, I listened to lawyers debate the different options for holding Bush and other high government officials accountable for their crimes, and I also listened to activists who had come to address the conferees.

One woman made a particularly strong impression. She was Lauri Arbiter, a diminutive woman wearing a black T-shirt with big white letters emblazoned across the front: "Arrest Bush." In riveting detail, she recounted her experience at the Republican National Convention in St. Paul only weeks earlier: how the police had put a gun to her head for no reason, thrown her and a handful of other antiwar protesters up against a fence and handcuffed them for forty minutes, then released them—for no apparent reason other than to terrorize the demonstrators. Another protestor had been arrested and placed in a cell with a black hood over his head, then beaten. Shades of Abu Ghraib in Iraq? What were they teaching police officers in St. Paul these days?

By the time the Republican convention was wrapping up, police had jailed more than three hundred protestors in the Twin Cities—all too often breaking up crowds with methods protestors and observing journalists found alarming. Amazingly, a number of protestors had conspiracy and terrorism charges brought against *them*. Amazingly, too, more than forty journalists were arrested.[18]

Lauri looked around the room at the lawyers imploringly. "If this happens in our own towns and cities," she said, "we have to stand up. Minneapolis was a laboratory. Our democracy is in our hands."

The audience sat in stunned silence, then burst into applause. Clearly, we were all in this together.

The dean of the Massachusetts School of Law, Lawrence Velvel, spoke next. "I agree. Lawyers and judges won't act unless there is a grassroots movement." But lawyers, he added, were important and necessary—especially respectable lawyers.

I saw my cue and went up to the mike. "I'm a lawyer, and I consider myself respectable. I'm not famous and I'm not a prosecutor . . . [but] I will seriously consider prosecuting George W. Bush for murder." Once again, the room erupted in applause, even though my words—"seriously consider"—were cautious, as if I couldn't believe I might be the first lawyer to take this step. "It's not easy for any lawyer to come forward," I continued. "Lawyers have to worry about their reputations, and their position if it's an elected position. But I think it has to be done."

Before leaving Andover, I sounded out Velvel about Bugliosi's theories. I had seen other lawyers show deference to Bugliosi, and activists clearly admired him. But what did the dean of the law school think? His response was positive. Bugliosi's approach had merit, he told me. When I told him I was thinking of running for attorney general, he wished me well. He could have dissuaded me, but instead I thought I saw a look of respect in his eyes.

I returned to Vermont and consulted with two more Progressive Party leaders, state legislators David Zuckerman and Chris Pearson. They approved of my taking up the prosecution plank. So, then, did my husband, Jerry. With this news, I called Bugliosi, who had flown to Washington, D.C., for a series of interviews.

"That's terrific," he said. "I've been hinting that someone was very interested, but I wouldn't give your name and I wouldn't even say it was a woman. Now I can do both!"

"So, Vince, do you think you could come up here and help me announce my campaign?"

"Sure. I had some interviews scheduled back in Los Angeles, but I'll cancel them. When do you want me to come up?"

"The sooner the better. Can you make it in a couple of days?"

"I'll see what I can do."

"Fantastic," I replied, reminding him to look out his window when his plane began its descent over the beautiful Green Mountains of Vermont.

Vince comes to Vermont

Kristina and I picked Bugliosi up at Vermont's "international" airport, in Burlington, on September 16. He had arrived two days before the press conference so that we would have time to prepare just how I would announce adding the prosecution of the president to my platform. We were a few minutes late and found him pacing outside the arrivals section looking for our car. His face brightened when he saw us honking and waving.

"You know," he said as he unloaded his suitcase into the car, "I don't have a cell phone and I didn't know how to reach you!"

"Sorry, Vince. Sorry, too, that it's a little chilly today." He was, as always, wearing a three-piece suit, with no coat. He would soon discover that Vermont, in many ways, was not California—beginning with climate (it's much colder than Los Angeles) and attire (jeans, parkas, and plaid shirts are more the norm).

"Did you look out the window, Vince?" I asked, hoping he might have marveled over the spectacular stretch of green hills and mountains that borders either side of Lake Champlain.

"Oh, no. I'm sorry. I guess I forgot. I was focused on my reading."

Kristina and I whisked him off to the Burlington Boathouse, a must-see stop on the city's waterfront. Again, he seemed oblivious to his surroundings. I would soon learn that Bugliosi tends to get very focused hours before a public event—and, in this case, days before. His penchant for intense concentration was key to his success as one of the country's most successful prosecutors, but he admits to losing out on some of the other fine things in life. When I later took him for a ride outside of Burlington, hoping that Vermont's rural landscape and quaint New England towns would make an impression, he graciously acknowledged the beauty of what he was seeing, especially after I told him that the *entire state* has been deemed a national historic site. But he confessed that Gail, his wife of fifty years, would have enjoyed the scenery a lot more. That was Vince. Honest and to the point.

There were other aspects of Vermont, though, that pleased Vince immensely. Among those was the fact that people in our tiny state had a tendency to take big stands, making it a suitable venue for the campaign to bring a wayward president to justice. One of the Vermonters he had already spoken with was Kurt Daims, a retired engineer who lived in the small but politically lively town of Brattleboro. Daims, a tall, thin man with a shock of gray hair and intense eyes, wanted to see liberal-minded towns like Brattleboro get more involved and empowered in opposing the actions of the Bush administration.

He had come up with the idea of getting Brattleboro to threaten George Bush and Dick Cheney with arrest if they set foot in Vermont. For days he stood on street corners seeking the required number of signatures to have his resolution placed on the town ballot, and soon other town residents were helping him out. On March 4, 2008, the town voted in favor of his resolution,[19] which began with the words, "Shall the Selectboard instruct the Town Attorney to draft indictments against President Bush and Vice President Cheney for crimes against our Constitution?" Brattleboro's self-styled "arrest warrant" resonated with the press and got reported all over the country. A film crew doing a documentary of Vince's book for the big screen arrived to cover the story and to talk to people who participated in the vote.

Opponents insisted that it would have no effect, since town attorneys did not have the authority to pursue indictments or arrests. The Brattleboro town attorney agreed and refused to carry out the resolution that was voted upon. Proponents acknowledged that the resolution was symbolic but asserted that it represented the frustrations of American citizens upset with the Bush administration for acting above the law, especially with its preemptive invasion of Iraq and torturing of detainees held in Guantánamo and Abu Ghraib without the protections afforded prisoners of war. In the absence of congressional action, proponents claimed, passing the Brattleboro resolution was their only recourse. They hoped it would serve as a model for other cities. Vince was clearly impressed, having raised this little act of rebellion to me the first time we talked on the phone. Getting Bush or Cheney arrested "would never happen," he assured me as we sat drinking coffee at the Burlington Boathouse, "but I still see Kurt as a hero."

I filled him in on a bit of Vermontania. "Vermonters are fiercely independent and they love to be groundbreakers for the rest of the nation," I boasted. "They will tell you that little Vermont, one of the smallest states in the nation, was the first to oppose slavery and sent more soldiers per capita into the Civil War than any other state."

More recently, I went on, Vermont was the first state to grant civil unions, paving the way for same-sex marriage in other states.[20] And, of course, it was the only state that had a truly viable third party, one that had governed the largest city in Vermont for over two decades and had six members sitting in the legislature.

"I don't know how to explain how special this state is," I said. "You can walk up to the governor or any other elected official and have a conversation on a first-name basis. Probably because of Vermont's small size and its natural beauty, people here feel connected—to each other and to the land. As you see, there's very little urban sprawl. We banned billboards decades ago. And there's a real sense of community. Every time Jerry and I cross the bridge over Lake Champlain from New York, we cheer when we see the sign, 'Welcome to Vermont.' "[21]

Then I told him of one of my favorite sayings about Vermont from a man who was born in Vermont and went on to be president of the United States:

> If the spirit of liberty should vanish in other parts of the Union and support of our institutions should languish, it could all be replenished from the generous store held by the people of this brave little state of Vermont. (Calvin Coolidge, 1928)

Calvin Coolidge was not exactly known for his liberal views, I explained, and I had yet to find out the precise reasons why he uttered those words,[22] but they are engraved on a marble plaque inside the Vermont statehouse. "Every time I go up there I stand in front of that plaque and marvel over those words."

Vince nodded approvingly.

"In fact," I added, "I actually had the opportunity to read those words in front of a gathering of impeachment activists at the statehouse when they were hoping to get a resolution passed by the legislature." To read those words, in front of those fine people, and in that context of trying to save our democracy, was for me a very memorable moment.

Unfortunately, that resolution never passed. The top Democrat in the Vermont House, Speaker Gaye Symington, nixed it before it was able to go anywhere. Once again, the fix against impeachment was in. By Democrats, no less.

But now Coolidge's words had a new relevance.

Lost emotions

After taking Vince on his introductory tour of Burlington, Kristina and I drove him to Robin Lloyd's place, a converted carriage house located behind her big, red Victorian home on leafy Maple Street just two houses away from the home where Grace and Calvin Coolidge were married. Vince would sleep in a large back room that Robin alternately used for meetings and out-of-town guests. As just one more in a string of coincidences, the first-floor apartment in her adjoining Victorian home had recently been vacated and no tenants were expected for at least two months. We turned this into our office—though we would soon invade her adjoining office as well and turn the whole carriage-house apartment-and-office complex into campaign headquarters.

Robin's home had always been a sort of "command central" for many progressives. It is conveniently located in the heart of downtown Burlington, the hub of Vermont's cultural and educational life with the University of Vermont, St. Michael's College, and Champlain College all located nearby and Middlebury College just an hour's drive away. But it also had the undeniable character of a well-used spot where political activists had long burned midnight oil in hopes of making change happen.

For the next forty-eight hours, Vince and I sat at Robin's dining-room table and went over the legal arguments for prosecuting Bush for murder. While I had already read them carefully and found myself accepting his basic premises, I realized I was now on the hot seat. What if the press asked a trick question? Best to use this unique session with Bugliosi to get the full flavor of how he had developed his arguments. Then we would tailor them specifically to Vermont's laws. Also, with Vince at my side, I knew I could refer very complex questions dealing with criminal law to him.

It became clear, in the course of our discussions, that there was an emotional underpinning to Vince's resolve to prosecute the president. Something deep down inside drove him to spend many hours researching his theories in the federal Ninth Circuit law library in Los Angeles during the week and the county law library on weekends. "You know, I'm a true-crime writer, not a political activist," he said when I first asked him why he cared so much. "I'm not like you and some of the other people I've met who commit their lives to fighting injustice in the political system, something I admire very much. But when something particularly egregious happens, like when the Supreme Court stopped the vote count in Florida and appointed George Bush president, or when Bush invaded Iraq on a lie, I just have to stop what I'm doing and jump in. That's what happened when the right wing tried to remove Clinton from office for having consensual sex in the Oval Office, and when the Supreme Court stole the election. The *nerve* of them."

He couldn't tell me the exact moment when he decided to write his book on prosecuting George W. Bush for murder, but several things deeply affected him:

1. Bush's cavalier attitude toward the war. Vince couldn't get over the thought that in the days and months after 9/11 and leading up to the war, and then during the war itself, Bush was having a lot of fun. He even brazenly told the media that he was one happy fella at the same time that American soldiers were being blown to pieces by roadside bombs in Iraq. Vince mentioned this frequently to me—and continues to do so to this day.

He wrote:

> The first inkling I got that Bush didn't care about the suffering of anyone, not just those dying in Iraq, was from an article in the September 22, 2001, *New York Times* just eleven days after 9/11. Though 3,000 Americans had been murdered and the nation was in agony and shock, the man who should have been leading the mourning was, behind the scenes, not affected in the tiniest way. The article by Frank Bruni said that "Mr. Bush's nonchalant, jocular demeanor remains the same. . . . In private, say several Republicans close to the administration, he still slaps backs and uses baseball terminology, at one point promising that the terrorists were not 'going to steal home on me.' He is not staying up all night. . . . He

is taking time to play with his dogs and his cats. He is working out most days."

Two months later, on December 21, 2001, Bush was telling the media, "All in all, it's been a fabulous year for Laura and me."[23]

The only pictures Vince put in his book are ones showing the suffering of family members and fellow soldiers who had lost loved ones and friends, juxtaposed with pictures of a laughing, back-slapping president. "Throughout the sea of blood," Bugliosi wrote, "and the screams and cries of men, women, and children, even babies, coming out of the hell on earth he created in Iraq, unbelievably, he laughed and joked, had fun, and enjoyed every day of his presidency."

Vince discovered a statement from former Lieutenant General Gregory Newbold, a three-star Marine Corps general, who said Bush's decision to invade Iraq "was done with a casualness and swagger that are the special province of those who have never had to execute the missions—or bury the results."[24]

2. Hussein had no reason to attack the United States. Applying common sense (and Vince has been dubbed the Master of Common Sense), he thought the notion of Saddam Hussein wanting to attack the U.S. or have some terrorists like al-Qaeda do the job was "ridiculous on its face," because all the evidence showed that Hussein wanted to live. He went on about this for several pages of footnotes in his book.

> I mean, here's someone who had two people, independent of each other, testing every morsel of food that he ate, who slept in a different bed every night; someone who owned forty palaces and loved his life as the supreme dictator of his country. Why would he do anything at all that could only jeopardize his existence? He would have nothing to gain and everything to lose.[25]

Hussein, Bugliosi believed, would not risk his life to drop a bomb on the United States or help anyone else do so, because he knew, for certain, that there would be instant retaliation. He could kill his own people, but he knew he would be annihilated if he did anything that would harm the United

States. "As Joseph Wilson, deputy chief of mission at the U.S. embassy in Baghdad from 1988–1991, wrote at the time: 'Hussein has long known that every terrorist act, and particularly a sophisticated one, raises the question of his involvement and invites blame.'"[26]

3. Bush, unlike other presidents, earnestly *wanted* to go to war in Iraq. Bugliosi first learned this from Helen Thomas, veteran White House correspondent who had covered the White House since 1960. Thomas had written about presidents for half a century, but "of all the presidents she had known, Bush was the only one who 'wanted to go to war,'" said Vince.[27] Bush thought that by being a war president it would make his presidency more popular. He was, sadly, right about that—at least at the beginning.

4. But most of all, it bothered Vince intensely that the president had sent young soldiers to their deaths while lying to them. He describes in his book how one soldier wrote home to his parents that he was happy to "take a bullet for him [Bush]" a week before he was killed by a roadside bomb. "Can you imagine that?" Vince wrote. "Willing to die for the draft-dodging,[28] arrogant son of privilege from Crawford."

Later, at Robin's house, Vince told us that, to this day, soldiers deployed to Iraq still find the stark image of the Twin Towers greeting them at the entrances of their bases as a reminder of why they must fight and, if necessary, die for their country.*

Vince pointed out that Bush, by lying to the American people that Saddam Hussein was an imminent threat to our country, had also stated by "unmistakable innuendo" that Saddam Hussein was involved in September 11. "Yet Bush knew that both of these assertions were lies," he said indignantly.

I don't know if it's Vince's Catholic upbringing (with its undoubtedly strong moral values on life and death; though, when I asked him, he did not necessarily think this was a factor) or what, but he just couldn't get over Bush's tricking American soldiers into war. To this day, he remains haunted by the thought of parents weeping over the graves of their loved ones due to a war that didn't have to happen. No less anguishing, for him, was the government's failure to properly arm the soldiers once they got over there.

---

*Sadly, he said, a 2006 poll of American soldiers in Iraq found that 90 percent thought Saddam Hussein was involved in 9/11.

"Can anything possibly be more abominable," he wrote in his book, *"than this very rich nation sending its young men off to war without providing them with the proper equipment?"*[29]

So this was the passion and the anger that motivated Vincent Bugliosi to write his book.

"My anger over the war in Iraq, some will say, is palpable in the pages of this book," he wrote. He was unapologetic then and his anger continues to this day, as the media focuses solely on whether Bush administration officials will be held accountable for torture of detainees ("some of whom are our proven enemies, let's not forget," he wryly points out) and ignores the issue of accountability for the ongoing war in Iraq, with thousands of American deaths and hundreds of thousands, some say a million, Iraqi deaths resulting.

Prep time: Then and now

I was curious to know how Vince had developed the legal framework for his case. He told me he had spent many months researching the issues in Los Angeles's law libraries.[30] His goal was to figure out how to apply conventional principles of American law, principles that had never been so applied in the annals of the American crime of murder, to the indisputable fact that President Bush had taken the nation to war on false pretenses. Indeed, can a president be prosecuted for murder if he takes the nation to war on false pretenses?

Two incontrovertible realities were already in place that told him that the answer to that question had to be yes. The first reality was that in America no one is above the law. "It is very clear," he told me, "that under the U.S. Constitution and in the Federalist Papers, once a president leaves office he can be prosecuted for any crime he committed while he was in office." That made sense. For example, that's the legal reason why President Ford, if he was to protect his predecessor, had to pardon ex-President Nixon. Otherwise, Nixon could have been indicted and tried for his crimes, just as his underlings had been.

Secondly, no federal or state murder statutes say that the crime of murder can apply only to certain people, not presidents or engineers or golf pros, or only if the killing occurs in certain places, like in a home or carried out on the street but not on the battlefield. There are no such distinctions.

Then, he had to deal with the inevitable question: How, if the president didn't personally kill someone, could he be charged with murder? Here, Bugliosi had some experience. He had been able to prosecute Charles Manson and several other members of his "family" for the 1969 murders of Hollywood actress Sharon Tate and six others when Manson was not even present at the murder scene.[31] Bugliosi simply relied on a legal principle called the vicarious liability rule, used in cases where the charge is conspiracy to commit murder.

"Each member of the conspiracy is liable for the crime, whether or not they were present," he explained. "If A is sitting in the getaway car while B killed a bank teller, A is liable. You follow?" Vince had a habit of saying "You follow?" after making a legal argument, whether talking to lawyers or nonlawyers.

"Sure, so far."

But then he threw out a novel twist.

"But, of course, I had to go one step further and explain how one of the co-conspirators (Bush) could be indicted for murder (of American soldiers) when none of his fellow co-conspirators committed the murder." He continued: "The doctrine of vicarious liability still applies. If a co-conspirator sets in motion a chain of events that he knows will cause the crime, he's as guilty as the person who pulled the trigger."

"So what happens," I asked, "if the person who pulled the trigger is an Iraqi, not an American?"

"That's when the doctrine of innocent agent comes into play. It states that a defendant who was not present at the commission of the act can be convicted of first-degree murder if the defendant engaged in acts that caused the perpetrators (in this case, Iraqi soldiers) to commit the murder."

By now, Bugliosi had become fully animated. "In invading Iraq in 2003, Bush caused Iraqis—either in self-defense or to repel an invader to fight back. They are the third-party innocent agents."

He stopped, and looked straight into my eyes. "I suppose you have heard of Cindy Sheehan, who lost her twenty-four-year-old son Casey in Iraq and then protested outside of Bush's Texas ranch?"

"Sure."

"She understood the concept without even reading my book. She called me one Sunday afternoon last June and said, 'The Iraqi insurgents didn't kill my son. Bush did. They were just repelling an invader, which they had every right to do.'"

"And I told her she was exactly right. The defendant, in this case Bush, is as guilty as if he had done the act himself. Under the law, he cannot immunize himself from criminal responsibility and wash his hands of all culpability." Vince had a habit of rattling off citations, and I knew that was important to establish credibility. He told me that the doctrine of innocent agent is codified in Title 18, US Code II (b): "Whoever willfully causes an act to be done which if directly performed by him . . . would be an offense against the United States is punishable as a principal." So, Vince concluded, George Bush cannot sit comfortably in his Oval Office while young soldiers are being killed in Iraq."

Once again, his indignation, his fury over the killings of young Americans and "hundreds of thousands, if not a million innocent Iraqis" was rising to the top.

We returned to the main legal issues that would present themselves in court—namely, why the killing of soldiers in Iraq was unlawful.

"As you know," he began, "to prosecute for murder, as in any crime, you have to show intent, or what's called in legal jargon 'malice aforethought.'"

"Right."

"And there are two types of malice: express malice, where Bush absolutely knew he would cause the death of soldiers by invading Iraq, and, at a minimum, implied malice, where all you have to show is an intent to commit a highly dangerous act with reckless and wanton disregard for the consequences and indifference to human life. You follow?"

"Certainly. Starting a war in Iraq would qualify."

"Neither of these states of mind would be criminal, however, if Bush had the legal justification that he started this war out in self-defense."

"That's the heart of the whole case, right?"

"Precisely. But I have documentary evidence that Bush knew that Saddam Hussein was not a threat to our country, that he did not intend to use weapons of mass destruction, and that those weapons were not even in evidence.

So there was no need to do a preemptive invasion. So his only defense for his actions falls apart. He did not act in self-defense."

He paused again, his face crinkling up as it does when he's trying to think of the best way to make an otherwise difficult point.

"I always felt that Saddam Hussein did not want to go after us," he said, returning to the central point that got him started on his crusade to bring Bush to justice. "Just judging by his actions, you could see he was a man who wanted to live! They found him hiding like a rat in the bottom of an eight-foot spiderhole. He told his captors 'Don't shoot!' for God's sake!"

Bugliosi, I was learning, had a way of seeing things for what they were. "I don't think I'm a particularly bright person," he had written in his book, "but at least in my professional life (I go through my private life blindfolded) I seem to naturally—and not as a result, I believe, of any special intelligence at all—see what's in front of me completely uninfluenced by the clothing (reputation, hoopla, conventional wisdom, etc.) put on it by others."[32]

Hmm. How did he read me? I wondered. During one of our breaks, I finally mustered up the courage to tell him that I never went to law school, that I got my license to practice law by being mentored in a Vermont law firm for four years and by "reading for the law" in preparation for taking the state and federal bar exams.[33] He never flinched. "Why, that's great!" he said, smiling at me. And whatever reservations he may have had about teaming up with me, he never let on.

Fortunately, I had the opportunity to prove I had some legal mettle that same day when we thought we had hit a snag in Vermont's conspiracy statute. For a space of about thirty minutes, my heart started that slow, sinking feeling as it occurred to me—and no doubt to Bugliosi—that his trip to Vermont might turn out to be a gigantic embarrassment because of the Vermont definition of conspiracy.

Up until that point, our plan for arguing for a a conspiracy charge against Bush came straight out of the book, so to speak. All we had to show was that Bush, sitting in Washington, conspired with one or more members of his team (say, Cheney and Rumsfeld) to commit an act (sending troops off to war in Iraq) to further the conspiracy to commit murder.

To land *jurisdiction* in Vermont, however, we had to show that some overt act had to have occurred in Vermont in furtherance of that conspiracy.

Bugliosi offered two such overt acts for starters. First, Bush announced on national television that war was imminent because Hussein was an imminent threat to national security—and directed his televised address at every citizen (and potential soldier) in the country, including into the homes of Vermonters. That was the first overt act to occur in Vermont. A second overt act involved the recruitment of Vermont soldiers in Vermont-based military recruiting centers, an act that linked directly back to Bush as commander in chief.

The relevant Vermont statute (13 VSA § 1407) reads that jurisdiction applies if "the defendant, while outside of this state, conspires with another outside of this state and an overt act in furtherance of the conspiracy is committed within this state *by any conspirator*." Uh oh. Did this mean we would have to find another conspirator in Vermont? To my relief, I found a subsequent section (1408) that helped clarify that question. "A conspiracy may be prosecuted in the county or territorial unit . . . in *which an overt act was done in furtherance of the conspiracy*." Phew.

In the course of researching, I also found a quaint Vermont homicide statute that seemed steeped in biblical meaning with a moral—if not an on-point legal—relevance to our case. That was 13 VSA § 2308, titled "False testimony with intent to cause death." The statute, which I first found cited in an 1868 Vermont case,[34] reads: "A person who willfully and corruptly bears false testimony with intent to take away the life of a person and thereby causes the life of such person to be taken, shall be guilty of murder in the first degree."

Bugliosi and I concluded that this would not necessarily help our case, since "bearing false testimony" as mentioned in the 1868 case meant lying on the witness stand, and Bush had not lied under oath. Still, the biblical commandment "Do not bear false witness against your neighbor" (Exodus 20:16 and Deuteronomy 5:20) is an exhortation not to lie, equivocate, or in any way deceive your neighbor.[35] Underlying both the ancient biblical and Vermont's legal prohibition is the theme that lying is a very serious wrong— *especially* when death results. Extrapolating from the old Vermont statute, we can give it a modern meaning: the president knowingly and intentionally lied to potential young recruits in order to induce them into going to war, knowing full well that soldiers die in war and that his lies would "therefore cause the life of such a person to be taken."

Off and running

Even with all the preparation, I could barely sleep the day before our September 18 press conference. This was not a good thing for someone who, in six hours, would be facing cameras and, no doubt, a barrage of hostile questions. My mind raced.

I'm about to challenge the president of the United States. For murder.

I've never run for public office before. I've never prosecuted a criminal case in my life.

Thank God Vincent Bugliosi will be with me. He's got credibility. He's a lawyer's lawyer, respected throughout the country. He'll be happy to serve as my special prosecutor should I be elected. That's a huge relief.

He says it will be the most important murder case in American history, and while I'm not ready to think that far ahead, I can't help but admire his courage. Surely, there's no one more capable. He's never lost a murder case.

Still, there are people who think even he's gone too far. Prosecute the president for murder? In Vermont? When Bush hasn't even set foot in Vermont?

But Bugliosi can handle it. And so can I. We've gone through every counterargument imaginable. We're ready.

I drifted off to sleep.

Kristina, who agreed to stay on in Vermont until after the press conference, woke me up at 7:00 a.m. An early riser, she was already cruising the Internet. "Your press release is just getting out there," she said. "People are already responding. It looks good."

8:00 a.m. After fussing with me, making sure I had my makeup on right and my suit on straight, Kristina hustled me out the door for our 40-minute trip to Burlington.

9:00 a.m. We arrived at Robin's house to pick up Vince. He emerged from the back room smiling, confident, and ready to go.

Once again impeccably dressed in a tan three-piece suit and matching silk tie, he walked spryly like someone with the boundless energy of a twenty-year-old. In his hand he carried a yellow legal pad where he'd handwritten all his legal arguments. Vince doesn't use a computer or the Internet, and we had already learned that he didn't own a cell phone. "I'm just one of those guys who can't get used to newfangled technology," he joked. Then he turned serious. "Are you all set? Have you worked out what you're going to say?"

"I'm ready," I said. We agreed that I would make some introductory comments about the race, letting reporters know that this was not a single-issue campaign, but that I had with me a distinguished guest who would assist me in one of my platform planks, the prosecution of George W. Bush for murder. I would then turn the mike over to him to expound on our legal arguments. He was all business now, so much all business that he refused all interviews until the press conference was over. Nothing was going to distract him from this, our opening salvo, which would set the tone of the whole campaign.

The press turnout, by Vermont standards, was reasonably good. In a medium-sized room on the second floor of a converted firehouse, I counted eight reporters, one TV camera, and several handheld videos. I realized we would be on the Web within a matter of hours.

The following morning, Kristina woke me up again. "I've just spent the past hour on the Internet" she said. "You've already got three thousand hits and it's growing every minute." By Vermont standards, those were big numbers.

But soon I would be besieged with emails from all over the country. Within a week, I had the names of people who wanted to work on my campaign, as well as calls from foreign media. It was beginning to get exciting. Now, all I needed was a campaign manager and a team of volunteers. The Little Campaign That Could was about to get off the ground.

CHAPTER FOUR

The Little Campaign That Could

The race for attorney general has never been much of a wave-maker in Vermont, but this year it was going to be different. Interview requests began to pour in from all over the country. Inquiries from the foreign press followed.

Vince called me on September 28. "There's a guy from German TV who wants to interview you for a short documentary," he said. "He's with the German equivalent of the BBC. He's okay. He interviewed me and I think you should do it, too."

Wow, I thought. This was good news. Still, I wondered what this German reporter was like. What did he think about the whole prosecution-for-murder part? I asked Vince for his read on the man.

"I think he was a little skeptical," Vince said, "but I told him all about you and he's anxious to meet you. He's going to fly to New York tomorrow and would like to call you from there to make arrangements and then he's going to Boston to interview Dean Velvel."

More good news. This meant that Larry Velvel, dean of the Massachusetts School of Law, was actually going public in his support for our campaign to prosecute Bush in the state of Vermont. Why else would he agree to be included in the documentary?

It occurred to me that there was something poignant—no, eerily appropriate —about the fact that of all the foreign reporters to take an intense interest in this story, it would be a German.

Only two weeks earlier, the Nuremberg trials of Nazi war criminals had hung heavily over the Justice Robert H. Jackson conference in Andover for "Planning the Prosecution of High Level American War Criminals." Justice Jackson, for whom the conference had been named, had been America's top prosecutor at Nuremberg, and Dean Larry Velvel, the convener of the conference, made it very clear to those in attendance that the principles embraced at Nuremberg, including condemnation of planning a war of aggression "incorporated the victors as well as the vanquished, Americans and not just Germans." Joshua Dratel, a lawyer and an editor of *The Torture Papers: The Road to Abu Ghraib*, followed up by quoting directly from Justice Jackson at the opening of the Nuremberg trial of Hermann Goering: "We must never forget that the record on which we judge these defendants today is the record on which history will judge us tomorrow. To pass these defendants a poisoned chalice is to pass it to our own lips as well."

I wondered then whether George W. Bush and his closest advisors knew what they had done to America, subverting the rule of law while assuming near dictatorial powers, launching a preemptive war against a sovereign nation under false pretenses, creating a whole new class of prisoners—"enemy combatants"—so they could be tortured with abandon, treating protestors as terrorists, and turning police forces into Gestapos. Did they have any inkling of how the poisoned chalice had touched their lips?

It all begged the question: Were Bush and his closest advisors bringing fascism to America? Author Naomi Wolf had chronicled in her book *The End of America: Letter of Warning to a Young Patriot* the ten steps that autocrats take "in order to close down a democracy or crush a pro-democratic movement." These ten steps taken together,* she argued, "are more than the sum of their parts. Once all ten have been put in place, each magnifies the power of the others and of the whole." Naomi had been going around the country warning citizens that the momentum launched by the Bush administration toward a home-grown fascism must be stopped. Even though the Democratic Party had regained control of both houses of Congress, "a breather is unearned," she said. "We can't simply relax now." I had conversed

---

*The ten steps she describes in her book are: 1) invoke an external and internal threat, 2) establish secret prisons, 3) develop a paramilitary force, 4) surveil ordinary citizens, 5) infiltrate citizens' groups, 6) arbitrarily detain and release citizens, 7) target key individuals, 8) restrict the press, 9) cast criticism as "espionage" and dissent as "treason," and 10) subvert the rule of law. These ten classic pressures, Wolf argues, "were set in motion by the Bush Administration to close down our own open society. These pressures have never been put in place before in this way in this nation" (Naomi Wolf, *The End of America* [Vermont: Chelsea Green, 2007], pp. 3 and 11).

with Naomi several times during my campaign and agreed with her whole-heartedly. I had been doing my own monitoring, too, clipping stories and putting them into a file folder that, by 2008, was 2 inches thick. I had titled it "Democracy in Trouble."

The German reporter, Dominique Gradenwitz, showed up the evening before our scheduled interview, giving us time to talk. He was at all times professional, maintaining a serious demeanor throughout the evening, his dark eyes probing mine for some insights into my *weltanschauung*—my world view. Was I sincere? How much did I believe in what I was doing? Did I really think I was going to pull it off?

I was equally curious about him. He looked to be in his thirties, maybe a generation younger than my own "politically aware" generation, but he seemed to be quite knowledgeable about the American political scene. He said he had spent some years living in the United States doing freelance productions for German TV. I figured I would ask his views about the right-ward political direction of the United States under the presidency of George W. Bush.

"Surely," I said at one point, "you must see parallels in this country to what the Germans were facing in the 1930s. We're watching our democracy go down the tubes. Bush is acting like he's the king, like he can do anything he wants. And the press and the Congress have literally let him get away with murder." He nodded gravely and pointed out that perhaps now Americans would have a better "structural" understanding of the dynamics that led to the growth of fascism under the Nazis. Wolf, too, pointed out in her book and lectures that many citizens in many democracies that slip into fascism fail to notice the growing restrictions on their freedoms—until it is too late. But, across the board, the basic steps taken to close down open societies are uniform. And the Bush administration had taken many of these steps by the time this reporter and I were talking.

As our conversation wore on, I could see that Vince was right: Dominique was highly skeptical of our chances of victory. But he wanted to give Vince and me our due. I figured most people felt that way. Dominique's short documentary—which featured Bugliosi, Dean Velvel, and me—would later air throughout Germany and Switzerland in October, prompting more responses and messages of good luck from Europe.

Gearing up for battle

To win support from Vermonters, though, I had to focus on other issues that concerned Vermont voters. I contacted a state's attorney (equivalent to a district attorney) for advice. He was an imaginative thinker who had dared to publicly oppose Vermont's draconian drug laws, so I figured he'd have an open mind about my campaign. Shortly into our conversation he let me know that he would not stray from his support of incumbent William Sorrell. Despite this caveat, he tried to be helpful. "The first thing people will want to know," he said, "is, why do you want to be attorney general?"

Why indeed? I had agreed to run for the position before I had even heard of Bugliosi's book. But the more I explored the AG position, the more I realized that it carried a significant amount of power and, if handled correctly, it could mean the power to do a lot of good. The Office of the Attorney General, with its eighty-some attorneys, had the authority to protect and defend the citizenry not just against high crimes, but also against fraud, discrimination, and pollution. I studied the home page of Sorrell's official Web site.

> Our mission is to implement and enforce Vermont's laws to improve the quality of life for all Vermonters. Whether this means enforcing our criminal laws to keep our cities, towns, and homes safe, or vigorously pursuing those who would foul our air, land, and water, it is the job of this office to bring the legal resources of the State to . . . protect our citizens.

"Vigorously pursue"—now that was a useful phrase to put up against the incumbent's actual record. My initial research indicated that Sorrell's approach was more laid-back than vigorous, especially when it came to addressing citizens' concerns about the health and safety risks posed by the Vermont Yankee nuclear plant in southern Vermont,[36] one of the oldest nuclear power plants in the country. (By comparison, the Massachusetts attorney general has been far more aggressive in raising citizens' concerns about their own aging nuclear power plant, the Pilgrim, to the Nuclear Regulatory Commission.)[37] Vermont had the unique distinction of being the only state in the nation where the decision to relicense or close Vermont Yankee in 2012 rested with the state legislature. This made Yankee—and Entergy, the big out-of-state corporation that owned it—a hot-button issue, and deservedly so.

I would soon discover distinct legal parallels between Entergy's mistreatment of Vermonters and Bush's mistreatment of Americans. Twisting the law to serve policy objectives was as much a part of Entergy's MO as Bush's. In both cases, I would get an education on how political power operated on the highest levels, whether governmental or corporate.

At this early stage, however, I had little to go on except Attorney General Sorrell's formal statements to the press and his official statements on his Web site. Clearly, he liked to see himself as a champion of protecting the environment. That came with his job description, of course. It was also an important issue in a state full of natural-born environmentalists. In September, 2008, Sorrell gave an interview that startled me in its implications. "When acid rain comes from Midwestern power plants and directly affects Vermont," he told a reporter, "if someone thinks I should put my head in the sand about that, that is ridiculous. I wouldn't be doing my job and the voters would rightfully turn me out of office."[38]

Now this was choice. The attorney general was effectively saying that the voters could run him out of office if he didn't deal with out-of-state polluters. Following that logic, I wondered what he would say about out-of-state government officials who also brought harm to Vermonters. Granted, the Midwestern polluter was subject to civil litigation, and Bush et al. to criminal prosecution—but still, the underlying principle was the same. Surely, if the criminal defendant conspired *outside* the state (in my case, Bush spreading lies on TV to convince American soldiers to go off to war) and caused harm *inside* the state (misleading Vermont soldiers to go to war on a false pretext, more than twenty never to return home alive), then how could Sorrell argue—at least in principle—that Bush could not be criminally prosecuted in Vermont under the well-recognized effects doctrine?[39]

In other words (I was tempted to argue), isn't what's good for Midwestern power plants also good for the president of the United States? Both "outsiders" caused harmful effects in Vermont and should be held to account. I decided to raise this in my debates.

In a related matter, Vermont, unlike Massachusetts and New York, had a shockingly bad record when it came to offering legal whistleblower protection to its workers. In fact, it ranked the lowest of all fifty states, offering no laws *at all* protecting whistleblowers, except for some recent legislation won by unionized nurses at Vermont's largest hospital. For a state that prided itself on being in the vanguard on so many social issues, this last-place rating was to me both unacceptable and unimaginable. Was Vermont's lack of whistleblower protection a reflection on the incumbent attorney general? In my research, I learned that a whistleblower in New York sued Entergy under state whistleblower laws and convinced a New York judge to rule in 2005 that Entergy wrongfully harassed and then fired the employee for reporting safety problems.

So, closing Vermont Yankee in 2012 and bringing whistleblower protection to Vermont would be two other big issues in my campaign. And there would be more, like investigating predatory bank lenders responsible for a rash of Vermont-based foreclosures, and examining local gas gougers who may have fraudulently increased the price of gas at the pump. (I discovered a huge disparity of gas prices between the northern and southern parts of the state. The question was, why?)

I was beginning to get psyched for this campaign.

Easing into the first debate—with boleros

Quarrels almost invariably develop among campaign workers, adding internal conflict to the pressures confronting a candidate from the outside. It all makes for a good story, but in my case, the personalities that became part of my campaign were the best thing about it. Beginning with Vince. Ever the gentleman, he sent me a package of "thank-you" gifts once he got back to Los Angeles—three of his previous books (on O. J. Simpson, the Supreme Court, and the Kennedy assassination)[40] and a collection of Latin love songs, or boleros, which he selected and released on CD. "It's a hobby of mine," he had told me. "Boleros are an integral part of the culture of Mexico and Cuba, where they originated. But they're heard all over Latin America. Every one of the songs in the collection is known to the people. They could be composed fifty to a hundred years ago, but they are still sung today, even by young people. Not like here."

So when the package from Los Angeles sat waiting for me upon my return to Vermont, I eagerly opened the slim envelope containing the CD of *Vincent Bugliosi Presents: Greatest Latin Love Songs of the Century.*

I read the little promotional packet that accompanied the CD.

"Vincent Bugliosi has put together, in my opinion, the best album of Latin love songs that I have ever heard," said Lucho Gatica who, Vince would later tell me, is the most famous bolero singer ever. (In the 1950s, Gatica sold more albums on the Capitol label than Frank Sinatra and Dean Martin together.)

Wrote bolero authority Nelson Henriquez, "Bugliosi's hobby and passion has been to search for the finest recording ever of each of these great songs, listening to more than a hundred different recordings of some of the more popular ones before finally deciding on the one for this very special album."

So here was yet another side to the famous prosecutor—the romantic who just had to go out and find the best of the very best recordings of all the great boleros. The embodiment of perfectionism, but this time, put in the service of culture.

Being an incurable romantic myself, I immediately got hooked. I *still* play the songs in my car, but during my campaign they served a particular practical purpose: they calmed my nerves as I drove to my debates.

The first debate in the campaign—in fact, my first debate ever—was located in the best possible setting for a neophyte TV debator: the studios of Burlington's Community Access TV, Channel 17, known for its liberal audience. (Burlington, remember, except for two short years had been under Progressive governance since Independent Bernie Sanders became mayor in 1981.) All questions had been posed in advance, so I figured there would be few surprises. Still, when I look back at the video of the debate, my behavior in the beginning was close to comical.

I looked unprepared. Two of my three opponents, the Democratic incumbent Sorrell and the Republican challenger (an open transsexual by the name of Karen Kerin) were sitting at the table with no notes, looking supremely confident. The third candidate, Rosemarie Jackowski of the Liberty Union Party from Brattleboro, was on the phone line. For the first ten minutes, I sat hunched over files, rustling through papers. Hey, I had to

field questions on a slew of subjects: Is Vermont a magnet for sexual preda-
tors? What would happen if a woman's right to choose shifted to state
jurisdiction? How would I deal with budgetary constraints? What were
my objectives as attorney general over the next two years? And yes, the
big one: Should the federal or state government pursue criminal charges
against individuals in government who may have violated laws in pursuing
the war in Iraq?

When the "big one" came up, I was warmed up—and ready—only to be
taken aback by the incumbent's unexpected attack on my character. Sorrell
accused me of violating my ethical duties as a lawyer. He said I was just
"throwing issues out there" and was not seriously pursuing justice. In short,
he accused me of violating the attorney general's oath of office.

Wow. I knew that politics could get dirty, but I was, nonetheless, inwardly
appalled. My opponent had just lashed out at me and questioned my integrity, which is something I value highly. I recall thinking: "He doesn't know
me and clearly doesn't understand why I'm in this race." I remembered—and
repeated—one of Vince's points: If you know a crime has been committed,
it is your *ethical duty to prosecute.* I emphatically described Bush's crimes and
questioned Sorrell's own "softness" on Bush and on other key issues in my
campaign, not the least of which was the need to retire the Vermont Yankee
nuclear plant.[41]

Karen Kerin, the Republican, scoffed at the notion that a federal officer
(Bush) could be tried in a state court. She insisted that the case would be
removed to a federal court. Had I had the time to respond to her, I would
have pointed out that if the federal government wanted to prosecute Bush,
all well and good, but there was nothing that indicated that was likely and
nothing that barred a state court from prosecuting him as well under the
well-established principle of dual sovereignty.[42]

A caller asked if I planned to spend taxpayers' money on the prosecution.
Vince and I anticipated this one. After all, with the way the economy was
going (the stock market had just begun its precipitous descent), this was a
legitimate question. I stated that I would supplement the cost of the prosecution by doing some fund-raising among private individuals, just like
New Orleans District Attorney Jim Garrison did for his prosecution of Clay
Shaw for conspiracy to murder in the Kennedy assassination. Sorrell looked

shocked and bewildered that I would try to raise money from private citizens. I wondered if he would raise this again, but he never did.

Putting the team together

October 7: One debate down, one more to go (at Vermont Public Radio) and only one month left in the campaign.

The Vermont press, having sympathetically covered our press conference, now seemed to shy away from my race. Was the novelty over? Or had editors gotten word from on high to retreat into silence? The three major dailies had declined to print my op-ed responses to the snarky put-downs by Sorrell and the Republican National Committee and ignored my letters to the editor. Disturbed but not surprised—after all, the press outside of Vermont had effectively blacklisted Bugliosi's book—Vince suggested I call up his friend Bob Alexander in Seattle, the gourmet coffee merchant who was selling *The Prosecution* on his Web site. "See if he can be your Web master," Bugliosi counseled. We figured if no one in the mainstream media would allow us to elaborate on our arguments, we'd post them on the Web site.

So I called up Bob Alexander and found a sympathetic ear. Like so many of the people who supported my campaign, he was disgusted with the Democratic Party's politically expedient inaction on impeachment, and equally disgusted over the mere thought of Bush actually getting away with murder for what he had done in Iraq. In July, 2008, Alexander had read Vince's book and was instantly galvanized into action. "Just when I thought Bush, Cheney, and Rice would walk away from their crimes, I read this book and thought, 'Here, at last, something could be done to help put right their horrible wrongs.'"

Up until that moment, he and his wife had been the relatively quiet proprietors of SuperBeans.com, selling gourmet coffee on the Web from Hawaii and elsewhere. After reading Vince's book and hearing him speak in Seattle, they were determined to get his book in front of as many people as possible. A friend called and asked if he could get a copy of the book to Seattle's local district attorney. "That's when I got this idea," Alexander told me. "Let's send this book, written by a preeminent prosecuting attorney, to every DA in the country. Another attorney would read what Bugliosi was writing about, and then maybe do something."

Bob and his wife set up a Web page, prosecutegeorgebush.com. Its mission statement: "There are 2,700 District Attorneys in the United States. We intend to send a copy of *The Prosecution of George W. Bush for Murder* to every single one of them." This came with a message to his coffee bean customers: "In lieu of buying coffee this month . . . please consider purchasing Vince Bugliosi's book instead."

Their site went up live on September 17, 2008—ironically, the day before Vince and I had our press conference. Shortly after, money started to pour in to their Web site. All it took was Vince appearing on the Mike Malloy Show, a progressive talk show that is part of Air America.

"Sure, I'll host your Web site," Bob said when I called and asked for help. Within a day, he moved it from my temporary location on the Vermont Progressive Party Web site. The party's director, Morgan Daybell, helped me set up a Paypal account, worked with Bob, and within a few days we were off and running.[43] Up went every article on the press conference. Up went my op-ed responding to Sorrell and the Republican National Committee. Up went a section for all the other issues in my campaign, plus a bio and links to other Web sites.[44] And in rolled the money for the campaign, over $30,000, mostly in small donations from out of state because Vince Bugliosi was giving out my Web address over the radio and at speeches every chance he could get.

Momentum—that's what every campaign needs, and now, within a matter of days, it was practically sweeping me off my feet. I was getting calls from people in Vermont and all across the country.

Probably the most helpful call came from Susan Serpa, leader of the Northeast Impeachment Coalition. Bugliosi had called her and urged her to support my candidacy, which she did.

Sue had no need for politics before the ascension of George W. Bush to the presidency. Like many women, she considered politics "a bad reason for good people to fight with each other." The daughter of a World War II B-17 bomber pilot, she was content to manage the finance department of a large Boston law firm and in her spare time kept up with a hobby of some thirty years: researching the genealogy of her Paine family links to the famous Revolutionary War patriot and pamphleteer, Thomas Paine.

The 2000 election season left her cold—she couldn't see much difference between Bush and Gore and ended up voting for Ralph Nader. But it didn't take long before she realized that Bush was not engaged in politics as usual. First, she got involved in environmental issues, then started going to antiwar protests. Next came Bush's assaults on the Constitution and disrespect for the rule of law.

"Here he was," Serpa later recalled, "violating the Sixth Amendment with the indefinite detention of even U.S. citizens without charge; then violating the Fourth Amendment by mining emails and phone calls and even library records without warrants, and then eroding the balance of power between the three branches of government by denying subpoenas and relying on signing statements to get his way."

She couldn't, she said, "sit by and silently witness the undoing of everything my ancestors strove to achieve." She vowed to do whatever she could to restore the rule of law. Inevitably, she got involved with the impeachment movement. "I have access to about two hundred thousand people on email," she told me. "So if you need to get a message out about your campaign, I'll be happy to help."

It didn't bother her at all that I was a Progressive. When Representative Pelosi took impeachment off the table following the Democratic victories in 2006, Serpa left the Democratic Party in disgust. She remained unaligned until September, 2008, when she attended the Republican presidential debates in Durham, New Hampshire, and discovered to her surprise and delight that it was filled with Republicans eager to take her "Impeach Bush and Cheney" buttons. "They felt the Bush administration had betrayed them and failed to support traditional Republican values," Serpa explained. She eventually registered as a Republican intent on working to take the party back from the extreme right-wing neocons.

By the time she and I talked in early October, she had become a high-profile and highly respected figure in the impeachment movement. I was, of course, eager to connect with her network of followers. We ended our conversation with her suggestion that I get in touch with another impeachment activist and friend of hers, Ralph Lopez.

"He's managed campaigns—even his own—and he has a lot of experience with the media. You might consider him for your campaign manager."

Ralph Lopez, it turns out, was a third-generation Mexican American, Yale graduate, and the son of a career Air Force man who had spent most of his life on military bases. He became disenchanted with the Bush administration in stages. He initially supported sending troops to Afghanistan to fight the Taliban because of 9/11, but became disturbed when Bush justified what appeared to be a long-term, open-ended war in Iraq based on lies. Lopez began writing in heavily trafficked political forums online, like Daily Kos. He ended up publishing a small book on impeachment with stories collected off of Daily Kos[45] and became the Northeast Impeachment Coalition's guru for creating riveting TV ads and getting them placed on YouTube as well as traditional media, like CNN and Fox News.

I called Ralph. He told me he'd love to come to Vermont and work on my campaign. In fact (no doubt tipped off by his friend Sue Serpa), he had created, on video, a draft campaign ad for me—featuring clips of Donald Rumsfeld lying about weapons of mass destruction, George Bush joking about not being able to find them, and actor Sean Penn going after both men with a searing one-liner (on the Letterman Show). Bush and Cheney, Penn said, were responsible for "deceiving people into a situation that is murdering young men and women from this country and others." Wow, I thought. Sean Penn used the word murder. But Penn went even further: Bush, Cheney, and the whole lot of them "should all be in jail." The Letterman crowd cheered. I got goose bumps. Lopez's ad impressed me.

I hired him on the spot, sight unseen. In mid-October he arrived in Burlington in Serpa's loaned 1998 Toyota, which was plastered with bumper stickers: "Republicans for Impeachment," "Democrats for Impeachment," and a big sign across the top of the back window saying "Honk for Impeachment." I could tell the moment I met this guy that he was the right man for the job. He rubbed his hands together with mirth, literally rolled up his sleeves, and said: "Point me to a computer." He had three weeks to pull my campaign together. He couldn't wait to get started. "Now *this* is a campaign worth working for," he said.

My journalist friend Kristina Borjesson returned to Vermont the same time Ralph arrived. She promised to be my press secretary and overall Girl Friday. Fortunately, she and Ralph seemed to hit it off. Ralph, with his curly black hair, dancing dark eyes and a mischievous smile, conveyed just the kind enthusiasm the campaign needed, but without pretense. "Here was this Yalie," Kristina recalls, who "came with the trappings of a serious progressive, including a rattletrap car with the gas-gauge needle perpetually hovering near empty and a big 'Impeach Bush' on the back window." And here she was, a blonde "Haitian princess" and former hotshot documentary maker driving around Burlington in the beat-up, bumper-stickered impeachment mobile doing errands in between hours hunched over her computer. For a long time, Ralph didn't realize that he was working with a top-flight journalist who had won an Emmy award for her work on CBS. She was just Kristina, "a high-energy, savvy, and super-intelligent woman" who struck him as very New York and very cool. "I knew people like her from having gone to Yale," Ralph would later tell me. "Kristina was what we'd call a 'live wire,' her elevator ran all the way to the top and then some. We had an easy kind of back-and-forth when we worked together, and between the two of us we would come up with one hell of a press release."

Ralph and Kristina would become the backbone of my campaign, reaching out to Vermonters, Americans, and (it seemed) the world.

Vince joined us in a few days. Hunkered down in Robin Lloyd's carriage house and adjoining first-floor apartment (HQ), we got down to serious work. While Vince and I did interviews and public appearances, Kristina and Ralph worked the phones and Robin's computers, Ralph focusing on creating and placing radio and TV ads with what money we had, Kristina lining up the interviews and answering, as "an advisor to Charlotte Dennett," what seemed like an avalanche of emails. The number of negative comments were tiny, but when they came in, Kristina was ready for them. Her son was a Marine, training to be a pilot. No one was going to out-patriot her.[46]

Ralph, we quickly learned, needed very little to keep him happy. He would stay glued to his station for hours. When he came up for food, it was for one kind only: "Ralph was a total pie hound," Kristina recalls. "Keeping him happy required massive daily doses of the stuff, preferably apple."

Robin, who stoically allowed her privacy to be constantly invaded and never complained (except when our cars blocked her driveway), kept a diary. Kristina, she observed, soon emerged as the chef for the group—drawing on her Scandinavian-Haitian heritage. "She cooks a piece of meat with rice and beans in the middle of the day, and people serve themselves when they wish.

No sitting around and eating together. Everyone is too busy. My house is the retreat from the business of the front office where Ralph Lopez reaches out to the world 24/7. 'You're the only one, Char, who is telling the truth,' he encourages her."

The Little Campaign That Could was now fully engaged.

The People's Attorney

As I drove to my second debate, this time on Vermont Public Radio, I once again shoved Vince's boleros into my car's CD player and turned up the volume. What was it about these beautiful songs that put my nerves at ease? I couldn't be sure, but I laughed to myself about Bugliosi's soft side. I remembered his admitting to me at one point that he'd been called "The Prosecutor with a Heart." On one of our many car rides together, he even mentioned having told mass murderer Charles Manson that he would give him a fair trial.

I arrived at the radio station fully prepared with talking points, thanks to some tips by Progressive Party Chairwoman Martha Abbott.

I noticed that the moderator did not ask me about my controversial campaign pledge to prosecute Bush, so I brought it up myself when it was my turn to question any of the three other candidates. Why, I asked Sorrell, could he say he would vigorously pursue polluters from outside the state when they did harm inside the state but could not bring himself to apply the same principle to high-level government officials who committed crimes outside the state that affected people inside the state.

He responded that I was confusing civil law with criminal law. I shot back that the "effects doctrine" was well recognized in criminal law.

He reverted to his old mantra, that the Vermont attorney general could not prosecute war crimes; they could only be prosecuted in the International Criminal Court in The Hague. I said "Wrong again—I'm going after Bush for murder, not war crimes."

I hammered him on Vermont Yankee and asked why Vermont had the worst record of whistleblower protection in the country. He seemed at a loss for words.

I ended the debate by describing myself as the People's Attorney:

"If you are losing your home because of predatory lending;

"If you want an *honest* assessment of Vermont Yankee's safety;

"If you can't pay your fuel bill because the heating company has treated you unfairly;

"If you've been discriminated against at work;

"If you've been the victim of inflated prescription-drug pricing, credit-card rip-offs, gas price gouging, and other forms of consumer fraud;

"And most of all, if you want George W. Bush prosecuted for sending Vermont's young soldiers to their deaths in Iraq: Vote for Charlotte Dennett, the People's Attorney."

People called me and sent me congratulatory emails: I had won the debate hands down, they said. But how many people had actually heard the debate? I had no idea.

I was flying blind.

The ad to end all ads

I continued to appear on radio shows that had been set up by Vince thousands of miles away. Donations continued to pour in from all over the country. A freelance reporter from the *Toronto Star* came to Vermont to cover our campaign. She walked into Robin's house just as Kristina, true to the Girl Friday role she had graciously offered to fill, was putting my hair up in curlers. We all laughed, conscious that my down-home, do-it-yourself campaign was in stark contrast to the carefully managed and fully wardrobed campaign of another female candidate for office also in the news: Sarah Palin.

Our spirits were high. We all felt momentum going our way. Susan Harman, another activist connected with the impeachment network, drove to Vermont from her home in Martha's Vineyard several times to pass out literature, organize events, and goad me to get "seasonal" pictures taken of me campaigning. She was indefatigable. Months later, she would spend hours researching which districts in all fifty states had lost soldiers in the war in Iraq to assist any future district attorney who might consider bringing a case against Bush.

With just two weeks left, we relied primarily on producing ads for cable TV and radio to reach voters across the state. Ralph's Sean Penn ad stalled on copyright protections, something I had worried about (as a writer) from the beginning. Ralph crafted a new ad, which did not pass muster. I began to doubt my new campaign manager. But Ralph, rather than fight me on this, hunkered down.

He stayed up all night working on a new ad, and by morning, presented it to our team: It was amazing, the kind of visual and emotional event that sent chills up your spine. To the sound of muted drumbeats, we watched Bush joking at an official press dinner about not being able to find the weapons of mass destruction. Next we saw an airplane hold full of flag-draped coffins. Then Bush again, accompanied by mirthful laughter as he looked under his lectern. "Those weapons must be somewhere!" Mournful music became louder, with heartbreaking scenes of families mourning their dead at gravesites and lowered coffins. Next, Bugliosi was giving his most dramatic testimony at the House Judiciary Committee about how Bush ignored the conclusion of the CIA about Saddam Hussein not being a threat, and lied a few days later to Congress and the American people in an official presidential white paper: "The conclusion of U.S. intelligence—that Saddam Hussein was *not* an imminent threat to the security of this country—was completely deleted! . . . Whether Republican or Democratic, all Americans should be outraged over what the Bush Administration has done. How *dare* they do what they did." With sixty seconds almost up, the ad faded to black, and then a stark statement in white letters appeared:

> "If elected, Charlotte Dennett will prosecute George W. Bush under the laws of the state of Vermont, which has lost more soldiers in Iraq per capita than any other state."

Pause, as the mournful music continued. Then, a new frame:

> "She will appoint Vincent Bugliosi as Special Prosecutor."

Pause.

> "Elect Charlotte Dennett Attorney General of Vermont."

We cheered Ralph and called out to Vince, who had arrived back in Burlington the night before. He liked it! The ad had struck an emotional chord with all of us. For Vince, this was important. He had shaped his entire case around an emotional as well as legal underpinning: the commander in chief had deceived us all, while sending innocent young men and women to war and to their unnecessary deaths.

Under pressure

As the campaign heated up, there were moments of hilarity that, in retrospect, show the kind of pressures we were feeling. Ralph recalls the evening he went out with Vince and others in the campaign and, during dinner, began to joke about the dangers of going up against the Big Boys. I wasn't at this dinner, but this is how Ralph remembers it:

> It suddenly hit us that what we were doing was nothing less than taking on, bar none, the most powerful men in the world, and that if our message took hold we would draw the attention, if we hadn't already, of perhaps some very dangerous people. We were out there on radio and TV and saying things that in many countries would cause you to disappear, or be put in jail, or what have you. We were simply exercising our right of free speech in a democracy and, to be sure, were maybe just gnats biting an elephant, but we didn't really know, in the end, what we were dealing with.
>
> Someone said something about the mysterious suicide of the D.C. madame Heidi Fleiss. It was well known that she had a little black book which was explosive—congressmen, senators, everyone—and that many of her friends knew that she was the kind of woman who would never commit suicide. Maybe she even said this beforehand. Then we talked a bit about Danny Casolaro, the independent reporter in the '80s who was found dead in a bathtub in Virginia—an apparent suicide—at a time when he was working on a story about Bush-family connections in the Iran-Contra scandal, BCCI bank, and

something that was emerging in his writing, which he was calling "the Octopus." Those who knew Casolaro said he was entirely too full of life to ever take his own life.

I, or someone, joked that perhaps there should be a standardized form when applying for a job such as we had, that you signed and that said "This is a statement to the world that I will never commit suicide, and efforts to say I have are false." You fill out tons of paperwork for any job anyway, like W-2s and background checks and company-policy statements. This could be a standard form particular to our line of work. Vince laughed and laughed, as we all did, but he especially seemed to enjoy it.

Probably Vince was so used to being alone in his daring crusades that it was refreshing for him to be able to find himself in the company of others who shared his passion for justice and were willing to take risks for it. And when I look back on it, I think it is precisely because we *knew* we were risking a lot—careers, reputations, even perhaps our lives—that we felt a special bond.

And, clearly, we were all exhausted. But with just two weeks left, we forged ahead. Our Little Campaign That Could now traveled to southern Vermont, to White River Junction, Brattleboro, then back to Rutland. The audiences were small, certainly by Vince's West Coast standards, and he began to wonder if Vermont was the progressive little state that we had all bragged about.

Where, he asked, were the throngs of ardent supporters? "I get standing-room-only crowds in California!"

I tried to explain: "Vermont is much smaller than California, Vince, and I barely had time to organize these events." Besides, I offered, the events were being videotaped and put on the Web. Still, the low turnouts privately worried me. Meanwhile, Jerry, who had been helping the campaign on weekends and was planting lawn signs all along the major southern towns, had been urging me to reach out to other interest groups on other issues. But I felt so overwhelmed by the prosecution issue that I could not adequately follow through.

We spent the night in the Rutland home of Jeff Taylor, who as a young lawyer prosecuted antitrust cases in Los Angeles not far from Bugliosi's office and now wanted to help. Angry over the political precedent set by Congress's refusal to impeach Bush, he had discovered an obscure rule of the House penned by Thomas Jefferson that stated that impeachment could be set in motion by a state legislature. Taylor's resulting "Rutland resolution" was resoundingly supported in state Democratic Party committees across Vermont and was adopted in the Vermont Senate, only to be defeated in the House by House Speaker Gaye Symington.[47] Taylor believed that not acting to hold Bush accountable would almost be "an act of dishonesty on my part if I did nothing about it." He offered to call Vermont attorneys to hold a forum for Vince and me, including the Vermont Bar Association, the University of Vermont, and the liberal Vermont Law School. Apparently, none responded in time.

Meanwhile, Taylor quietly told Bugliosi that Sorrell was quite popular in Vermont, part of a venerated Democratic Party family, and that our chances of winning were very slim. Neither Vince nor I let this advice deter our resolve.

We met for an hour with the editors of Vermont's leading independent newspapers, hoping that they would, if not endorse us, at least give us a fair hearing. The editors listened politely and asked intelligent questions. But our efforts were in vain. Only after I lost the election did one of those papers, *The Barre-Montpelier Times Argus*, publish something, an editorial anticipating more moves to prosecute high-level government officials, without mentioning my race in their own state.

Vince and I got a more cheerful reception at the home of Ben Cohen, one of the founders of Ben & Jerry's Ice Cream. He and Jerry Greenfield, both of whom endorsed my campaign, invited Vermonters to hear us speak. After the event, Ben and Jerry posed for a round of picture-taking with Vince and me wedged between them. We were quite the jovial foursome, and Vince thought this was a great coup. He thought we should post the picture as widely as possible and even include it in a half-page ad in *The Burlington Free Press*. But I declined to put the happy picture of Vince and me with Ben and Jerry in the ad, explaining that the subject of the ad was far too serious. Was this a mistake? I'll never know. It's the one move Vince disagreed with. "If Ben and Jerry are extremely popular among the citizens in Vermont, as I keep hearing, you have to get that picture out there," he said.

William Sorrell refused to accept our challenge to debate him on the jurisdictional issue. So, on Vince's last day in Vermont, the two of us held our own press conference outside of the Pavilion building in Montpelier, which houses the office of the attorney general.

Sorrell, predictably, was nowhere to be found. We had explained, in our press release, that we were there to give Sorrell one last chance to debate us on whether the ex-president could be prosecuted in Vermont. The only mainstream press to appear was WCAX, a CBS affiliate. The station, which had originally called us for an interview for its Sunday talk show, *You Can Quote Me*, had instead sent its lead reporter, Brian Joyce.

WCAX, known for its Republican leanings, is called by savvy Vermonters WGOP. When Joyce started firing questions at us, he seemed to be hitting us with a Republican-inspired counteroffensive: If you are going to go after Bush, you will have to go after the Democrats too, because they signed off on Bush's war.

This would be raised by Republicans on the national scene over and over again in later months, especially when the issue of torture became a hot issue.

Once again, Bugliosi was quick on his feet.

Joyce: "In Vermont, if you have information about a murder conspiracy, and if there are accessories after the fact, then Vermont law demands that you must charge them at the same time. Since Congress went along with the Bush administration with this war, are you planning to charge members of Congress as accessories?"

Bugliosi responded that fraud vitiates consent. "Members of Congress were misled. It wasn't Congress who put soldiers in their graves. It was Bush."

Besides, he added, in order to be charged with being an accessory after the fact, two other things had to be shown. One, that the members of Congress had had knowledge that Bush took the nation to war on a lie and, secondly, with that knowledge, Congress then took affirmative steps to help him avoid arrest and prosecution.

Bugliosi put the onus back on the reporter. "What affirmative steps did they take to help make sure that Bush was not arrested?"

Joyce: "There is no arrest warrant."

That didn't prove anything, Bugliosi said. "You have to show they took an affirmative, active step to help the defendant avoid arrest. Do you have any evidence of this?"

No answer.

The reporter let up, and in the broadcast eliminated this exchange. The viewer saw Bugliosi and me stating that the president was not above the law and should be prosecuted. But the broadcast omitted entirely our claim that Vermont had jurisdiction and ignored that we had challenged Sorrell to a debate on this very issue. The last thing the viewer heard was Sorrell's statement that Vermont did not have jurisdiction. So much for a debate. Sorrell got the last word; and the last word, once again, made our cause seem foolish.

This episode alone showed that media distortions were to be expected in any effort to prosecute high-level officials.

Bugliosi decided to return home, figuring (rightly) that he could do more good boosting the campaign and fund-raising on the West Coast, where, I had told him from previous experience, the media were less controlled. If we weren't going to get the local media coverage we sought, we could at least raise more awareness of our campaign west of the Mississippi. Vince's radio appearances out west continued to work wonders with listeners, who responded to his appeals for money by sending me campaign donations right up to the last day of the campaign.

The final few days were a blur of last-minute interviews and appearances.

Our campaign had hoped to make one final media event on the last day of the campaign with a joint press conference with the Progressive candidate for Congress, Iraq war veteran Thomas Hermann; Carlos Arredondo and his wife, Mélida, active members of Gold Star Families for Peace; and myself. Arredondo had made international news in 2004 over the death of his son in Iraq. He became so distraught when Marines came to his Florida home with the tragic news that he rushed to his garage, grabbed a can of gasoline and a lighter, ran to the Marine van, and set fire to himself and the van. The Marines pulled him from the burning vehicle, but not before he suffered second- and third-degree burns over much of his body. After his year-long recovery, he and his wife became outspoken critics of the war in Iraq. They appeared at the Andover conference, where they spoke and displayed, on large posterboards, pictures of their son, his letters home—even a picture of him lying in his coffin. They had warned me at the Andover conference in September that finding Gold Star families to publicly oppose the war was very difficult[48] and that this was still the situation. The night before the press conference, Mélida called to say that Arredondo had been involved in a minor accident with his truck in New Hampshire. He would not be able to come to Vermont as planned.

This was disappointing news, as it would have put a human face to the suffering as a result of the war in Iraq. As it was, there was very little press coverage of the war during the last months of the 2008 elections, an inexplicable omission considering the widespread opposition to the war in both Vermont and the nation. Only later, after talking to other progressive candidates, would I realize just how complicit the mainstream media had become in backing the issues defined by the two-party candidates, while ignoring the antiwar candidates.

One of the candidates I spoke with was Cindy Sheehan, the nationally known mother who had set up Camp Casey outside of Bush's Texas ranch in 2005 to protest her son Casey's death in Iraq. That action had turned her into an instant media celebrity. But when she ran for Congress against Nancy Pelosi in California in 2008, she was confronted with an entirely different situation. Just getting her name on the ballot had been a huge challenge, requiring ten thousand signatures from voters. After a Herculean effort involving countless speaking engagements, meetings with civil organizations in Pelosi's district of San Francisco, and getting help from scores of grassroots organizers, Sheehan succeeded in becoming the sixth person in the history of California to be listed on the ballot as an Independent. She was thrilled, thinking that at last she would give voters in her state the chance to challenge the powerful Speaker of the House for failing to end the war in Iraq or to get impeachment hearings going against Bush and Cheney.

"I am even more convinced now than I was a year ago that the people of San Francisco are ready," she told Linda Milazzo of The Huffington Post, "to lead the way to step outside of the dated two-party system and elect someone who truly represents San Francisco values, not party loyalties and criminal activities."[49]

But once her campaign got off the ground, Cindy Sheehan discovered the same thing I did: Local media, so vital for covering the issues she wanted to raise to voters, just backed away. "When I was going up against George W. Bush, I had half the country behind me," she told me. "When I went up against Nancy Pelosi, I got no support. . . . I knew that 63 percent of the people of San Francisco favored impeachment of Bush, but we were shut out by the press."[50]

I was amazed. Here was a woman who had been covered all over the country for her vigil outside Bush's ranch in Crawford, Texas—but when it came to directly challenging a very powerful member of Congress, she found herself iced out.

Cindy and I found something else in common in our two campaigns: the incumbents' refusal to debate us. If you put the two phenomena together, you can understand why we did not garner as many votes as we had hoped. Both of us were in a four-way race against a powerful Democratic Party incumbent. Both of us ran in liberal areas. In fact, in San Francisco, over 60 percent of the voters favored an impeachment resolution in 2006, a percentage identical to Vermonters' known opposition to the war in Iraq. Yet Cindy only got 17 percent of the vote; I got only 6 percent. In both cases, the incumbents won handily.

"We tried very hard to get our message out, but it is very hard when the media do not listen to your message," Cindy had told the *San Francisco Chronicle*.[51] And the incumbent's refusal to debate, for her, was a slap in the face, a show of disrespect.

I couldn't have agreed more. Some might say, "That's politics." I would say, "That's just one more lesson in what to expect from taking on the powerful."

Does that mean we shouldn't keep trying? Absolutely not. Cindy and I discovered yet another thing in common: We both felt the need to write a book about our experiences. Hopefully, our combined knowledge will add a few more steps to victory on the accountability trail.

CHAPTER FIVE

What Does It Take to Prosecute the Powerful?

Before Election Day, Ralph and Kristina, my stalwart campaign workers, returned to their home states to vote. Jerry and I were alone, sitting in Robin's kitchen in front of the TV when the results began to trickle in around 9:00 p.m. We watched WCAX, Vermont's CBS affiliate, and that meant watching its veteran anchorman, Marselis Parsons, the man who had inexplicably canceled our appearance on the local Sunday talk show, *You Can Quote Me*. He announced, without a hint of emotion, that William Sorrell had easily won reelection, noting that the Progressive candidate, with 40 percent of the returns in, had received only 4 percent of the vote. "This is the candidate who vowed to prosecute George W. Bush for murder," he said, looking down at his papers as if—as if what? As if to say, "We always knew this was a lost fringe cause. In fact, he had done his part to make sure it was."

I was stunned, as was Jerry, by the poor showing. That low? In Vermont? How was it possible? Everyone I had met on the campaign trail had given me high-fives. "You got my vote!" they invariably said. By 10:00 p.m. the results were up to 5.7 percent, and the final tally would be 5.9 percent, but that was small consolation. To be sure, I was a "third-party candidate" in a four-way race, but even tough campaigns have a way of building up the candidate's hopes that miracles can happen.

I felt like I had betrayed my supporters, but most of all I felt like I had betrayed Vince Bugliosi. Here I had bragged about what a great little progressive state Vermont was, and Vermonters gave me only 5.9—well, let's round it off and say 6 percent of the vote.

Later that evening, around 11:00 p.m., Jerry and I were heading over to a Progressive Party gathering in downtown Burlington when we heard wild cheers coming out of Nectar's bar. Obama had been proclaimed the winner in the presidential race (with Vermont the first state to declare, with what would turn out to be the highest percentage next to that of Obama's original home state of Hawaii). Within minutes, hundreds, then thousands of students were streaming down to Burlington's central Church Street. Filling the streets, they shouted "Obama! Obama!" with such jubilation that we were as shocked and happy by this display as we were stunned and dismayed by my own results. We were both supporters of Obama, and his victory took the edge off my defeat.

I spent the next month trying to make sense of my campaign. Where did we go wrong? What happens next? What role would I play?

As noted earlier, many factors played into the campaign results. But three stood out: Democrats, invigorated by the Obama candidacy, voted a straight ticket; Sorrell had misrepresented our legal arguments to the media; and we simply didn't have enough time or money to reach enough voters.

The last point may have been one of the biggest factors. One of our campaign volunteers, the ever-imaginative Kurt Daims of friendly Brattleboro, sent an email about an informal exit poll he had done on election day. On that day, only 10 percent of respondents in Brattleboro had heard of me. By the same token, only one in five voters knew the incumbent by his name. His conclusion: "This was definitely a party-line election. The voters may have been so excited about Obama that they voted Democratic for everything."

Other than the small consolation that 10 percent name recognition was an improvement over 4 percent from an informal poll he had done on October 18, it seemed pretty clear that one public appearance in Brattleboro and a radio interview had had only limited success.

I asked Ralph Lopez what he thought about our TV ad coverage, and he said that in order to have a major impact on voters, you have to really *saturate* the airtime during the last couple of months of an election, running your ad over and over again throughout the day, preferably on network television. Vermont's cable TV market, where we ran our ads, was not that large, and the ads ran only three times a day. Then Ralph reminded me of something: The Brattleboro cable TV station had refused to accept our ad. Of all places! I couldn't help but think if the ad had run, we would have picked up a lot more votes from Brattleboro, the town that voted to arrest Bush if he stepped foot in Vermont.

Friends consoled me that I should be pleased by the fact that seventeen thousand Vermonters voted for me—and for the prosecution of Bush for murder. "That's not bad for someone getting into the race as late as you did," they said. I thought about Kurt Daims's belief that since 60 percent of Vermonters strongly disapproved of Bush, I would win the campaign if I just focused on the prosecution issue alone. Neither of us had factored in the short time we had to reach voters, and I think Jerry was also right that I should have reached out to more people on other issues like the environment, women's issues, and how to deal with sex offenders.

As time went by, I would discover other factors that hurt my campaign indirectly. I learned, for instance, that Bruce Fein, a former Justice Department lawyer under Ronald Reagan—and, despite being a Republican, a fierce critic of the Bush administration (he testified the same day as Bugliosi at Representative John Conyers' July, 2008, hearings)—had been highly critical of Bugliosi. Fein, Bugliosi learned, was at a fund-raising party at Sean Penn's house for Independent candidate Cindy Sheehan (then running for Congress against Representative Nancy Pelosi), and in a conversation with West Coast activist/Sheehan supporter Cynthia Papermaster had discouraged Papermaster from showing any support for my campaign. Bugliosi had asked for some support, especially since the war in Iraq was an issue common to both our campaigns.[52]

Fein, Bugliosi later told me, insisted that President Bush had immunity from prosecution. But when Bugliosi challenged him on this, Fein refused to debate. "He got the law all wrong," Bugliosi told me. "Remarkably, he cited a civil case, *Nixon v. Fitzgerald*,[53] to me about presidential immunity, which I told him was not applicable to criminal cases *at all*."

Wrong about the law, then refusing to debate? That sounded familiar. In fact, it was identical to what I had confronted with my opponent, William Sorrell. Bugliosi showed me where Fein had jotted down "Read *Nixon v. Fitzgerald*" in the margin of his, Bugliosi's, book. "He told me that Bush had complete immunity as the two of us sat next to each other on July 25 before the House Judiciary Committee."

When I brought up his exchange with Fein again, in January, 2009, it was clear to me that he was still upset. Not only because Fein, a highly respected constitutional lawyer, got the law wrong, but because he had apparently interfered in my campaign by persuading possible supporters to stay away. "I can't allow you to do this," Bugliosi had told Fein. "The decent and honorable thing to do is for the two of us to have a debate."[54] Not surprisingly, it never happened.

Velvel points the way

Recovering from a campaign defeat is like recovering from any loss: You go through stages—denial and disbelief, perhaps some anger, and eventually acceptance. After a few weeks of rest and recovery, I found myself traveling to the Boston area and decided to pay a side visit to Dean Lawrence Velvel at the Massachusetts School of Law. As a major backer of my campaign, he deserved to be briefed. I wanted to tell him how hard we had all tried, how beautifully we had all worked together, and how disappointed we were with the results. I still felt that I had let down a wonderful group of people who had been working on the prosecution issue ever since that historic September conference in Andover.

The conference had been held in a hotel, so this was my first opportunity to see Velvel's law school. Two things struck me right away: It was new and nicely landscaped—a modern-looking, three-story, red-brick building set comfortably among trees and shrubs; and its adjoining parking lot, at 6:00 p.m., was full of cars. The impression I got was of a welcoming rather than intimidating law school that catered to night students.

Velvel, who had been waiting for me in his office, looked more like a Vermonter than a law-school dean. He was dressed in blue jeans and a flannel shirt. He listened quietly as I briefed him, telling him about our ups and downs and the many obstacles placed in our path by my opponents, along with an increasingly indifferent, if not hostile, media. To my surprise, he gave me words of encouragement. He told me he had failed many, many times in his life. Great movements often take years, even decades, to build, he said. That's what happened with the civil rights movement, the labor movement, and the women's movement. So take heart, he said. Big things start small. I thanked him for that, and ended up adding that insight in thank-you notes to my supporters.

Before I left, I asked Velvel about himself: "Who *are* you, anyway?" I asked with a smile. "How did you dare hold a conference for lawyers on the subject of prosecuting high-level officials—while they were still in office?" He gave me a book describing the origins of the Massachusetts School of Law and a huge, four-part memoir chronicling his growing disillusionment with the legal profession.[55] As I skimmed through them later, I quickly understood that Velvel was as unusual as the conference he sponsored. He was deeply affected by the civil-rights movement and the Vietnam War and had been irritating the establishment ever since. His biggest claim to fame was what he was doing now: heading up a law school for working-class students who otherwise would never have a chance of attending one of the nation's elite American Bar Association–approved law schools. Now it all made sense.

Velvel would subsequently send me the CDs of the September conference, and these verbatim discussions would act as a touchstone for me as I tried to figure out what options remained for anyone who deeply cared about holding a lawless administration accountable for its crimes.

Were prosecutions—at the very least, for war crimes—the way to go? If so, should they occur in Washington, D.C., on a federal level, or in any of the separate states, or abroad? If not prosecutions, what about congressional investigations or truth commissions, like the one in South Africa?

As these other options were passionately debated back in September at the Andover conference, a lawyer from England gave his perspective on what lay ahead. Philippe Sands, an intelligent-looking man with closely cut hair and wire-rimmed glasses, was clearly no average lawyer. He was the author of *Lawless World*, a fascinating account of the evolution of international law and how it has achieved new legitimacy in holding war criminals accountable, and *Torture Team*, an exposé on Donald Rumsfeld's authorization of torture in 2002. His crisp, concise delivery that Saturday revealed that he was as comfortable discussing the law—whether international, British, or American—as he was wary of prognosticating outcomes or rendering his own judgments on Americans as a British lawyer.

Sands did not want to prejudge what would happen in the U.S. regarding possible prosecutions of high-level officials. Nor did he feel comfortable anticipating what would happen if the lawyers who advised high government officials should or would be prosecuted for engaging in a conspiracy to commit torture (by counseling their bosses in how to skirt laws against torture).

But what I found most compelling—and hopeful for the future—was Sands's anecdote about his experience as counsel for Human Rights Watch. He had been talking with the lawyer representing Chilean dictator Augusto Pinochet during Pinochet's extradition hearings in England in 1997. "Pinochet's lawyer admitted that it never occurred to him that his earlier advice to Pinochet, to sign the UN Convention Against Torture in 1984, would actually remove Pinochet's immunity from extradition to Spain years later," Sands said. (In 1998, Pinochet was arrested in England on ninety-four counts of torture against Spanish citizens during his last year as head of state in Chile. Both Chile and the UK, by signing and ratifying the Convention, had waived all immunities for those accused of the crime of torture.) Sands's point was this: "You never know what will happen. This happened twenty-five years ago and ten years after Pinochet left office. Things take time. There is a lot of evidence already on the crimes of the Bush administration, but it will take time for things to come out and it takes time to figure out how to proceed."

So, now, with my campaign for attorney general behind me, it began to dawn on me that my campaign for accountability—and for democracy—was not yet over.

Probing the powerful

"Know your enemy" is a powerful adage for anyone engaged in struggle, whether military or political. I decided that if I were going to be part of a movement that would inevitably engage the powerful on a national level, I would have to investigate who was on which side on the prosecution issue. In other words, I needed to know who wanted to prosecute for war crimes and torture, and who believed in prosecuting for murder and conspiracy to commit murder, and who wanted nothing to do with prosecutions whatsoever.

By the time Americans gave Obama his landslide presidential victory in November, one thing was becoming clear: Even if, assuming for the sake of argument, the American people wanted to prosecute George W. Bush for sending troops to war on false pretenses, members of Congress were staying clear of the war and all that devolved from that war, including a murder charge against Bush. President-elect Obama had already made it clear that he intended to send more troops to Afghanistan, so many Democrats felt uncomfortable addressing war in general, and specifically the "good war" in Afghanistan (the war purportedly being fought to get the Taliban for harboring Osama bin Laden and committing terrorist acts against their own people). Between the September, 2008, primary and the November elections, the wars in Iraq and Afghanistan seldom came up.

During the much-watched first one hundred days of the Obama administration, the ongoing war in Iraq had become virtually invisible and the war in Afghanistan was beyond debate. Liberal lawyers (many of whom were politicians and vice versa) thought that going after Bush and Cheney for authorizing the crime of torture was the more practical way to go, something I well understood. You've got to pick your battles, and the public's revulsion over torture, already evidenced post–Abu Ghraib, was easier to tap.

Waterboarding, which involved submersing a suspect in water to create the sensation of drowning, was a form of mock execution and was clearly a violation of the UN Convention Against Torture. Both Bush and Cheney had *admitted* in December, 2008, to authorizing waterboarding, the same time that the Senate Armed Services Committee put out a bipartisan "Inquiry into the Treatment of Detainees in U.S. Custody" that was so explicit and so clear as to who was responsible that even *The New York Times* called for criminal prosecutions against top officials. "We can understand that Americans may be eager to put these dark chapters behind them," the *Times* editorialized on December 15, 2008, "but it would be irresponsible for the nation and a new administration to ignore what has happened. . . . A prosecutor should be appointed to consider criminal charges against top officials at the Pentagon and others involved in planning the abuse."[56]

Prosecuting for murder, on the other hand, took a lot more explaining, especially since the murder charge was being aimed at the president while he served as commander in chief. And especially when many Americans still believed that Saddam Hussein needed to be removed.

That Americans wanted *some* kind of reckoning after eight years of lawless and undemocratic behavior in the Bush administration was clear. Even before the Obama administration took over in mid-January, 2009, appointing a special prosecutor to investigate Bush-era crimes was the number-one wish-list entry on Obama's official Web site.

On the day after his inauguration, President Obama seemed to be acknowledging the depth of the American people's sentiments when he signed two executive orders, one declaring an intent to close Guantánamo and the other banning torture. But he did not ban renditions, or kidnappings of suspected terrorists to foreign prison sites where their fate was uncertain, despite his ban on torture. This "oversight" caused a flurry of anxious speculation among human-rights activists. Was it a sign that he would actually hold on to some of Bush's policies with regard to detainees? Their concern turned into alarm when on February 9, Obama's own Department of Justice urged a federal appeals court to *dismiss* a lawsuit brought by the American Civil Liberties Union against a subsidary of Boeing for its role in transporting five kidnapped men to secret prisons where they were tortured. Citing the Bush-era mantra of "state secrets," the DOJ's lawyers argued that national security would be undermined if the lawsuit were permitted to continue.

The American public, on the other hand, seemed ready to give Obama's new attorney general, Eric Holder, time to get a grip over his department, which during the Bush administration had come under congressional scrutiny for its firings of U.S. Attorneys deemed to be disloyal to Bush's conservative agenda. As I watched speculation mount in the press and on the Web as to what kind of attorney general Eric Holder was going to be, I realized that I, too, had become intensely interested in what would happen next.

In short, I was hooked on accountability. Not just because I'd been privately chronicling the growing threats to our democracy, but also because my campaign had tapped into a national angst, a palpable desire by thousands of Americans to bring the president and his ilk to justice. Would this movement succeed? If so, how and when?

It was around this time that I decided to write a book about my experiences, both as a candidate and as a postelection accountability advocate. I would follow the ride, wherever it took me.

I began by doing a closer study of the four key players in the Democratic Party—those who, if given the nudge, could play a major role in prosecuting the higher-ups in the Bush administration, if not for murder, at least for torture: President Barack Obama, Attorney General Eric Holder, and the chairs of the House and Senate Judiciary Committees—John Conyers and Patrick Leahy, respectively. All had subpoena power, and the congressional chairs of the two committees could ask Holder to appoint a special prosecutor.

1. President Obama: Holder's boss, leader of the Democratic Party, and, to quote George W. Bush, The Decider

Presumably, Obama was—and is—on the side of the righteous, although his prevarications on any kind of criminal prosecution both immediately before and after his inauguration were frustrating and, it seemed, deliberately vague.

Right before his inauguration: Obama had made his famous hedging statement: "We are still evaluating. . . . We're going to be looking at past practices and I don't believe anyone is above the law. On the other hand, I also have a belief we need to look forward as opposed to looking backwards. . . . My orientation is going to be moving forward."

In other words, maybe he would, and maybe he wouldn't. Best reading: If he wanted his attorney general to prosecute Bush administration officials for their authorization of war crimes after "looking at past practices," then it would be the AG to take the lead—because no one "is above the law." But he, the president, could still move forward and get on with other business.

At the inauguration: "Our time of standing pat and protecting narrow interests and putting off unpleasant decisions, that time has surely past. . . . Our Founding Fathers drafted a charter to ensure the rule of law. We will not give up those rules for expedience's sake."

This was vaguely promising. The upholder of the rule of law was, in fact, Holder. And with a *USA Today* poll finding in early February that a majority of Americans favored some form of an investigation into Bush-era abuses (with only one-third opposed), Holder had to be feeling the pressure to prosecute.

2. Eric Holder: The Implementer and Upholder

Holder, at first, was just as careful as the president, beginning at his confirmation hearings in mid-January: *"No one is above the law, and we will follow the evidence, the facts, the law, and let that take us where it should."*

Or, as Obama said, "We're . . . looking at past practices"—*"but we don't want to criminalize policy differences."*

This sounded like a nod to conservatives and the CIA, both adamantly opposed to any prosecution whatsoever. It didn't seem to matter that the real issue here was violating the laws against torture. Forget about "policy differences"; the Bush administration had broken the law.

Holder also sounded a bit like Obama when he said on the campaign trail that he didn't want to engage in a "partisan witch hunt." "One of the things I think I'm going to have to do is to become more familiar with what happened that led to the implementation of these policies."

Now this sounded like he was in favor of some kind of investigation. As in, "What led to the torture policies?" And at least here Holder did not mince words. He stated, flat out, at his confirmation hearings, with prodding from Vermont Senator Patrick Leahy, that waterboarding was torture.

Since torture violated the UN Convention Against Torture, of which the U.S. was a signatory, people in the Bush administration were engaging in illegal behavior. And if anyone cared to doubt Holder and prevent his confirmation, he could fall back on some mighty powerful corroborating evidence that torture had been authorized at the highest levels.

The first significant corroborating evidence had come in on December 16, when none other than the vice president himself admitted, on national TV, that he approved of the torture of alleged 9/11 mastermind Khalid Sheikh Mohammed. Cheney was unapologetic. "I got the process cleared," Cheney said, sitting comfortably in front of a cozy fireplace across from an ABC reporter. "The agency came to me and told me what they wanted to do; I supported them." The program, he went on, had been "remarkably successful"—a view subsequently disputed by others, including some of the interrogators themselves, who insisted that the best information they got was not from torture, but from developing a rapport with the detainee.[57] But no matter. He, Richard B. Cheney, did not for a minute think it had gone too far. Did he think waterboarding was appropriate? "I do." It was all justified, in his mind, because of 9/11.[58]

Now this was ballsy. Why admit to such a thing? For one thing, Cheney no doubt knew that a lot of Americans believed that anyone associated with 9/11 deserved torture or worse, regardless of the notion that one is judged innocent until proven guilty. (Indeed, average Americans I spoke with continued to believe the detainees had what was coming to them even after learning, in April, 2009, that some of the "high-level" detainees had been tortured—in the case of Khalid Sheikh Mohammed, 183 times in the course of one month—to get them to say whatever their torturers wanted them to say.) Cheney also admitted to torture because his involvement in authorizing it would all come out anyway a week later in the Senate Armed Services Committee "Torture Report."

Besides Cheney's confession and the "Torture Report," two more events seemed to point the attorney general in the right direction, toward prosecution.

On December 18, *The New York Times* ran its extraordinary editorial calling for a special prosecutor "to consider criminal charges against top officials at the Pentagon and others involved in planning the abuse."

Then, only two days before Holder's confirmation hearings, Judge Susan Crawford, a lifelong Republican who had been appointed by Defense Secretary Robert Gates to preside over Guantánamo cases, made a stunning admission to *The Washington Post*: She had refused to allow a trial of one of the detainees because she believed he had been tortured. Evidence obtained through torture could not be admitted into a court of law.

Conclusion: If Holder had a mind to prosecute, there were people in high places willing to help him out.

But as I was quickly learning (at least on the issue of prosecutions), nothing said the week before—by any high-level Obama administration official—could be interpreted as the final word on the matter. Everything was in flux. One week later, Holder met privately with Senator Christopher Bond (R-Mo.), the Vice Chairman of the Senate Select Committee on Intelligence. Holder reportedly assured Bond, according to an article in the conservative *Washington Times*, that he would not go after "former Bush officials involved in the interrogations program." According to Bond, "I made clear that trying to prosecute political leaders would generate a political firestorm the Obama administration doesn't need. . . . He gave me assurances that he would not take steps that would cause major disruptions in our intelligence system or cause political warfare . . . [and that he would] not look backwards to prosecute intelligence operatives who were fighting terror and kept our country safe since 9/11."[59]

Holder's alleged "assurances" reportedly convinced Bond to vote in favor of Holder's nomination. This, in itself, caused a firestorm and received an immediate denial from an aide to Holder and a rebuttal from Vermont's Senator Patrick Leahy. "It would be completely wrong if a senator said, 'I'll vote for you if you promise to withhold prosecution of a crime. No senator would make a request like that. It'd be improper,'"[60] Leahy said.

Conclusion: Republicans love to raise these subjective arguments, like "don't do it because it will hurt our national security" or "it will divide the country." But the law is the law, and Holder had made it clear he would abide by the law. Whether or not he gave personal "assurances" to Bond (and only the two of them know what was actually said), Holder may have decided not to go after the people who "just followed orders," i.e., CIA interrogators following orders from on high. But this did not necessarily mean he was going to nix prosecutions altogether.

At this point, I was as much in the dark as anyone else. All we—and by we, I mean lawyers, journalists, and activists in the accountability movement—could do was speculate. To me, Holder's words and actions suggested that he actually wanted to focus on the people who gave the orders. And that would be Bush and Cheney, because Bush and Cheney had admitted that they had authorized torture.

But then again, what if Bush and Cheney came up with a defense that they were just relying on legal advice?

I went back and looked at what Bush said on February 9 in an interview with Fox TV about the capture of Khalid Sheikh Mohammed in early March, 2003:

> I'm in the Oval Office and I am told that we have captured Khalid
> Sheikh Mohammed, and the professionals believe he has information
> necessary to secure the country. So I ask what tools are available for
> us to find information from him and they gave me a list of tools,
> and I said are these tools deemed to be legal? *And so we got legal*

opinions before any decision was made [emphasis added]. And I think when people study the history of this particular episode, they'll find out we gained good information from Khalid Sheikh Mohammed in order to protect our country.

By Bush's account, he got legal advice first, and only afterwards proceeded to approve the "enhanced interrogation" of this top al-Qaeda suspect. It would take another two months—with the release of more torture memos in April—before most of us began to realize that torture by the CIA was occurring *before* Bush got his legal advice, and that the supposed "good information from Khalid Sheikh Mohammed" was highly suspect because it had been induced by repeated waterboarding—some 183 times in the month of March alone. But for now, it seemed that the battle over prosecutions would focus on the role of Bush's lawyers and not the top men in the Bush administration, and that meant inside the Office of Legal Counsel, inside the Department of Justice.

Apparently Bush's third attorney general,[61] Michael Mukasey, had seen it all coming back in early December when he told a group of reporters: "There is absolutely no evidence that anybody who rendered a legal opinion . . . did so for any reason other than to protect the security in the country and in the belief that he or she was doing something lawful."[62]

When I look back on this "period of transition" between Obama's election and his inauguration, I recall feeling dazed, almost overwhelmed by the flurry of revelations. It was hard to keep up with the back and forth between the incoming and former administrations. If Bush and Cheney were squirming as the noose seemed to be closing around their necks, they were doing everything in their power to act unfazed, even cocky, about their behavior in the White House.

Each side seemed to be working overtime to make their case to the national press, knowing that it was the main conduit to the court of public opinion.

Remember, by January 7, Obama's Web site had shown that the top issue among his supporters was the appointment of a special prosecutor to investigate wrongdoing by the Bush administration. The top issue. Which says something about what a movement can do—if adequately informed.

Was Obama publicly acting like the reluctant bride while privately encouraging his subordinates in the Department of Justice to carefully dribble out evidence to prepare for the ultimate trial? Holder had clearly walked into a hornet's nest when he took up his post at the DOJ as attorney general. The question was, how was he going to swat down the hornets? And could he emerge unstung?

Meanwhile, what was going on up on the Hill?

3. John Conyers: Chair of the House Judiciary Committee

On January 7, 2009, two days after "prosecutions for criminal behavior" had become the top issue on Obama's Web site, Congressman John Conyers announced his intention to seek congressional approval of a "blue ribbon panel" of "outside experts" to probe, among other things, "unreviewable war powers, torture and wiretaps."

His staff in the House Judiciary Committee had just completed an enormous undertaking, a 350-page *preliminary* report on the abuses of the Bush administration that would eventually be published (in March 2009)[63] under the provocative title *Inside the Imperial Presidency: Lessons and Recommendations Relating to the Presidency of George W. Bush*. It had probed every imaginable abuse: the politicization of the Justice Department; various assaults on individual liberties (torture, extraordinary renditions, warrantless surveillance); the misuse of executive-branch authority (overuse of presidential "signing statements," which often contradicted legislation); expanded political control by the White House over rule-making and lack of transparency; retribution against critics (the infamous "outing" of CIA agent Valerie Plame after her husband questioned the rationale for the war in Iraq); and the abuse of various executive privileges like the overuse of state secrets to withhold information sought through the Freedom of Information Act.

Second among the Judiciary Committee's *fifty* recommendations was the creation of a blue ribbon commission "to investigate the broad range of policies of the Bush administration." The makeup of the panel would be bipartisan, with no more than five members from each political party. It would have a budget of $3 million and subpoena power. After one year, it would file its list of recommendations.[64]

Would prosecution be one of them? Conyers had already demonstrated that he possessed both the will and the motive to prosecute. He had previously called on Attorney General Mukasey to appoint a special prosecutor to investigate war crimes. Mukasey had refused, saying there was no legal basis to "prosecute current and former administration officials for authorizing torture and warrantless domestic surveillance because decisions had been made on the basis of national security."[65]

But why would Conyers choose a commission over the more direct route of prosecution, especially with all the evidence that was coming in that the highest levels of the Bush administration had authorized torture? The most aides on Obama's transition team would divulge was that this commission was not intended to *prevent* a criminal investigation by the Department of Justice. But by the same token, these same aides let it be known that Obama was also open to the idea of a truth commission as a way of "ascertaining the facts." Which, of course, was an allusion to Senator Patrick Leahy's proposed Truth and Reconciliation Commission—a commission that, like South Africa's postapartheid Truth and Reconciliation Commission, would subpoena people to air the truth, but not bring criminal charges.

4. Patrick Leahy: Chair of the Senate Judiciary Committee

Like John Conyers, Patrick Leahy is one of the most senior members of Congress. (Conyers began serving in 1965, Leahy in 1974.) The two men have worked the system for decades, and as fellow Democrats and respective chairs of the House and Senate Judiciary Committees, they keep in touch. It was clearly no coincidence, then, that on the same day (January 9) that John Conyers announced his plans for a blue ribbon commission to investigate, among other things, "unreviewable war powers," the Senate Judiciary Committee—under Leahy's supervision—released three Justice Department memos on the president's war powers written by lawyers who advised the White House.

Leahy was no stranger to releasing information to the public when he felt it was in the public's interest. Back in January, 1987, in his capacity as vice chair of the Senate Select Committee on Intelligence, he had leaked a draft report on the Iran-Contra affair to a reporter.[66] The Republicans got wind of what Leahy had done and turned his leak against him. Leahy would subsequently resign from the Senate Intelligence Committee, ruefully acknowledging that "although the report was unclassified, some will use this as an example."[67] From then on, Republicans would scornfully refer to the senator from Vermont as "Leaky Leahy."

Now, more than twenty years later, Leahy was the top man in the Senate Judiciary Committee, and there was no one holding him back from making public previously unreleased Justice Department memos that would put the Bush administration in a bad light. Those memos were written by two lawyers who worked in the Office of Legal Counsel: Jay Bybee and John Yoo.

One of the memos was a lengthy, October 23, 2002, document stating that the president had the right to order force to protect America's national interests. It also stated that declaring war would be justifiable if the president determined that Iraq had helped the perpetrators of 9/11. The significance of this memo (discussed later in this book) would be lost in the furor over torture.

Over the next month, the names Yoo and Bybee would become grist for the anti-Bush mill[68] as word got out that an internal ethics investigation within the Justice Department was nearing completion on whether this secretive enclave of powerful, pro-Bush lawyers was supplying honest legal advice, or was shaping the memos to fit a policy already made, all the while covering up any illegalities.

Whither prosecution?

With all this rash of new information coming out, it was time for me to consult with some experts.

I caught up with Michael Ratner, president of the left-liberal Center for Constitutional Rights on February 5, shortly after he argued strenuously on *Democracy Now* for prosecution and against a truth commission. A mild-mannered, sweet-faced man whose distinctive bald head and large glasses make him instantly recognizable on TV, he had become a go-to guy for media who wanted to know what experts thought the Obama administration should be doing, as opposed to what it actually was doing. For him, the Obama administration was under both an ethical and legal obligation to begin criminal proceedings. As he said earlier that morning on TV, "Having Cheney admitting that he was one of the architects of waterboarding, Holder saying it's a violation of the anti-torture statute, and the Convention Against Torture saying there's an absolute obligation to begin a criminal investigation, the Obama administration is in violation [of these laws] if he doesn't commence an investigation of Cheney, of Rumsfeld, and others."

It wasn't enough for Obama to sign an executive order stating his administration would no longer torture, Ratner said. "Our fundamental rights, the right against torture—to be free from torture, should not be dependent on the length of the president's arm. The only real deterrent is prosecution."[69]

I interviewed him later that day. "That was a nice analogy about the president's arm," I said to him. "But what about those legal memos from Yoo and Bybee? How do you go after Bush and Cheney when they're going to say their lawyers advised them that what they were doing was legal and in the interests of national security?"

Those memos, he replied, were "modeled to fit policy," not to give honest legal advice. "Besides," he added, "the law against torture was written for times like these, not for normal times. And the ban against torture is absolute. What happened was flatly illegal."

But practically speaking, what did he think about the chances of prosecuting Bush, Cheney, and the whole gang for war crimes?

It couldn't be done by a normal prosecutor within the Department of Justice, he said. The place was filled with bureaucrats and prosecutors still loyal to Bush. Given the rampant and well-documented politicization of the Justice Department, "you can't clean it up and make it fair" in time. Appointing an independent special prosecutor seemed more likely to him—someone like Special Counsel Patrick Fitzgerald, who prosecuted top Cheney aide I. Lewis (Scooter) Libby and "did things the vice president didn't want." "What do you think of Bugliosi's approach to prosecuting Bush for murder?" I asked.

"Highly original," he said. "As a strategy, it has potential." In Washington, Ratner explained, the CCR had "a very limited pool of people to call upon in the Obama administration to try to convince them to take up a criminal prosecution." In fact, it really came down to the president and the attorney general. Ratner expected right-wing Republicans to call into question the alleged "independence" of any independent prosecutor chosen by Attorney General Holder.

Of the two thousand–plus district attorneys in the U.S., Ratner mused, "perhaps someone could be found who had a conscience."

That was a good reason to call Bugliosi. I reached him on February 7.

Torture or murder: Which path for prosecution?

"Vince, what do you think about all this back and forth on torture and the possibility of war-crimes prosecutions?"

Vince was indignant. "I'm not condoning torture, but I think *The New York Times* reported that there were twenty-four known torture victims. You compare twenty-four victims to over four thousand American dead and a million Iraqis in their graves, and there is no comparison. Torture takes a back seat to murder. I'm profoundly offended that all you hear is torture, torture, torture—and of members of al-Qaeda, no less—and not one word about the murder of thousands of our soldiers and innocent Iraqis. So it annoys me that there's so much emphasis on torture. If there are to be torture prosecutions, they should be secondary to murder prosecutions."

"I agree. But that seems to be where the emphasis is now. So, do you think there will be a war-crimes prosecution?"

"The whole question is criminal intent. If the former attorney general under Bush said that waterboarding was not torture or that waterboarding was not violative of the Constitution and the Geneva Conventions, it would be extremely difficult to prosecute those who relied on the attorney general's advice. And that would include Bush and Cheney. If they could say, 'Look, we're not lawyers, we rely on the opinions of lawyers in the Department of Justice,' as you know, you can't prosecute people who thought they were doing the right thing. Their lawyers will argue that their behavior was not unlawful. And I can tell you that most federal judges accord a lot of respect to the attorney general."

"Well," I responded, "I heard on *Democracy Now* back in December[70] that there is evidence that the torturing occurred before there were legal briefs. An Air Force vet named Matthew Alexander cowrote a book called *How to Break a Terrorist,* and in it he said the Defense Department authorized torturing before they got any memos from the Justice Department approving what they were doing." (I had not yet fully digested that the internal inquiry within the DOJ was already zeroing in on this issue.)

Vince replied: "If it can be shown that the White House was urging torture and torture took place before Yoo's memos, then that will knock down the defense. Otherwise, the courts give a lot of deference to an attorney general's opinion."

Vince's comments got me going. I began to examine press reports following the release of the Yoo and Bybee memos and found that one reporter was already scouring the Office of Legal Counsel memos for examples of criminal intent.

He was Robert Parry, a former *Newsweek* reporter who had covered the Iran-Contra hearings and now posts regularly on the Web site that he and his son created to effectively prevent censorship, which they call Consortium News. (Parry, I would soon learn from interviewing him, had had some searing experiences at *Newsweek* over not only Congress's but his own magazine's aversion to getting to the bottom of the Iran-Contra arms-for-hostages scandal. He had been burned more than once. Now he was casting a critical eye not only on the Yoo memos but on how the Obama administration, Congress, and the press would deal with them.)

In a long critique that he wrote on February 3, 2009, for Consortium News ("First, Jail All Bush's Lawyers"), Parry reminded readers that Holder's oath of office requires him to support and defend the U.S. Constitution and that means seriously considering "prosecuting crimes committed by the Bush administration, including its torturing of detainees." He also suggested that Holder begin with Yoo and Bybee, the lawyers whose memos "justified" the torture. Not only did they provide what Parry called "paper cover for both the interrogators in the field and the senior officials back in Washington," he wrote, but Yoo's own book showed that it was "policy concerns, not legal logic" that drove the memos.

"It was far from obvious that following the Geneva Conventions in the war against al-Qaeda would be wise," Yoo wrote in *War By Other Means*, published in 2006: "Our policy makers had to ask whether [compliance] would yield any benefit or act as a hindrance."

These and other statements in Yoo's own words, Parry concluded, were damning. Clearly, "lawyers from the Justice Department's OLC weren't just legal scholars handing down opinions from an ivory tower; they were participants in how to make Bush's desired actions 'legal.' "[71]

Congress, Parry continued, was already hot on this trail of "whether the OLC lawyers were honest brokers or criminal conspirators." Two senators— Dick Durbin (D-Ill.) and Sheldon Whitehouse (D-R.I.)—had written the Justice Department's internal watchdog agencies in February, 2008, to launch an investigation into the role that Justice Department officials played "in authorizing and/or overseeing the use of waterboarding by the Central Intelligence Agency . . . and whether those who authorized it violated the law." At issue was the fact that having lawyers devise a legal argument for an illegal act does not make that act any more legal—especially, as Senator Whitehouse pointed out, if the lawyers were persuaded to develop a particular opinion.

A case in point, Parry continued, was the issue of waterboarding. In August, 2002, Yoo and Bybee devised a novel and narrow definition of torture that attempted to get the torturers off the hook:

> The Yoo-Bybee legal opinion[72] stated that unless the amount of pain administered to a detainee led to injuries that might result in "death, organ failure, or serious impairment of body functions," then the interrogation technique could not be defined as torture. . . .
>
> Whitehouse said the Bybee-Yoo memo was "beyond malpractice" and "raises the specter that these things were overlooked" just to advance policy.

Now this was intriguing, especially since my own senator from Vermont, Patrick Leahy, suddenly came up with the idea of putting together a bipartisan "truth commission" to look into the Bush-era abuses. It seemed to me that there was already ample evidence of lawbreaking by Yoo and Bybee inside the Department of Justice.

Equally intriguing, why was Leahy proposing Whitehouse, a first-term senator from Rhode Island, as one of the people he chose to speak in favor of his truth commission, when Whitehouse, a former prosecutor, already knew where the evidence lay? Why didn't they skip the truth commission and get on with calling for a special prosecutor? What did they know that we didn't?

CHAPTER SIX

Leahy's Truth Commission
and the Jersey Girls

Senator Leahy's proposed Truth and Reconciliation Commission had barely hit the press in early February when I began to get calls and emails from leaders of the accountability movement. All had felt burned by the failure of the national impeachment drive, but they were willing to think and act strategically with this latest proposal from a leading Democrat. Some, like my campaign media guru, Ralph Lopez, thought the truth commission was worth considering. Others, like William Crain, a co-coordinator of Progressive Democrats of America in Montana and a Vietnam War veteran, saw it as nothing more than "milquetoast." Leahy himself had described his idea as a middle ground between appointing a special prosecutor and doing nothing. Crain wanted Leahy to know that "we need to step up to the plate with the Constitution. Laws have been severely broken and there are consequences to *pay*. We don't want reconciliation. We want justice!"

Leahy's office had just announced a petition drive for his proposed truth commission, and Crain—who belonged to a local group that favored prosecutions, not truth commissions—was worried that it might "get a lot of signatures from well-meaning folks who have not heard of us." He was right. The petition was already circulating on the Internet and getting a highly enthusiastic response. (It would eventually get one hundred thousand signatures.) This would not be the first time that accountability activists who favored prosecutions found themselves outmatched by the communication power of elected officials who had their own agenda.[73] Sue Serpa, responding to a flood of queries, proposed a meeting between Leahy and his Vermont constituents to see what he realistically hoped to accomplish. I spoke with Vermonter Dan DeWalt, accountability activist *par excellence*, and we agreed that he should be the one to approach Leahy and request the meeting. After all, it was DeWalt who had laid the groundwork for the impeachment movement, a special movement that took off in Vermont towns during Town Meeting Day in 2006 and soon spread throughout New England. His work inspired *The Nation* writer John Nichols to devote the last chapter of his 2006 book, *The Genius of Impeachment*, to Vermont's daring experiment in impeachment. "It was appropriate indeed," Nichols wrote, "that the first opportunity for American voters to express their sentiments on the question of whether to impeach members of the Bush administration for high crimes and misdemeanors came at a New England town meeting in a community chartered two years before the Declaration of Independence was drafted."[74]

Vermont's insurrectionists

Dan DeWalt—a carpenter, musician, and freelance journalist living in the tiny Vermont town of Newfane (population 1,704)—decided, shortly into George W. Bush's second term, that he just couldn't take it any more. His government was acting immorally and illegally, and he felt he had to do something about it. So, as a member of the town selectboard, he drafted an impeachment resolution that would go before the annual town meeting in March, 2006. The resolution charged Bush with misleading the nation into war, lying about his government's use of torture, and ordering his government to engage in domestic spying. It also called on the U.S. House of Representatives, as well as the Vermont legislature, to take up the matter of impeachment. The people of Newfane voted resoundingly for the resolution, 121–29. DeWalt was ecstatic. "In the U.S. there are only a few places where citizens can act in this fashion and have a say in our nation," he told the press.[75] News spread fast, inspiring four other towns that were holding their meeting the following day to take up the issue and approve it by voice vote.

By Town Meeting Day a year later, impeachment was on a tear across Vermont. DeWalt and other activists had brought "Peace Mom" Cindy Sheehan into Vermont prior to Town Meeting Day to barnstorm the state in a bus dubbed the "Yellow Rose of Texas." Accompanied by three Iraq war vets from Vermont and author John Nichols, they crisscrossed the state, meeting Vermonters and explaining the importance of impeachment.

They made thirteen stops. At each stop, they followed the same routine. First, the vets would speak. Adrienne Kinne,[76] an Arabic linguist for ten years, had become disillusioned with the Iraq war when she learned that our intelligence community was getting false information about Iraq's WMDs from exiled Iraqis like Ahmad Chalabi, who had political ambitions and stood to benefit from the invasion of Iraq and the overthrow of Saddam Hussein. Adrienne told her superiors, only to be accused of being unpatriotic. She eventually left her unit and at the time of the tour was working in a VA hospital in Vermont. She told her audiences about soldiers suffering from post-traumatic stress disorder. Sheehan, who would later write about the tour, described Adrienne's stories "of soldiers who were driving down the road in a sandy country that they had no business being in . . . and who awaken to find themselves covered in blood with body parts in their laps, not knowing if it was their own or one of their buddies."

Vets Matt Howard, a Marine, and Drew Cameron, a soldier, told equally horrifying stories about lack of body armor, poor food rations, and the soldiers' despair over the killing of innocent women and children. They told of miserable conditions in the nation's underfunded and poorly staffed VA hospitals and of soldiers committing suicide, because, said Sheehan, "even if the harmed soldiers wanted to, they can't get a bed in a VA facility." It was positively criminal. The vets would tell Vermont audiences that the illegal occupation of a country had created more damaged veterans who couldn't get adequate care when they returned home.

Writer John Nichols would talk next, speaking passionately about the history of impeachment, how it found its way into our Constitution six times, and how it reflected the Founders' way of ensuring that no branch of the government, especially the executive branch, became too powerful.

Then Sheehan, the aggrieved mother of a young man killed in the early days of the war, would bring the event to its heartbreaking conclusion. What she had to say about her son Casey's death invariably moved her audiences. But so did her anger that the primary architects and implementers of the Vietnam War—including President Lyndon B. Johnson, Defense Secretary Robert McNamara, and Secretary of State Henry Kissinger—"left their offices to go on to lead happy and healthy lives of ease." If even one of them had been impeached or imprisoned, she said, "maybe George Bush would not have thought he was above the law and maybe he wouldn't have felt so comfortable leading our country into disaster in a war [like the one] he spent a lot of time avoiding himself."[77]

While DeWalt, Sheehan, and the war vets crisscrossed the state on their "Democracy Tour," other activists began pressing the Vermont state legislature to pass an impeachment resolution based on Rutland lawyer Jeff Taylor's remarkable discovery of the *Manual of Parliamentary Practice* written by Vice President Thomas Jefferson in 1801. Section LIII, 603, allows for various routes to impeachment, including state legislatures calling on the U.S. House of Representatives to set impeachment in motion. DeWalt had made reference to that avenue into his town meeting impeachment resolutions the year before, and then Taylor had popularized it further by getting what became known as the "Rutland resolution" adopted among many of Vermont's county democratic committees.

When Town Meeting Day came, thirty-seven Vermont towns voted for impeachment. Once again, Vermont made national news.

Buoyed by these results, and by the subsequent adoption of a somewhat amended version of the Rutland resolution by the state senate, some four hundred Vermonters, including DeWalt, descended on the Vermont state capitol in April, 2007, urging the Speaker of the House to back an impeachment resolution. Speaker Gaye Symington found herself fending off questions from citizens who had packed into the House chamber and overflowed into the galleries. She spoke against impeachment, claiming (as many Democratic Party leaders did) that impeachment would get in the way of the presidential race. She called for a vote and defeated the resolution, having joined in a coalition of Republicans and middle-of-the-road Democrats. DeWalt and his followers were deeply disappointed, accusing her of putting the "Democratic Party above the Constitution" while "misread[ing] the threat of the Bush administration." But DeWalt remained defiant. Describing the dramatic events of the last few weeks in The Huffington Post, he wrote:

> Last week's events in Vermont were nothing less than the occasion of actual sovereignty being exercised by the hands of the People. And the People like the feeling that comes with having been heard. Symington's tortured arguments and political machinations shattered

more than a few illusions about how our citizen legislature works. But at the same time, these are lessons that will not be lost. The citizenry is aroused, educating itself, and has become a force to be reckoned with. Our neighbors are getting the idea. When will our leaders?[78]

The ultimate test would come one year later, when DeWalt put together a group of five Vermonters, each of whom had a following within Vermont's own accountability movement, to meet with Senator Leahy.

In addition to DeWalt and me, the group included:

- John Nirenberg, a sixty-year-old academic who walked 450 miles in the dead of winter, starting on December 1, 2007, from Faneuil Hall in Boston and ending up in Washington on January 12, 2008, to deliver a letter to House Speaker Pelosi urging her to put "impeachment back on the table." His walk inspired Dan DeWalt and thousands like him in the impeachment movement. Dan helped publicize Nirenberg's walk, writing in OpEdNews.com that the Vermonter felt ashamed over his country's embrace of war, torture, and repression. "John decided to take this walk entirely on his own," DeWalt wrote, "with no organization or infrastructure supporting the journey or helping to publicize it. But within days, activists, citizens, and organizations came on board and have helped him to connect with a network of Americans who will be joining him in their towns when he comes through."[79]
- Kurt Daims, the creator of the resolution calling on Brattleboro, Vermont, police to arrest either Bush or Cheney if they entered the state. Kurt presented the resolution in January, 2008, to be placed on the Brattleboro ballot for town meeting in March, 2008. It caused an uproar locally and made news around the world because the selectboard approved the resolution. Daims became an instant celebrity.[80]
- And Martha Hennessy, the granddaughter of Dorothy Day, the famous founder of the Catholic Worker movement, which is still active today. Hennessy had frequently traveled from her Vermont home to protest against torture in Washington, D.C.

A week before our scheduled meeting with Leahy, set for March 30, 2009, the five of us went over our talking points and concluded that we were effectively groping around in the dark. It seemed that there was already plenty of evidence to convince Attorney General Eric Holder to appoint a special prosecutor.

Holder's own Justice Department had recently released nine Bush-era memos that showed plans for a military takeover of our democracy.[81] The memos, formulated by the Office of Legal Counsel, had caused a huge outcry and demands for prosecution, at least in the blogosphere. Glenn Greenwald, a civil litigator and Salon.com blogger who was widely read by accountability activists, wrote on March 3, 2009, that we now had solid evidence that the Bush administration had created "a whole regimen of secret laws that vested tyrannical, monarchical power in the president. . . . What kind of country has secret laws?"[82]

And scarier still, it seemed like nothing was going to be done about it. As Greenwald sadly observed, "If our political class had its way, even the bits and pieces we've now seen would continue to be hidden in the dark. Most of the specific individuals who initiated these measures may no longer be in power, but the institutions and the political and media elites who enabled all of it haven't gone anywhere. They're now actively working to keep as much as possible concealed and to insist that nothing should be done about any of it."

If Leahy was not part of this political class, then what, we wondered, was his truth commission all about? It simply made no sense to us.

We reviewed the failure of impeachment efforts. It seemed that at every turn Democratic Party leaders gave a reason why impeachment was a bad idea: either the timing wasn't right; or impeachment might provoke a Republican backlash; or it was more important to channel Democratic Party energies into getting Democrats elected to Congress; or, after those elections (in which Democrats regained control of Congress), it was more important to get a Democrat in the White House.

We concluded there might be another reason for the party's disaffection with impeachment: Some powerful Democrats had been compromised through their cooperation with the Bush administration in the war on Iraq and the torture policies that emerged. The brouhaha over what House Speaker Pelosi learned or did not learn from secret CIA briefings over its planned torture program had not yet erupted, but it was already widely known that she knew torture was happening and never spoke out against it. This suggested some degree of Democratic Party complicity with the Bush administration, a degree that might prove embarrassing down the road. As Dan DeWalt pointed out, "no other explanation made sense."

We wondered whether Leahy ultimately wanted to go after the big guys, as he claimed, or whether he was just "seeking the truth" for political play-time. One thing seemed certain. Whenever the subject of prosecution had come up, Senator Leahy would find a way of shooting it down. Right after the November elections, for instance, he told Vermont Public Radio that prosecutions were "not going to happen"—at least "not in the United States."

Then, on February 10, only days after *USA Today* released a nationwide poll showing that a majority of Americans wanted a criminal prosecution, Leahy announced his truth commission, which appeared to be a kinder, gentler alternative to prosecution. His reason? *"Prosecutions take too long,"* he had told MSNBC's Rachel Maddow. "You're going to have people, some people, will say, let's go ahead and prosecute everybody. That can take ten to fifteen years." (But who, some of us wondered, wants to prosecute everybody? Most people would be happy with the top guys.)

Even when he allowed the possibility of prosecuting someone who refused to testify, or who perjured themselves, he kept presenting prosecutions as a last resort. A truth commission was preferable, he said, because it would act faster than a trial, it would get wrongdoers to fess up by granting immunity, and it would deter future wrongdoers by being "very, very public," thus sending a message: "You try the same thing, you are going to be found out, you are going to be prosecuted."

As if a very public trial wouldn't send the same message.

We asked ourselves what good would come out of the information his commission would gather without any action to hold the wrongdoers accountable.

We wondered if the senator was living in a bubble, perhaps unaware of the true depth of anger over what the Bush administration had done to our country, and the fact that Bush and his co-conspirators in crime—Cheney, Rice, Rumsfeld, and others—might get away with it without even a slap on the wrist.

We mulled over possible downsides to prosecutions at this time. Much had already been made of the fact that they could divert the new president from other important issues, like shoring up Wall Street and preventing an economic collapse. We listened carefully to Kurt Daims, who thought the Democrats had a genuine and perhaps well-placed fear of humiliating and/ or antagonizing the right wing. Obama himself had made it clear he did not want to be accused of fostering a witch hunt.

We also considered the possibility that Leahy's truth commission would never get off the ground because of lack of Republican support.

I personally felt conflicted about this meeting. Leahy's office had been helpful to me when, in my quest to find out more about how my father lost his life, I had filed a Freedom of Information Act (FOIA) lawsuit to force the CIA to release my father's World War II papers. I respected Leahy as one of the country's foremost champions of open government. In March, 2005, Leahy helped create Sunshine Week as a direct challenge to the Bush administration's obsession with secrecy and long delays in processing FOIA requests. That same month, his office encouraged me to submit written testimony to Senate hearings on FOIA, which I did shortly before filing my lawsuit.[83]

On the other hand, I was concerned that Leahy wanted his truth commission to be modeled after the 9/11 Commission. By most serious accounts, the bipartisan 9/11 Commission was flawed at the outset, so mired in making compromises between Republicans and Democrats that its final report was deemed a whitewash. The final 2004 report merely pointed to "systemic failures" in intelligence and "lack of imagination" without assigning responsibility to any individuals in the Bush administration.[84] I recalled William Raspberry of *The Washington Post* describing it as a "childlike explanation of what went so tragically wrong." Ray McGovern, a twenty-seven-year veteran of the CIA, described the report as an effort to "exculpate anyone in the establishment. Mistakes were made, but no one is to blame."[85]

Not a very reassuring precedent for millions of people who now wanted to bring the president and his top advisors to justice. Were the powerful going to get a reprieve, once again?

And were our elected officials—even our liberal senator Leahy—simply looking for ways just short of prosecution to scold the criminals, expose them, get information from them, act like they did something useful, but in the end, let them off?

These were the questions we wanted answered.

An unsettling discovery

Whatever concerns I had about Leahy's truth commission were only magnified when Leahy held a hearing on March 4 on his now-renamed Nonpartisan Commission of Inquiry. The title seemed to address Republican concerns about a "witch hunt," but one of the three people Leahy invited to speak for his commission deepened my alarm: He was John Farmer, who, Leahy said, was "senior counsel and team leader for the 9/11 Commission."

Farmer, predictably, saw no immediate need for a special prosecutor. Instead, he favored a "bipartisan commission, with staff, timetable and a budget, as well as subpoena power and offers of immunity, [which] could provide a factually based narrative." This narrative, in turn would provide "policy makers with something to debate."

Debate? How about *doing something*? And what were the chances of getting a bipartisan committee to go after the Bush administration when Republicans seemed to be digging in their heels?

As our meeting with Leahy drew near, I tried to look at the truth commission through the eyes of a hard-nosed prosecutor. There was the law—torture is illegal—and then there were practical considerations about implementing the law, like a judge's reluctance to second-guess opinions produced by the Justice Department, as Vince Bugliosi had warned me. I had already experienced similar warnings in my FOIA case: Judges, I was told, will hardly ever second-guess the CIA when it argues that it won't turn over documents for national security reasons, even when the documents are half a century old.

But then something unexpected occurred. A letter from four 9/11 widows from New Jersey began circulating the Internet and landed in my in-box. The letter was addressed to Senator Leahy, and it raised a number of questions about his truth commission. The signers, Mindy Kleinberg, Lorie Van Auken, Patty Casazza, and Monica Gabrielle, called themselves, interestingly enough, 9/11 Advocates for Truth. But they are best known as The Jersey Girls.

Their letter, while polite, had an edge to it. They suggested that Leahy's planned inquiry—which he claimed would cover the politicization of the Justice Department, the wiretapping of U.S. citizens, the flawed intelligence used to justify the invasion of Iraq, and the use of torture at Guantánamo—was misguided. In fact, it was unnecessary. Why, they wondered, would the senator want to form another commission when he could simply investigate these charges as part of his responsibility as chair of the Senate Judiciary Committee? And why would he want to model it after the 9/11 Commission, whose commissioners seemed to have agreed at the outset that their role was to "fact-find, not fault-find." The result of their inquiry, the Jersey Girls wrote, was that "no individuals [were] held accountable for their specific failures." Instead, individuals found to be incompetent at best were left in their jobs—or worse, promoted.

The more I read, the more disturbed I became. Their letter said the hearings yielded very little evidence. "Many individuals were not sworn in, critical witnesses were either not called to testify or were permitted to dictate the parameters of their own questioning, pertinent questions were omitted, and there was little follow-up. Whistleblower testimony was suppressed or avoided altogether." Some of the report's final recommendations were based on "distortions and omissions."

The Jersey Girls' final observation was devastating. "It could be surmised that holding no one accountable was more important than uncovering and disclosing the truth."[86] Which was another way of saying the 9/11 Commission was a cover-up.

I suspected they knew and understood a lot more than even their letter implied. The journalist in me was intrigued. For it seemed that the more I had probed the issues involved in any potential prosecution of high-level Bush administration officials, the more I kept stumbling into 9/11. It was Bush's stated reason for sending troops to Afghanistan and Iraq. It was cited as the reason for torturing detainees. It was the reason why we had to have warrantless wiretaps, even of American citizens. Every affront to our democracy under Bush was linked back to 9/11. I had even begun to wonder if this event stood at the core of all the hand-wringing in Congress, the prevarications about what to do, the back and forth with no sign of accountability.

Perhaps by meeting the Jersey Girls before meeting Leahy, I could raise their concerns directly to the senator and gain further insights from him. After all, he was one of the most powerful and senior senators on the Hill and rapidly becoming a congressional leader on the issue of accountability.

Meeting the Jersey Girls

I arranged to meet two of the four Jersey Girls at the Colonial Diner—off Exit 9 from the New Jersey turnpike. I found them sitting next to each other in a booth—Lorie Van Auken, a petite, short-haired brunette with glasses and a very alert look on her face, and Mindy Kleinberg, a well-coifed blonde with big, expressive, green eyes. I knew when I went over and shook their hands that we would hit it off. We had a lot in common, even though our quests for the truth were separated by over sixty years.

They wanted to know what happened to their husbands. I wanted to know what happened to my father. Each of us had experienced the pain and frustration of stonewalling by government officials. As I talked, I found Lorie examining me carefully, no doubt wondering if she could trust me.

"Sounds like you're dealing with the state secrets privilege," Lorie finally said. I'd been explaining the CIA's refusal to turn over some 1947 documents about my father's plane crash for reasons of national security. "I don't know if you know about it," she added, "but it all started with a plane crash, right around World War II."

"Yes, I'm familiar with it,"[87] I said, thinking to myself, *Jeez, this lady is sharp.* What a way to start a meeting: on the subject of state secrets. And yet, it was a perfect segue into what Mindy and Lorie had been through. The Bush administration had repeatedly blocked inquiries about 9/11, arguing "state secrets" and "national security" as reasons to withhold vital information, including information by FBI whistleblower Sibel Edmonds about warnings received in May, 2001, of a planned terrorist attack by Osama bin Laden using planes against four U.S. cities.[88]

Only recently, Lorie and Mindy had met with President Obama and other 9/11 families about his intentions to close Guantánamo. Most of the people there, they told me, wanted him to keep Guantánamo open, fearful that some of the 9/11-connected detainees would be released before being brought to justice. Some didn't want the prisoners brought to the U.S. and tried in a regular court. Apparently anxious to quell their concerns, Obama said he would be open to the idea of having the detainees brought to swift justice in some kind of military commission. Other family members, including Lorie and Mindy, had no problem with closing Guantánamo, agreeing with Obama that its continued existence sent the wrong signal to the rest of the world. It had been linked to torture and Abu Ghraib and its image was not helpful. Keeping it open would just serve as a recruitment tool for more terrorists.

Lorie and Mindy had an additional reason for meeting the president. They wanted to hold him to his pledge of ensuring transparency. They had worked on a steering committee of twelve families to get the 9/11 Commission off the ground, and now, having been disappointed in the Commission's final report, they were seeking more information. They asked Obama to declassify and release twenty-eight pages withheld from the first 9/11 investigation report, called the Joint (Congressional) Inquiry. "You can see most of the report online," Mindy explained to me, "but those twenty-eight pages deal with foreign countries and that information remains classified." They wanted to know which foreign countries were involved in the 9/11 attacks, and how. And they didn't want the information just for information's sake. "We were determined to find out everything we could," Mindy explained to me, "so a disaster like this would never happen again."

As we talked, I realized that these two women had become self-educated experts in how to seek information from various government bureaucracies. I asked them at one point if there were many other families like them seeking answers. "We're a diverse group dealing with a myriad of issues," Mindy said. "Some of the families trust their government implicitly. Others are frustrated by loopholes in the official explanation of what happened. There are groups dealing with victims' issues. There are groups involved in planning the memorial. People do what they need to do. But we all respect each other."

As for Lorie and Mindy, investigating 9/11 was their way of doing justice to their deceased husbands while wanting to keep the nation safe. "Who else would do this 24/7?" Lorie asked with a sardonic smile. There wasn't a hearing they hadn't watched or attended or a report they hadn't read.

Which is precisely why they had a problem with Leahy's call for a truth commission.

"Every one of the areas Leahy is going to cover has *already been covered!*" Mindy exclaimed.

She showed me an index of all the hearings in the last three years that covered the very subjects Leahy wanted his truth commission to address—torture, wiretapping, flawed intelligence, and so on. The index ran on for *19 pages*. I skimmed through some of them. Sure enough, here were some of the subjects they covered:

- Restoring the Rule of Law (Senate Judiciary Committee, September 15, 2008);
- How the Administration's Failed Detainee Policies Have Hurt the Fight Against Terrorism (Senate Judiciary Committee, July 16, 2008);
- Department of Justice to Guantánamo Bay: Administration Lawyers and Administration Interrogation Rules (House Judiciary Committee, June 18, 2008);
- Warrantless Surveillance and the Foreign Intelligence Surveillance Act (House Judiciary Committee, September 18, 2007).

And on and on.

Now, granted, a lot of new information had been released since the summer and fall of 2008—especially those incriminating memos on torture written by Bush's Office of Legal Counsel. More would assuredly come out, too. But the point Mindy and Lorie were emphasizing was this: Hearings had been held, recommendations had been made, and nothing happened. Why would it be any different with a truth commission?

As for the 9/11 Commission itself, the two women elaborated on what they had put in their letter to Leahy. They had spent years, they said, pressing Congress to do a thorough investigation and encountered resistance all along the way. "Bush didn't even want any hearings," Lorie reminded me. "We had to push for them. "

Even after they got their hearings, they felt repeatedly betrayed. They prepared lists of questions for the commissioners to ask witnesses. "But they wouldn't ask them!"

When they objected, they were put down as being "complainers."[89] A few of the more conservative family members accused them of being paid Democratic Party operatives. "In fact, we were simply citizens trying to get the truth," said Mindy. "I couldn't go to sleep at night if I didn't think I had tried all I could."

Lorie and Mindy described efforts by the State Department to keep the 9/11 families speaking in one voice. One State Department designee suggested how happy they should feel about going to war because of 9/11. "Our response," Lorie said, "was, 'Are you kidding? Our husbands died in 9/11 and you think we're going to feel good about going to war, watching more people die in a country that had nothing to do with 9/11?'" They were not alone in this. Another independently minded group would form the Families for a Peaceful Tomorrow to oppose the war in Iraq.

The true depth of the Jersey Girls' anger and feelings of betrayal emerged after a *New York Times* reporter, Philip Shenon, published a book titled *The Commission: The Uncensored History of the 9/11 Investigation*. The book turned out to be a scathing indictment of the 9/11 Commission and confirmation of everything the girls had already suspected about the commission and its work.

Shenon's book gave weight to one of their major concerns: that the man hired to be executive director of the 9/11 Commission, Philip Zelikow, had direct ties to the national security apparatus of the Bush administration. With growing alarm, they had discovered that Zelikow was choosing the direction of the investigation, including who would be called as witnesses and who would not and what information would be considered or not. In March, 2004, the family steering committee had issued a statement discussing Zelikow's conflicts and requesting his resignation. On several other occasions they asked for his immediate resignation. It never happened.

When Shenon's book came out, they put out a statement in February, 2008, reiterating their earlier concerns:

> One of the [book's] most egregious revelations . . . is the fact that Philip Zelikow was hired as the Executive Director of the 9/11 Commission despite his direct ties to the Bush Administration. In 2000–01, he served as a member of Condoleezza Rice's National Security Council transition team. . . . Furthermore, he was a member

of the President's Foreign Intelligence Advisory Board from 2001–03, where Zelikow drafted most of the 2002 "National Security Strategy of the United States," creating the preemptive Iraq war strategy.

It seemed to us, that allowing an individual with this much involvement in the Bush administration to run the investigation might give the appearance of impropriety and could ultimately taint the Commission's findings.

And yet, in February, 2009, Senator Leahy and others were touting the work of the 9/11 Commission as if it were something to be emulated.

By the third hour of my conversation with these two remarkable women, I felt appalled by the degree of disrespect shown to them as 9/11 widows. No doubt the umbrella of "national security" had been lowered over them. But I vowed that if I ever got the chance to personally address any of those 9/11 commissioners, or anyone who supported Senator Leahy's truth-commission sequel, I would say this: "Put yourselves in the shoes of the family members who lost a spouse or a child in those attacks. Wouldn't you want to know everything that happened leading up to that fateful morning? And once you found out, wouldn't you want the perpetrators and the criminally negligent to be punished?"

Mindy handed me the documents we discussed during our meeting, including their critique of the 9/11 Commission and their nineteen-page index of hearings, and asked if I would share them with the group of Vermonters who planned to visit with Leahy in a few days. I said I would be happy to do that.

As I got ready to leave, the three of us agreed that we had all experienced, in our frustrated efforts to get at the truth, what they only half-jokingly called "Political Betrayal Trauma." It's actually a diagnosable disorder, they told me. "PBT—that's what happened to us."

Meeting with Leahy

On March 30 our day of reckoning with Senator Leahy had finally arrived. I met up with the other four Vermonters in a Brattleboro café and the five of us walked down Brattleboro's narrow Main Street until we reached our designated meeting place with the senator. It was an old, renovated hotel called *The Latchis*. We emerged from the second-floor elevator and walked down a dark corridor lined with barred windows to a conference room. We felt like we were in a renovated prison and joked, somewhat nervously, about being led to a torture chamber. Torture was very much on our minds at the time.

In recent weeks, protests against torture had erupted in several major cities as a result of the release in early February of the Yoo-Bybee "torture memos." Scores of activists wearing orange jumpsuits and black hoods demonstrated in front of federal buildings. I felt proud that we had in our midst Martha Hennessy, the granddaughter of Dorothy Day, whose progressive Catholic Worker House was now playing a major role in organizing these protests. Back in 2006, while Bush was still in power, Catholic Workers from Washington, Baltimore, and New York held vigils outside the Department of Justice, and on the first day of Lent called for repentance by reading an extraordinary passage from the Book of Isaiah that began: "Your hands are stained with blood, your fingers with guilt, your lips speak falsehood, and your tongue utters deceit."

By the time we were meeting with Leahy, the antitorture movement had grown into a large "100 Days Campaign" led by Amnesty International and scores of other peace groups, including Witness Against Torture, a group founded by the Catholic Worker organization. They wanted to make sure the new president held true to his promise of closing Guantánamo and ending torture and human rights abuses. Every day, between 11:00 a.m. and 1:00 p.m., peace activists in the D.C. area sponsored film and discussion series, met with members of Congress, and on Thursdays engaged in "creative action" (civil resistance and street theaters). Martha had participated herself, walking outside the White House in her orange jumpsuit while on a nine-day fast and, still wearing her jumpsuit, visiting the offices of Vermont's congressional delegation. She would later confess to me that the experience walking the halls of Congress was disheartening. "None of my Congressmen were available. I felt really disconnected, like walking in the halls of the deaf, dumb, and blind. I really didn't feel like my witness meant very much."[90]

President Obama had acceded to only one of their demands: He issued an executive order to ban torture the day after his inauguration. But he had not yet set a date for closing Guantánamo. Nor had he agreed, as implored, to hold an independent commission to investigate torture and other abuses. After his own Justice Department had released nine Bush-era documents earlier in the month detailing secret plans to unleash the U.S. military on American citizens if need be, the mood in the accountability movement was restive. Demands for prosecution had become louder and more insistent, with some lawyers and activists (Michael Ratner of the Center for Constitutional Rights and writer Naomi Wolf, for example) describing the Bush administration's behavior as nothing less than treasonous.[91]

Senator Leahy was far too cautious to acknowledge publicly anything like treason. But we knew he was appalled over the repressive actions of the previous administration and had gone to great lengths as head of the Senate Judiciary Committee to try to keep them in check. He even made a cameo appearance in the latest Batman movie, *The Dark Knight,* where he said, in one of his more memorable one-liners: "We won't be intimidated by thugs!" Leahy, in short, seemed to have a heart beneath his rather steely exterior, and it was his heart we wanted to appeal to.

He appeared on time, looking very much like the distinguished statesman, a stand-out in his well-tailored suit in an otherwise drab setting. A tall (over 6-foot) Irishman, slim, his bald dome neatly fringed with grey, Leahy took up the first five minutes of our precious thirty minutes talking about his success-ful efforts at getting the place restored. We bit our tongues on that one, then went around the room introducing ourselves. His staff had obviously not done any advance work on who we were and at one point Kurt Daims said, only half jokingly, "Well, you could have googled us!"

Dan DeWalt started things off. He was all seriousness, his dark hair pulled neatly away from his somber face, his body hunched over his prepared statement. He had worked hard on this. It meant a lot to him. "We are not coming here out of anger," he began—at which point Leahy interrupted, "I don't mind if you're angry." Unfazed, DeWalt continued. "We come out of concern for the future of our country. We are deeply concerned about dangers to our democracy, with the trend going to executive power and damaging our Constitution."

Now Leahy was silent, listening intently. "We are a nation of laws," Dan went on. "Why not have the system of justice take its course? It seems to many Americans that the rich and the powerful have a different system of justice, and they're getting away with torture, murder, fraud, and Ponzi schemes."

Dan handed Leahy a copy of the draft complaint that Lawrence Velvel's Robert Jackson Justice Committee had formulated, charging the Bush administration with war crimes. Leahy acknowledged it, as well as a recent revelation that a Spanish judge would pursue an indictment of Bush's lawyers if Eric Holder did not.

Martha Hennessy spoke next. She hoped her approach might resonate with a fellow Catholic. She informed Leahy that she was the granddaughter of Dorothy Day and handed him a prayer card with words from her grandmother. She saw him put it in his shirt pocket, close to his heart. "She's with us today," she said, and Leahy seemed genuinely touched. He thanked her, acknowledging his admiration for her grandmother.

Then Martha shared a personal story. She had been handcuffed for twelve hours straight, been denied water, and then was detained for thirty hours back in January, 2008, after participating in a demonstration outside the U.S. Supreme Court against the torture of detainees. She realized that compared to the conditions in Guantánamo, her experience had been a cakewalk—but, still, it did make her feel closer to understanding what the detainees had gone through. Then she handed Leahy a letter from a prisoner in Guantánamo who complained of a double standard in the U.S. for those who got justice and those who did not. Many inmates, she said, had been tortured and left to suffer in their prison cells for years, wondering whether they would be put on trial or released. Most of them, she added, were now deemed innocent. "I just wanted to give you a personal face to our efforts at accountability."

Leahy was gracious in accepting the letter. He knew about the injustices in Guantánamo and had raised this issue during committee hearings. But in the little time we had left with him, he chose to focus on his background as a prosecutor for eight years, with the highest conviction rate in Vermont's Chittenden county. He was not against prosecutions per se, he said. But prosecutions seldom went above midlevel people. "We don't want another Abu Ghraib," he said. "You know, 'boy did we get those corporals and privates.' So many on high never get touched. It's like the war on drugs—'let's get those black kids on cocaine.'"

So it seemed that prosecutions were definitely out. As for his truth commission, he was equally blunt. "I can't get one Republican to support it," he said, and without bipartisan support, "it's not going to happen."

We were stunned. Even though we heard hints of this, we couldn't quite believe it.

When my turn came around, I returned to the issue of prosecutions. I thanked him for his staff's help on my FOIA case, said I admired him for his fine work on the Senate Judiciary Committee, then told him that I, too, had a personal story to impart: I had read, on the Internet, a letter to his office from the 9/11 widows from New Jersey expressing their frustrations with the 9/11 Commission and urging him not to replicate that model. "I met with them, and they gave me these documents." I turned over the nineteen-page index of hearings and some letters they had written to the Senate Judiciary Committee complaining of inaction on the subject of accountability.

He looked mildly startled and hesitated a moment before accepting them. "You have probably seen some of these already," I added, "but I just wanted to reiterate, on their behalf, that a lot of the information that you want your truth commission to gather has, in their view, already been answered." I pointed to the lengthy index of hearings. "They say there have been hearings up the ying yang, that they've monitored all of them, but nothing has come of them."

He immediately cut me off. "There will be no truth commission," he said firmly.

"We should at least be glad," he added, that "we were able to get Alberto Gonzales to resign as attorney general"—a resignation that Leahy had been crucial in obtaining.

At that, he stood up to leave. Our time was up. As he began to leave, Dan got in one more comment.

"Senator, we have lost faith in Congress," Dan said.

Leahy, surprised, turned around. He was clearly offended. "Then I've failed, haven't I?" And with that he left the room.

His aide, Chuck Ross, came back to the meeting. He wanted to assure us that no one had done more to defend the Constitution than Senator Leahy. "You should see what it's like to take leadership in an unfriendly environment."

DeWalt shot back, "Understood, but he's our senator, and who else can we turn to? When you're down in the engine room and the boat is sinking, it doesn't matter how good of an engineer you are. You need to get up on top and do some steering. This is no ordinary time with no ordinary future."

Now Ross was clearly on the defensive. "He has been persistent in the face of obfuscation," he said. "He got rid of Gonzales." He paused, and then, in a moment of apparent exasperation, added "He's all you got." With this, he, too, exited the room.

What? Leahy was all we had to protect the Constitution? We were supposed to be satisfied with Gonzales's resignation as punishment for years of gutting the rule of law? It took about five minutes for all of this to sink in.

Then John Nirenberg broke the silence. "If he's all we've got, then this is not a healthy situation."

I thought back to my meeting with the Jersey girls. They had warned me that nothing was likely to come out of our meeting with Leahy. And they were right. What did this all mean? Was Leahy, by his loyal aide's reckoning, the last man standing in Congress? Was his "getting rid of Gonzales" his last hurrah? I had to know. In the group report that we submitted to the blogosphere on our meeting, we had concluded that he had "the air of a man beaten down by the system."

Soon, after some additional probing, I realized that Patrick Leahy was that and more—a symbol of weakened senatorial power that all Americans would be remiss in ignoring.

Is he really all we have?

Reviewing Patrick Leahy's record in Congress is like getting a crash course in the decline of a republic in the age of empire. He arrived in Washington in 1974, just after President Nixon resigned in disgrace over the Watergate scandal. At age thirty-four, Leahy was one of the youngest members of Congress, and he was full of youthful idealism. "There was a sense in the Senate among both Republicans and Democrats that the government had gotten off course and that we had a responsibility to find out what happened," he told a *New York Times* reporter in November, 2008.[92]

His senior colleague from Idaho, Senator Frank Church, had convened a special probe into domestic spying (one of Nixon's legacies) and had interviewed over eight hundred officials and held twenty-one public hearings into the abuse of power by the FBI and the Central Intelligence Agency. Americans were rapidly getting an education in the most secret machinations of their own government, and it was not pretty. The Church Committee hearings would bring about some major reforms aimed at curbing domestic spying, and since the effort was largely bipartisan, it is small wonder that Patrick Leahy may have thought that in 2009 he could somehow replicate that era and its spirit of bipartisanship.

But much had happened over the span of forty-five years, and by the time George W. Bush took power, there was no disputing that he had taken command of an "imperial presidency" that disregarded the reforms of the Church Committee era and sought to undermine the power of Congress. Patrick Leahy himself had to sadly acknowledge to *The New York Times* that the blossoming power of the Senate, which had grown and thrived during his early years in Congress, had now withered on the vine.[93]

Still, as Leahy rose in power and seniority, he tried to do his best. He knew that Vermonters (who elected a self-proclaimed democratic socialist, Independent Bernie Sanders, to Congress in 1990 and helped propel Howard Dean into a bid for the presidency) expected bold action from their elected representatives. In the year 2001, Leahy and the other senator from Vermont, Republican James Jeffords, shifted the entire balance of power in Washington. The upset began in May, with Jeffords's decision to defect from the Republican Party and become an Independent. That dramatic move gave the Democrats majority control of the Senate for the first time since the Republican Revolution of 1994. *Time* magazine darkly called it "one of the most successful covert operations in American political history."[94]

By July, 2001, the conservative *National Review* had Leahy pegged as the nation's "nastiest" Democrat, nastier and more liberal than Ted Kennedy, Christopher Dodd, Joe Biden, and John Kerry put together.[95] "When Jim Jeffords pulled his big switch [from Republican to Independent]," conservative columnist Jay Nordlinger reported, "Leahy landed a big job: chairman of the Judiciary Committee. It's a job Leahy has always wanted; and a Republican nightmare has begun."

Nightmare in the judiciary

Actually, their nightmare was already underway when, beginning in January, 2001, Leahy presided over the confirmation hearings of John Ashcroft for attorney general. He repeatedly exposed the Missouri senator's ultraconservative background, stunning Ashcroft's followers. "Our reaction," one member of the Ashcroft team told Jay Nordlinger, "was Wow! I mean holy Moses! The guy's trying to slay us!'" Ashcroft ultimately prevailed, Nordlinger added, "but not before being tarred before the nation as a racist, reactionary nut."

After the hearings, Leahy's final words of warning were prophetic in terms of what Ashcroft's confirmation signified for America:

> Running through [the nominee's] record [we find] disturbing, recurrent themes: disrespect for Supreme Court precedent with which he disagrees; grossly intemperate criticism of judges with whom he disagrees; insensitivity and bad judgment on racial issues; and the use of distortions, secret holds, and ambushes to harm the careers of those whom he opposed or for political gain.

Seven months later, following the attacks of September 11, John Ashcroft became the chief architect of the USA Patriot Act. Leahy immediately saw its inherent dangers and succeeded in adding a sunset provision for certain governmental powers that could adversely affect civil liberties. Reported Salon.com, "Senator Leahy emerged as perhaps the biggest obstacle to the sweeping law-enforcement powers sought by the Bush Administration and Attorney General John Ashcroft." Once again, Leahy seemed to sense what was coming.

What he surely could never have anticipated was being one of two U.S. senators to receive a letter laced with anthrax within weeks of the September 11 attacks. The other senator was Senate Majority Leader Tom Daschle, the same senator who, with Leahy months earlier, had helped convince Vermont's Senator Jeffords to leave the Republican Party in May, 2001.[96]

One can only imagine how unnerving this must have been for Leahy and his staff. "I come from Vermont where these things don't happen," Leahy told Salon. But if the anthrax-laced letter was designed to intimidate—if not kill—him, he did not let on.

In June, 2004, Leahy went on the offensive against Ashcroft again, this time for the attorney general's apparent role in approving torture at Abu Ghraib and Guantánamo. Leahy's Senate Judiciary Committee immediately convened oversight hearings on torture and probed whether superiors at the highest level (including President Bush) may have approved of the torture in violation of the Geneva Conventions.[97]

Leahy became particularly indignant over the fate of detainees with no connection to terrorism who had their rights denied them. They had been "rounded up on the basis of their religion or ethnicity, held for months without charges and in some cases . . . physically abused," he said. Many of these noncitizens were Muslims. Leahy, who had previously exposed Ashcroft for his racist opinions, was now revealing the attorney general, without using the "r" word, for his racist policies.

Ashcroft would soon become such a lightening rod for attacks from Democrats that he quietly slipped away—but not into oblivion—following Bush's reelection in 2004. Even with Ashcroft out of office, Leahy was not ready to let bygones be bygones.

In April, 2005, when the sunset provisions of the Patriot Act came up for review, the senator seized on the opportunity to expose the Bush administration's penchant for secrecy.

> We know the government is using its surveillance powers under the Foreign Intelligence Surveillance Act more than ever, but everything else about FISA is secret.
>
> We have seen secret arrests and secret hearings of hundreds of people for the first time in U.S. history; detentions without charges and denial of access to counsel; misapplication of the material witness statute as a sort of general preventive detention law; discriminatory targeting of Arabs and Muslims; selective enforcement of the immigration laws. . . . Such abuses harm our national security as well as civil liberties because they serve as recruiting posters for terrorists.[98]

Up to this point, with both the House and the Senate controlled by the Republican Party, Leahy seemed hamstrung by policies he could not change. But there was one area where he could fight back: by strengthening the Freedom of Information Act, which allows citizens to get access to government information. There had been serious cases of government delays in responding to FOIA requests over the past decade, and he aimed to repair the damage.

"FOIA," Leahy said in a statement announcing Sunshine Week, "helps hold our government accountable." Four years later those words take on a new relevance, for if it weren't for FOIA, groups like the ACLU would not have obtained some of the torture memos that would be the undoing of the Bush administration.

At this point of my review of Leahy's record on accountability, I could not fault the man. His run-ins with Republicans were genuine—so genuine, in fact, that Leahy earned a famous expletive from the far-right Republican pooh-bah himself, Dick Cheney. The occasion was the U.S. Senate class photo in June, 2004. Cheney, then serving as constitutional presider over the Senate, was present, but was seen talking only to Republicans. When Leahy went up to him and suggested he talk to Democrats as well, Cheney muttered back, "Go fuck yourself!"[99] Which, of course, only endeared Leahy more to his Vermont constituents.

As I would soon learn, Leahy's greatest challenge as Congress's shiner of light on the far right was yet to come, in the seemingly mild-mannered persona of Alberto Gonzales, the president's lawyer who would soon become the nation's next attorney general. Talk about having the fox guarding the chicken coop!

Getting Gonzales

Alberto Gonzales, the grandson of Latino immigrants, seemed to be the epitome of the American success story. He was the kid who started out selling soft drinks at football games in Texas and ended up joining George W. Bush in the White House.

But on this opening day of Gonzales's nomination hearings for attorney general, you could almost feel Leahy's sense of foreboding. The nominee may have defended his friend the president as White House counsel, Leahy reminded Gonzales, but now he was expected to serve the people and enforce the law. The attorney general "cannot be worried about friends, colleagues, and benefactors at the White House," Leahy warned—and then launched into a speech that summarized all the horrors of the previous four years, aptly reduced, right at the onset, to two sentences: "The job of attorney general is not about crafting rationalizations for ill-conceived ideas. . . . We have now seen what happens when the rule of law plays second fiddle to a president's policy agenda."

This was a loaded statement. Leahy was saying that everything the previous attorney general had done—along with his loyal minions at the Office of Legal Counsel in the Department of Justice—was to help shape policy around a political agenda, rather than offer independent advice on the president's legal options.

Leahy launched into a lecture about the torture scandals at Abu Ghraib and Guantánamo, because, as he reminded Gonzales, "these hearings are about a nomination, but these hearings are also about accountability."

He ended his preamble by hoping that "things will be different if you are confirmed, Judge Gonzales."

They weren't. In fact, by the end of the first day of nomination hearings, Leahy became so frustrated with Gonzales's refusal to give clear answers on the administration's definition of torture that he held up a thick file before the cameras. Inside the file, he said, voice shaking with indignation, were all the unanswered letters and questions addressed to Gonzales. "If he's confirmed," Leahy predicted, "I'm sure he'll feel that he never has any duty to answer them."[100] And Leahy, who voted against Gonzales's confirmation, was right.

Over the next four years, Leahy and Gonzales would face off again and again as more evidence of the Bush administration's unconstitutional policies leaked out to the press and the public.

In January, 2007, now Senate Judiciary Chairman Leahy's usually calm demeanor exploded, his bald and befreckled head literally shaking back and forth in anger as he grilled Gonzales on the "extraordinary rendition" (kidnapping by U.S. agents) of Canadian citizen Maher Arar to a torture chamber in Syria.

"I'm somewhat upset," Leahy confessed. Then he began jabbing his finger at Gonzales. "We knew damned well if we sent him to Canada he wouldn't be tortured; he'd be held and he'd be investigated. And we knew damn well that if he went to Syria, he *would* be tortured. And," he added, his voice rising, "it's beneath the dignity of this country, a country that has always been a beacon of human rights, to send someone to another country to be tortured!"

Gonzales just sat in his witness chair, looking a little embarrassed and chagrined, like a naughty puppy. I would have blown my top, too, if I had had to confront someone who acted as if these illegal activities were nothing more than having a doggy accident on the kitchen floor.

By July, 2007, after Gonzales refused to answer some sixty questions, Leahy had reached his limit of endurance. He was so used to Gonzales's stonewalling that he sent the attorney general his questions—on the politicization of the Justice Department, on warrantless wiretapping, and on omissions and inconsistencies in Gonzales's previous testimony—in advance.

It was a highly unusual move—and it worked. Now, when Gonzales appeared yet again, on July 24, he had no excuse for not remembering.

This time, however, Leahy looked tired and subdued. When he addressed Gonzales, he talked about the crisis of leadership in the Department of Justice, with whom he had worked for a number of years when he was a prosecutor in Vermont. They had never shown any political leanings, he said. They acted like professionals.

"You say morale is good," he said, then stopped before saying, "You're wrong." Instead, he launched into a quiet speech about trust.

"You came here seeking our trust. Frankly, you've lost my trust." He paused, realizing the gravitas of the moment. "I've never said that to any cabinet member before—not even anyone with whom I disagreed. I hope you can regain the trust of the hardworking people at the Department of Justice. They deserve better. Once the government shows disregard for the independence of the justice system and rule of law, it's very hard to regain the people's faith."

He ended by saying he took no pleasure in saying what he did. The hearing ended, and just as it did, voices heard in the Senate chamber yelled out, "Resign! Resign!"

A month later, Gonzales did. This must have been, for Leahy, one of his finest moments.

In the months to come, when confronted with harsh opposition from left and right to his "bipartisan" truth commission, there would be times when he would have to consider it the last of his finest moments.

Most people would probably agree. But Jersey Girls Mindy Kleinberg and Lorie Van Auken saw the Senate Judiciary hearings in a different light. The senator from Vermont had done a fine job of exposing the wrongdoing of the Bush Justice Department, but they already knew all of this. What they wanted was justice and accountability as well as the truth, and they weren't finding it. Instead, they felt they were witnessing a once-noble institution, the Senate, becoming a mockery of democracy. Here's an excerpt from a letter they wrote on July 26, 2007, to all members of the Senate Judiciary Committee:

> The Attorney General, a man who supposedly personifies America's rule of law, obfuscated, committed perjury, and belittled the very institution, the Congress, which makes America a great democracy. Over and over, we publicly witnessed Gonzales' refusal to answer questions posed by you. . . . We want to know: Is it not a crime to mislead and outright lie to the Congress? We are watching the U.S. Congress . . . making itself irrelevant. When the Executive Branch alone is allowed to act without any oversight, or any accountability, then what we will become is a dictatorship. . . . And once . . . Congress is unable to perform any oversight, whether it is due to the lack of will or complicity, you will no longer be needed. . . .

What Mindy and Lorie sensed, just by watching those hearings, was a serious crisis in America's constitutional history. Gonzales's behavior was symptomatic of the total disdain with which the Bush administration regarded Congress. The move away from democracy toward dictatorship was actually more advanced than even they had realized. And the people who made it happen were all, every single one of them, lawyers.

CHAPTER SEVEN

Lawyer Hoax: The Stealing of America, and the People Who Fought Back

As we all know, there are lawyers and *then there are lawyers*. Lawyers like to joke among themselves that everyone loves to hate them—until they need them. But let's face it. Lawyers in this country (not all, but enough) have earned themselves a pretty nasty reputation as liars and thieves. "What's the difference between a lawyer and a catfish?" goes one typical lawyer joke. "Answer: One is a slimy, bottom-dwelling scum sucker. The other is a fish."

The lawyers who helped George W. Bush and his team break the law will go down in history as some of the most despicable in living memory. As will be shown in this and the following chapter, they justified war when war was not necessary; they justified torture even though torture was a crime; they turned the president into a dictator and Congress into a hollow shell. And they did it all under the guise of legality, to justify policy—and shield themselves, their bosses, and the people who acted on their legal opinions, from prosecution.

In my journey on the ragged path to accountability, I was relieved to find some very good lawyers, indeed brave lawyers, who were taking on the bad ones even while most of the legal community remained silent.

The first place I found them was in Andover, Massachusetts, at the same venue where I first met Vincent Bugliosi, in September, 2008. Lawrence Velvel, the dean of the Massachusetts School of Law, had organized a conference for lawyers and activists because, as Velvel would later tell me,[101] "the mainstream media at that time refused to talk about war crimes. So holding a conference was a matter of frustration."

Velvel had had many past encounters with bad lawyers. In his younger years, he spent time in Washington, D.C., in private practice—and later wrote a scathing, somewhat fictionalized memoir spanning his entire legal career.[102] Like so many young lawyers fresh out of law school, he had started out believing in the pursuit of social justice. Along the way he discovered corruption, cheating, and opportunism, causing him to conclude that honesty and serving the greater good of society were actually liabilities on the way to a truly successful law career, at least in Washington, D.C. Still, he stayed the course, never giving up on his core beliefs. He went on to become a law-school dean at a school that catered to working-class students, and through this vehicle he was able to take on the powers that be by holding the 2008 conference provocatively titled "Planning for the Prosecution of High-Level American War Criminals."

Velvel financed the whole thing himself. I asked him why. "All I'm willing to say," he replied, "is this: We have twenty-five hundred students, and among them, only twenty hated the idea that George W. Bush could be responsible for war crimes." But that was enough to cause him some grief. "They set up a Web site, and nineteen to twenty people wrote negative comments—which they also sent to the trustees—saying I should be fired."

The conference survived, as did Velvel and his job. In those days, Velvel could afford to take risks. "That was before I got burned by Bernie Madoff," he told me. Fortunately for us, he was able to pull off this important conference just in time, before being victimized by the Ponzi-scheme rip-off artist whose crimes will forever remain a symbol of the excesses of the Bush years.

When Velvel introduced a conference panel on "The Actions of Bush Administration Lawyers," he couldn't resist injecting a little grim humor: "And now, here's a panel for everyone who despises lawyers."

People laughed, though many were startled by his introduction. Here was a "man of the [legal] cloth" who was choosing to castigate members of his own profession.

"I'm referring to the lawyers who had "memo'd up" for the Bush administration," Velvel went on, "the lawyers who wrote the corrupt legal memos giving attempted cover to Bush's actions and have since been rewarded by federal judgeships, cabinet positions, and highfalutin professorships."

It occurred to me that some of the other panelists, like Velvel, might suffer some grief from publicly challenging the Bush administration. These lawyers had already seen how the Bush administration had driven good U.S. attorneys from their jobs simply because they were not adequately loyal to the

Bush agenda. What kind of response might these lawyers' *"disloyalty"* evoke, if not from their more conservative colleagues, then from government offi-cials in the future? Bush was still in office and Obama's victory, while likely as the economy began to tank, was not a certainty when these attorneys convened in Andover in September.

Yet when I interviewed them later on, I learned that they weren't in the least bit nervous. For one thing, they had already assembled plenty of evidence to bolster their cases against the Bush lawyers, thanks to memos released to the public through lawsuits, leaks, and FOIA requests. They also came with baggage—the good kind, acquired over years of fighting the good fight in the courts. Their stories cover the gamut of what good lawyers should do, from flying multiple times to Guantánamo to help a client, to trying to bring Chilean dictator Augusto Pinochet to justice, to suing Donald Rumsfeld for war crimes, to bucking the brass and exposing Army domestic spying on protestors—in the Vietnam War era and now. All should be recognized as early heroes in the accountability movement.

When I asked panelist Christopher Pyle, a gray-haired, goateed consti-tutional law professor at Mount Holyoke College, how he felt about going public with his critique of the Bush lawyers, he turned the question around: "Perhaps you should ask me how I feel about my government torturing people." This was his way of saying he was not easily intimidated, and when I questioned him further, I found out why.

In 1970 he had taught law at the U.S. Army Intelligence School and while there discovered that his division was engaged in unlawful domestic spying on civilian antiwar protestors. That, he knew, was a violation of the First Amendment. He proceeded to recruit 125 of his students—all counterin-telligence agents—to share what they knew with members of Congress. He supplied their information to Senator Sam Ervin of the Subcommittee on Constitutional Rights, which prompted further hearings, including the Church Committee hearings on intelligence abuses. Twenty-five of his students would eventually sign on to a legal brief submitted to the U.S. Supreme Court. "We lost 5–4 (the conservative Justice Rehnquist delivered the deciding blow), but we were able to get U.S. army intelligence to disband its domestic intelligence division and burn the records of those spied upon."

Now, some thirty years later, the still-youthful-looking Pyle was leading off the panel at the Andover conference. He got right to the point. "Bush's torture policy," he said, as he leaned slightly into the podium, his face grave, his brow knitted in genuine concern, "is the work of attorneys."

How, then, did the Bush administration lawyers pull it off, I wondered. And why? As Pyle and his co-panelists laid out the answer to this question, I was not prepared to agree with their assessments at this point, or their conclusions—that Bush and Cheney's lawyers were criminals deserving of prosecution or, at the very least, disbarment or impeachment. But I listened, carefully.

Their work began, Pyle explained, in November, 2001, when they helped the president create a new judicial system called military commissions. Thousands of suspected terrorists had been rounded up in Afghanistan during the first two months of the U.S. war in Afghanistan, and the top lawyers in the Department of Justice had decided to try them in military commissions outside the jurisdiction of either the federal court system or the military justice system of courts martial. "There could only be one reason to have military commissions," Pyle said, "and that was to [use them to] admit evidence obtained by torture. Otherwise, courts martial would have worked fine, and they are provided for under the Geneva Conventions [which outlaw torture]."

A "normal" court system would not countenance evidence obtained by torture, because such evidence was notoriously unreliable. Tortured people said what their torturers wanted them to say. Pyle did not go into details on what the Bush administration wanted the detainees to confess to. That would be up to us to find out. But he did say that back in November, 2001, the Bush lawyers—Alberto Gonzales in the White House, John Yoo and Jay Bybee in the Office of Legal Counsel, and Cheney's lawyer, David Addington—*anticipated* that people would be coerced to make self-incriminating statements and that these statements would be used against them in what would later be commonly referred to as a kangaroo court.

The legal memos that followed, issued by some of the same above-named lawyers beginning in December, 2001, and January, 2002, effectively acknowledged that the interrogators might get in trouble if they coerced statements out of the detainees. So, to cover up the torturers' illegal activities, the lawyers came up with bogus legal defenses, which, Pyle said, sounded more like "the advice of mafia lawyers"[103] than the kind of dispassionate advice expected from respectable law firms. Rather than objectively recite the state of the law, Bush's lawyers "left out huge chunks of the law"—most notably the well-established law set by the U.S. Supreme Court in *Youngstown Sheet and Tube Co. v. Sawyer* (1952)[104] that rejected sweeping claims of presidential powers. Rather than adhere to established precedence and the rule of law, the Bush lawyers single-handedly *redefined* the law.

The purpose of their memos, Pyle continued, was to alter American law and military practice regarding treatment of prisoners. Since their bogus opinions would never survive the light of day, they were done in secret. Their ultimate intent was to reassure CIA operatives that they could, as Pyle put it, "beat the hell out of the detainees and get them to confess to something they didn't do." The lawyers also tried to protect their bosses in the White House and the Pentagon from liability, offering them the unprecedented defense of "my lawyers said I could do it."[105]

Concluded Pyle, Bush's lawyers "were accomplices in a criminal conspiracy to violate the law" and, as such, "they should be punished." Within six months, the culpability of the Bush administration lawyers would become a matter of national debate as more of their so-called torture memos were released to the public pursuant to a Freedom of Information lawsuit brought on by the American Civil Liberties Union. The memos caused a storm of controversy, igniting an accountability movement that is as unprecedented in American history as the memos themselves.

Joshua Dratel, next on the panel, is a defense attorney who has the distinction of being one of the first, if not the first, private lawyers to defend a detainee at Guantánamo. He made fourteen trips to Cuba and became exposed to the military commission system firsthand ("This system is illegal; its sole purpose is to convict," he told me, "just like in a Star Chamber").[106] Over the years, he amassed such a volume of "torture memos" from leaks and FOIA requests that he assembled a book with co-editor Karen Greenberg called *The Torture Papers: The Road to Abu Ghraib.*

As a defense attorney, he knew full well that Bush's lawyers would argue that they were giving the best advice they could under very trying circumstances. He also knew that Bush, Cheney, and Rumsfeld, among others, would resort to a "my lawyers said I could do it" defense, but it wouldn't be that easy. If it could be proven that the lawyers, in their 2002–03 legal memos, were simply papering over illegalities which had *already occurred,* then these administration officials had no defense at all. Besides (and here Dratel quoted a Velvel blog), "you can't rely on an 'advice of counsel defense' when you told [the lawyers] what advice to give."

Philippe Sands, the British law professor and author of *Lawless World* and *Torture Team,* followed with the final *coup de grâce.* Speaking with the calm assurance of someone who had spent years tackling these issues in the courtroom and the press (most notably through his involvement in the indictment of Chilean dictator Augusto Pinochet) he noted that Article IV of the UN Convention Against Torture stated that complicity in torture policies, without actually physically carrying them out, is itself a criminal act.

What was to be done?

All these conclusions were stated as hypotheticals and were discussed in the briefest of terms due to time constraints. I would learn more about the specific charges against the lawyers as more incriminating evidence began to pour in after Obama's election. But even in the fall of 2008, it was clear to me that these top-ranked lawyers were confident that they had the goods on the Bush torture team. The inevitable question was: How would justice be served? Dean Velvel, not one to sit on the sidelines, suggested impeaching Jay Bybee, who still held a government job serving as a judge for the Ninth Circuit Federal Court in California. His proposal would gain traction in the coming months in the wake of Bybee's "torture memos" being released in April. Yoo, teaching at Berkeley, could be subjected to dismissal, but only after being convicted of a crime. All could be disbarred if well-crafted ethics complaints were brought to their respective bar councils.

Velvel also vowed to put together a Justice Robert Jackson Committee—named after the fearless Nuremberg prosecutor—to prepare a criminal complaint for war crimes against all the top people in the Bush administration, including the lawyers. He had said at the outset that he would "pursue the guilty as long as necessary, and, if need be, to the ends of the Earth." And he wasn't kidding, suggesting imprisonment and even capital punishment for the worst offenders, a fate that was "visited upon top German and Japanese war criminals in the 1940s."

That was, in fact, precisely what happened at Nuremberg. And Velvel was not alone in this assessment: "Lawyers have been prosecuted and imprisoned in the past," wrote legal affairs editor Scott Horton of *Harper's* magazine, "for issuing opinions like the opinions that were issued here that enabled torture . . . and the violation of the laws of war."[107]

Would Bush's lawyers—and their superiors—ever be prosecuted for war crimes? It was much too early to tell. But justice deferred had a way of creeping up on war criminals, as has been shown in England, Spain, Argentina, Brazil, and Uruguay where war-crime investigations are now going at full pace for acts committed by dictators decades ago. Pyle, in his new book, *Getting Away with Torture*, points out that Bush "was so fearful that he might be prosecuted after leaving office" that he personally visited Capitol Hill to lobby for the 2006 Military Commissions Act, a piece of legislation that would legalize, *ex post facto*, acts of brutality by American interrogators like dog attacks, sensory deprivation, and waterboarding.[108] Bush claimed he wanted to protect soldiers from unjust prosecution. Perhaps what he really had in mind was protecting himself and his closest associates. No wonder Dick Cheney, after leaving office, would fight back with every defense he could muster once the Obama administration came into power.

The Andover conference closed with most everyone agreeing that the fastest route for pursuing justice was to demand an independent special prosecutor. Panelist Laura Rótolo, a Boston-based lawyer with the American Civil Liberties Union, reported that the ACLU had written a letter to Congress giving ten reasons why this should happen. (And two senators, Dick Durbin of Illinois and Sheldon Whitehouse of Rhode Island, did in fact ask the Justice Department to conduct an internal investigation of the Bush lawyers.)

Rótolo had a particularly compelling reason for wanting to hold the Bush administration lawyers accountable. She had been born in Argentina, and as a young girl had lived through a *coup d'état* that brought into power a dictatorship and eventually the subsequent disappearances of thirty thousand people—students, activists, young people, people involved in politics. She had been lucky, she explained. She and her family were able to escape to the U.S. as immigrants. Years later, when lawsuits were brought in Argentina over these crimes, she decided to go to law school. "My sister and I didn't want what happened in Argentina to ever happen again."

But just how far would Congress go? Only a few seemed to have any stomach for it. The respective chairs of the House and Senate Judiciary Committees agreed on the need for accountability, but differed on their approach. Representative John Conyers, chair of the House Judiciary Committee, had been very active in gathering information on the Bush lawyers through hearings. In the spring of 2008, he had read an article by Philippe Sands in *Vanity Fair* that was one of the first to describe in graphic detail the physical and mental suffering of some of the "high-end" detainees. Conyers, according to Sands, was so appalled that he called a hearing on the responsibility of the Bush lawyers for the torture policies. From these hearings came some valuable evidence, including the fact that it was Jim Haynes, the top lawyer for the Department of Defense, who had initiated the torture policy. It was Haynes who also stopped the usual practice of having a legal review of the OLC legal opinions by military lawyers before they were approved.

Conyers would be one of the few high-ranking members from the House of Representatives to call for a special prosecutor. Representative Dennis Kucinich of Ohio was another. But they were exceptions.[109]

In the Senate, there was Senator Russ Feingold of Minnesota and Patrick Leahy, chair of the Judiciary Committee, who clearly suspected what Bush's top lawyers were up to. Remember, Leahy had lectured Gonzales during his nomination hearings: "The job of Attorney General is not about crafting rationalizations for ill-conceived ideas. We have now seen what happens when the rule of law plays second fiddle to a president's policy agenda."

But for all his scolding in Senate hearing rooms, Leahy consistently maintained a certain deference, a decorum suggesting he would not, or perhaps could not, cross the line into outright accusation of fellow lawyers of criminal behavior. It was as if there were some unspoken understanding among the patrician senators—including the lawyers on the Senate Judiciary Committee—that you could go only so far, you could not betray those of your own class by allowing them to be thrown in jail. The Senate is often referred to as a club, and now I understood why.

It certainly seems that a truth commission was as far as Leahy wanted to go. And for all his insistence that he wanted to see the people on top get their just desserts (not the little guys who always seemed to get the raw end of a criminal investigation), the fact is that truth commissions in places like South

Africa *never* punished the top people. In fact, one of the biggest complaints about the truth commission coming from black South Africans was that it weighed more in favor of the guilty than the victims. The top architects of the apartheid regime were given amnesty in exchange for their testimony and never even got a slap on the wrist for their criminal repression of the vast majority of South Africans.[110] Wrote William Kentridge, director of the highly acclaimed Jane Taylor play *Ubu and the Truth Commission*, "A full confession can bring amnesty and immunity from prosecution . . . for the crimes committed. Therein lies the central irony of the Commission. As people give more and more evidence of the things they have done they get closer and closer to amnesty and it gets more and more intolerable that these people should be given amnesty."

Oddly enough, Senator Leahy's protégé, Rhode Island senator Sheldon Whitehouse, seemed much more intent on pursuing the prosecution track— beginning with an inquiry into the role of the OLC lawyers.

It got me to wondering: Were Conyers, Leahy, and Whitehouse really all working in concert but trying to see which approach would ultimately find a way around a barricade of Republican opposition?

The Randolph massacre

Of the three of them, my own senator's actions struck me as the most perplexing. Only months later would I learn that Senator Leahy, the seeming champion of accountability, put the kibosh twice on Vermont's grassroots impeachment effort.

The first time occurred in 2006, when Jeff Taylor's "Rutland resolution" was rapidly gaining acceptance at different statewide town democratic committees. When it reached the statewide meeting in Randolph, however, it got a very different reception, at least from the party's leadership. According to impeachment activist Bruce Marshall, Leahy aide Chuck Ross—the same Chuck Ross who had told us "He's all you've got" at our meeting with Leahy—uttered some very discouraging words that caused impeachment activists to conclude that their senator was very much opposed.[111] Then the party leaders voted to cut Section 603 out of the resolution. Vermont's irreverent political columnist

Peter Freyne had caught it all, titling his regular column for Vermont's *Seven Days* magazine "The Randolph Massacre."

> The Democratic Party State Committee pulled off the dirty deed on Saturday when it officially gutted a pure-Vermont original! The so-called Rutland Resolution would have dared to pressure the Democrat-controlled Vermont legislature to officially request the U.S. House to commence impeachment proceedings against the most incompetent, dishonest and dangerous president in American history.

It didn't seem to matter, Freyne pointed out, that the overwhelming majority of the party's grassroots who attended the meeting were in favor of the Rutland resolution. They were overruled by their leaders.

They ended up with a watered-down resolution, but one that Speaker Gaye Symington defended as a "strong statement on impeachment." But Freyne wasn't buying it. He politely suggested to Symington that "[by] removing all reference to Section 603 from the final product and the call for legislation actions, the Dems had removed the meat from the bone. . . . Without the legislature's official imprimatur, the resolution passed by the state party on Saturday is nothing but junk mail in the eyes of Congress."[112]

Impeachment activists were upset, but not deterred. They went on to get the Rutland resolution before the legislature the next year, in 2007. Once again, House Speaker Symington shot it down.

Human rights and the first one hundred days

Human-rights lawyers had every reason to be apprehensive at the start of Obama's first one hundred days in office. They had actually seen the physical and mental toll that the Bush torture policy had exacted on their clients imprisoned in Guantánamo and elsewhere. They had plenty of good evidence of OLC malfeasance in the form of memos leaked and released in recent years. And they had powerful corroboration from Major General Antonio M. Taguba, the Pentagon's chief investigator of Abu Ghraib, that "there is no longer any doubt as to whether the current administration has committed war crimes. The only question that remains to be answered is whether those who ordered the use of torture will be held to account."

Everyone knew that the chain of command went right to the top. But how would those at the top be held to account? People in the human-rights community wanted to give President Obama the benefit of the doubt as he grappled with the legal minefield he had inherited over the issues of detainees. But it wasn't enough for them to see Obama sign executive orders foreswearing torture, repudiating OLC memos, and promising to close Guantánamo in a year. They wanted more demonstrative proof that Obama was going to hold true to his word, close Guantánamo, get the detainees a fair hearing, and go after the lawbreakers.

Candace Gorman, an attorney from Obama's hometown of Chicago, was paying particularly close attention. She knew Obama as a moderate, not the flaming liberal the press had widely portrayed him to be. As Illinois's junior senator, he had supported the Detainee Treatment Act of 2005 that denied the right of detainees to have their habeus corpus petitions heard in a federal court. As legal challenges went back and forth, with judges issuing rulings (some favorable to detainees) and the government responding by issuing stays, she had anguished for three years as her clients remained stuck in legal limbo. One of her clients, a middle-aged man who she believes was falsely accused by a deranged cellmate of being one of Osama bin Laden's bodyguards, was in failing health, having suffered for two years in solitary confinement from December, 2006, to November, 2008. She would never forget seeing him curled up in a fetal position, freezing in a highly air-conditioned room and barely able to talk.

Despite her reservations about Obama's voting record, she was overjoyed by Obama's election and encouraged by some of his appointments to run the Office of Legal Council. She was feeling hopeful, especially after the U.S. Supreme Court had ruled in July, 2008, in a 5–4 ruling in *Boumediene v. Bush*[113] that detainees had the same rights as American citizens to challenge their detentions in U.S. federal courts. It was an extraordinary decision, one that seemed to reaffirm the greatness of American democracy. "The laws and Constitution are designed to survive and remain in force in extraordinary times," the decision read. "Liberty and security can be reconciled; and in our system they are reconciled within the framework of the law. The Framers decided that habeas corpus, a right of first importance, must be a part of that framework, a part of that law."

But before long her hope began to fade as "everything continued at a snail's pace." Her efforts to get evidentiary documents declassified were being met with worse resistance since Obama's election, thanks to bureaucratic maneuvers adopted by the Department of Defense. For some strange reason, the high-level detainees—the ones Donald Rumsfeld called the worst of the worst—were actually getting processed and released, while the "nobodys" were still languishing in their prison cells.

Gorman is deeply involved in the accountability movement, and for over two years now has been chronicling her ongoing efforts—and frustrations (as well as others')—in a blog devoted entirely to Guantánamo.[114]

Much of her information would shock her readers. Here's how she began a blog that was published by The Huffington Post titled "Guantánamo Five Years Later: The Graveyard of Human Rights" on January 11, 2007, the fifth anniversary of the opening of Guantánamo: "The road to Guantánamo started with the bounty flyers. Thousands upon thousands of flyers in various languages were dropped in Afghanistan, Pakistan, Yemen, and who knows where else, offering huge bounties for 'murderers and terrorists.' Thousands of men were turned over to U.S. forces on promises of "wealth beyond your dreams."[115] Six months later, she would be happily reporting that Mohammed Jawad, one of the youngest detainees who had been taken prisoner when he was only twelve years old, had been released on a judge's orders. But "it's not," Gorman wrote, "because [the government] conceded that it had lost its case (the only evidence they had was tortured out of him").[116]

While Gorman was trying to draw attention to the plight of Guantánamo detainees, the lawyers who had brought the *Boumediene v. Bush* case, including Michael Ratner at the Center for Constitutional Rights (CCR), were putting pressure on the Obama administration by launching a "100 Days to Restore the Constitution" campaign. The CCR began sending out "white paper" pamphlets to the public on the different areas that sorely needed addressing, like "Ending Arbitrary Detention, Torture and Extraordinary Rendition," "Reigning in Presidential War Powers," "Protecting Dissent," and "Stopping Warrantless Wiretapping."

Educating and interacting with the public is something that Ratner and other CCR attorneys do as a matter of course. It's part of their mission. Ratner and a small group of lawyers founded the nonprofit back in the 1960s to help the civil-rights movement. It soon expanded its mission over the years to protect the constitutional rights of all Americans, and beginning in 2002 it became the first law firm to defend the rights of detainees at Guantánamo. Its commitment, as one of its white papers says, is "to the creative use of law as a positive force for social change."

Ratner has consistently called for the prosecution of the Bush "torture team." His political outlook and his strategies for bringing that team to justice were clearly shaped by his early years defending Guantánamo detainees. "It's the firsthand experience working with detainees that influenced my thinking," he replied when I asked him why he took such a hard line on prosecutions. "When you represent tortured individuals, you can't just throw up your hands and say a truth commission is okay, but not prosecution." Prosecutions serve as a deterrence in a way that a truth commission can never accomplish.

CCR started out very small, its lawyers shunned by the legal community when they first began representing the detainees at Guantánamo. In those days, the detainees had been presented by the Bush administration and a compliant media as presumed guilty. "We were treated as legal and political pariahs," Ratner wrote in his book, *Guantánamo* (one of the first to be published on this subject). "I got the worst hate mail I have ever received. I got letters asking me why I didn't just let the Taliban come to my house and eat my children."[117]

Gradually, as they worked their way through the lower courts, they won respect and help from other lawyers. Then, in July, 2008, the U.S. Supreme Court came in with its landmark decision in *Boumediene v. Bush* affirming the rights of detainees to be heard in federal courts. It was the kind of breakthrough CCR needed. Today, CCR's headquarters in lower Manhattan occupies three stories, employs forty-five lawyers (up seventeen in the last three years alone), and works with six hundred cooperating attorneys on the remaining two hundred detainee cases. Its central conference room during the summer is buzzing with young interns hunched over a bank of some twenty computers, all eagerly writing briefs and memos dealing with human-rights abuses around the world, racial and economic justice, and the rights of prisoners at Guantánamo in Cuba and at the detention center at the Bagram Airbase in Afghanistan.

Ratner, who is Jewish, is acutely conscious of Hitler's policies toward prisoners. During the early Guantánamo years, he began to see parallels to Nazism where powerful right-wing lawyers inside the OLC created new laws by fiat just as Nazi lawyers had done during World War II. In *Guantánamo* he singled out White House Counsel Alberto Gonzales for authoring the infamous January 25, 2002, memo recommending that the Geneva Conventions not be applied to the Taliban and al-Qaeda, thus providing the green light to torture. Gonzales knew that what he was doing was illegal. He even admitted, in writing, that his memo would "substantially reduce the threat of domestic criminal prosecution" of administration officials for war crimes.[118]

Ratner showed how Jay Bybee, with assistance from John Yoo, came up with a new definition of torture, applying it in their August, 2002, memo only to those cases that involved "serious physical injury, such as organ failure, impairment of bodily functions, or even death." And then there were the Pentagon's top lawyers, who devised a new term, "enemy combatants," and applied it to all people picked up anywhere in America's so-called war on terror. As "enemy combatants," these detainees would not be given the protections of prisoners of war established by the Geneva Conventions. Instead, they would be thrown into detention centers with no right to a lawyer or right to be charged. There wasn't much difference, in other words, between Bush's detention centers and the Nazis' "interrogation camps."[119]

No wonder Ratner was concerned.

I asked him about some anticipated defenses the Bush administration lawyers might use, like protecting the nation's security in a time of war.

"They may bring up national security," he replied, "but it's not a valid legal defense. What would happen if we put Pinochet up on the stand and he would testify that 'Operation Condor killings and kidnappings were justified because our national security was endangered'?"

In short, it wouldn't fly, at least not if judges applied the strict letter of the law. "The torture ban is absolute."

Recently, judges have begun to express concern for how some of the detainee cases have been handled by federal prosecutors. "I just encountered it today with my *Arar v. Ashcroft* case," Ratner told me back in February, 2009, referring to the rendition of a Canadian citizen to Syria where he was tortured to make false confessions. "The judge said 'You can't just pick someone up and take him away like that!'"

But in Congress and the White House, all hopes for prosecuting the torture team seemed stalled.

Ratner didn't have to look far for a reason. Just weeks after Obama was elected, Obama had chosen a former Bush appointee to head up his intelligence transition team. John Brennan had been closely associated with Bush's war on terror and torture policies. As deputy executive secretary to the CIA Director George Tenet, he had also overseen both the extraordinary renditions of detainees to various CIA "black sites" around the world and the torture programs in Iraq. Amazingly, Brennan had actually been Obama's first choice to head up the CIA until protests from influential bloggers, including Glenn Greenwald, reportedly convinced him to think otherwise.[120]

When *Democracy Now* host Amy Goodman asked Ratner back on November 17, 2008, for his reaction to Brennan's appointment, he said he found it "extremely, extremely disturbing." Brennan, to his mind, along with CIA Director Tenet, should be prosecuted for war crimes instead of helping the Obama administration shape its intelligence team. Five months later, he would learn just how disturbing Obama's decision had been.

The week from holy hell

By the middle of April, when the Obama administration was attempting to put its most positive spin on its first one hundred days, I began to see the convergence of human-rights lawyers, bloggers, and activists around a single issue: long delays by the Justice Department in releasing four highly anticipated torture memos to the American Civil Liberties Union. Freedom of Information regulations required their release, but Eric Holder kept stalling for time. As the final deadline for their release, April 16, approached, you could practically feel the electricity in the air. One way or another, there would be a showdown, one that would shake out all the players on both sides of the battle over the soul and security of the nation, with accountability proponents on one side, Republicans and the CIA on the other, and Obama and Holder seemingly caught in the middle.

What was becoming known as the accountability movement seemed to emerge out of nowhere as a force to be reckoned with, with mixed results at the beginning, and profound ramifications in the long term.

Glenn Greenwald helped jump-start the showdown with a provocative column on April 6, 2009, titled "There are no excuses for ongoing concealment of torture memos." It was a breathtaking piece, sure to capture the attention of the White House and the attorney general. Greenwald is a modest man when you talk to him, but the fact is, as columnist Marc Ambinder wrote in *The Atlantic*, "The White House does not give a scintilla of attention to its right-wing critics, [but] it does read, and will read, everything that Glenn Greenwald writes."[121] So do congressional staffers on the Hill—and, often, their bosses. And journalists and bloggers also pay close attention to his news and views.

Not only did Greenwald score the Obama administration for repeatedly delaying the release of the four torture memos—what he called "the Rosetta Stone for documenting war crimes committed not by low-level CIA agents but by the highest-level Bush DOJ officials"—but he also revealed (with appropriate credits to earlier reports by *The New York Times'* Scott Shane, *Newsweek's* Michael Isikoff, and *Harper's'* Scott Horton) that the person orchestrating the antidisclosure campaign was none other than John Brennan, Obama's first choice to head the CIA and now Obama's top White House counterterrorism advisor.

But it got worse. Greenwald suggested that the Republicans were engaged in blackmail.

"Today," Greenwald wrote in his April 6 blog, "Scott Horton—citing an anonymous Obama DOJ source and an anonymous Senate GOP source— claimed that Senate Republicans are now 'blackmailing' Obama by threatening to filibuster the confirmation of two Obama legal appointees (Dawn Johnsen as head of the OLC and Harold Koh as State Department legal counsel) unless Obama agrees not to release these OLC memos."

Johnsen had openly condemned the legal shenanigans of Bush's OLC lawyers, and Koh was a strong advocate of international law. Clearly, the Republicans were waging a very vigorous war to keep the prosecution net from closing in on the Bush lawyers.

Still, Greenwald reacted with a bit of journalistic skepticism. Was Horton's source, he wondered, trying to shift responsibility onto the Republicans, rather than onto the Obama administration for its delays in disclosing the memos? In the end, it didn't matter. "There is absolutely no justification whatsoever to continue to conceal these memos, and the fact that the GOP will stomp its feet and obstruct nominees doesn't come close to constituting an excuse for ongoing concealment."[122]

Then Greenwald went in for the kill on his blog, showing the irony of an Obama administration withholding documents when Johnsen, as well as Obama's acting OLC chief, David Barron, and his number-three OLC official, Marty Lederman, had in 2004 signed their names to a memo affirming that the OLC should be transparent and "publicly disclose its written legal opinions in a timely manner, absent strong reasons for delay or nondisclosure." Presumably, Greenwald wryly noted, "Those principles are equally applicable now that Obama, rather than Bush, occupies the Oval Office."

Greenwald ended that particular blog with a warning. Keeping the torture memos secret, he said, "will constitute the most extreme complicity yet on the part of the Obama administration in the last administration's war crimes. It was Obama who chose to place someone like Brennan in a position of high authority in his administration. That Brennan is now working with Bush-following Republicans to hide evidence of war crimes is, quite obviously, no excuse for continuing to hide it."[123]

Obama reportedly anguished for weeks over whether or not to release the torture memos, even staying up late at night conferring with aides while on a trip to Europe. Finally, on April 16 he gave Eric Holder the go-ahead to release the memos. There were four in all. One, written in August, 2002, by Jay Bybee, gave an elaborate description of the types of torture that the CIA could engage in, including waterboarding. Three others, written in May, 2005, by OLC lawyer Steven G. Bradbury, reassured the CIA that its methods were still legal despite prohibitions in international law against "cruel, inhuman or degrading" treatment.

They caused a sensation. The memos, commented *The New York Times,* contained passages "describing forced nudity, the slamming of detainees into walls, prolonged sleep deprivation and the dousing of detainees with water as cold as 41 degrees [which] alternate with elaborate legal arguments concerning the international Convention Against Torture."[124] The memos, the *Times* article went on, also "laid out with precision how each method was to be used."

The ACLU immediately put out a press release. "Through these memos," said Jameel Jaffer, Director of the ACLU National Security Project, "Justice Department lawyers authorized interrogators to use the most barbaric interrogation methods, including methods [like waterboarding] that the U.S. once prosecuted as war crimes."[125]

The ACLU urged the Department of Justice to appoint an independent prosecutor to investigate torture under the Bush administration. This was a big step, one that CCR's Michael Ratner applauded. "We are a much smaller outfit than the ACLU," he told me, "so when they did this, this was big. We were delighted."

Releasing memos that put CIA interrogators in a bad light was, no doubt, precisely what the CIA feared. And Obama was now acutely aware of the CIA's angst, because on the day he ordered the memos released, he also put out a statement assuring the CIA that "those who carried out their duties relying in good faith upon legal advice from the Department of Justice . . . will not be subject to prosecution."

A few days later, Obama went out of his way to visit CIA headquarters in Langley, Virginia. He met personally with a roomful of CIA employees and reassured them he would not go after CIA interrogators for following legal advice. They cheered him. You could almost hear him breathe a sigh of relief. Salon.com writer Mike Madden wryly observed: "Were they clapping for the new president at Langley because he won't punish them, or because they don't have to torture anyone anymore?"[126]

Michael Ratner was not impressed. "Since when," he blogged, "did legal advice make torture into a lawful technique?" And since when could a president decide whom to prosecute? "It is not his decision to make," Ratner stated. "Whether or not to prosecute law breakers is not a political decision. Laws were broken and crimes were committed." The worst thing that could happen, said Ratner, was that legal advice could be validated as a get-out-of-jail-free card and then be employed by "every petty dictatorship to protect its abusers."[127]

Human-rights lawyer and *Harper's* contributing editor Scott Horton was equally miffed. It seemed to him that amnesty was being granted before a full investigation of all the facts had occurred. And there were facts already known that shot holes in the "reliance on legal advice" defense, namely, that the CIA was using torture techniques *before* the "legal cover" memos were written in August, 2002.[128] "What's really going on here," he told *Democracy Now*, is that "CIA agents were acting in reliance on directives that came [not from the lawyers, but] from the White House . . . that go all the way up the ladder to Vice President Cheney and President Bush." It seemed to Horton that President Obama wanted to obscure that linkage. Glenn Greenwald weighed in by disagreeing "vehemently" with anyone—including Obama— who believed that prosecutions were unwarranted. "These memos," he wrote, "describe grotesque war crimes—legalized by classic banality of evil criminals and ordered by pure criminals—that must be prosecuted if the rule of law is to have any meaning." Like Ratner, he believed that the decision of whether or not to prosecute "is not Obama's to make; ultimately, it is Holder's and/or a special prosecutor's." Sensing the seriousness of Obama's concession to the CIA, Greenwald made a special appeal to the citizenry "to demand that the rule of law be applied."

And the citizenry responded, prompted in particular by the news that Obama's chief of staff, Rahm Emanuel, told ABC news on April 19 that *no one*—neither CIA operatives nor those who "devised policy"—would be prosecuted. "It's time for reflection," Emanuel had said. "It's not a time to use our energy and our time in looking back . . . in anger and retribution."

Suddenly, retribution, for war criminals, was becoming a dirty word.

A citizen's revolt

People in the accountability movement were shocked. How could this be? Was Obama really going to let off the people who authorized and engaged in this depraved, indeed criminal, activity?

The blogosphere went bananas. Code Pink, a women-run antiwar group that took its name, mockingly, from the Bush administration's color-coded warnings of terrorist threats, mobilized its nationwide network by urging members to send messages of protest to Congress, the Department of Justice, and the White House. And they were likely to be listened to. They had become so well known on Capitol Hill that when they weren't there raising hell, holding up antitorture signs during congressional hearings, marching outside the White House in orange jumpsuits, and staging daily vigils outside the Department of Justice, even Attorney General Holder had taken notice. On one such occasion, Holder was reportedly overheard saying, only somewhat in jest, "Where's Code Pink? I guess I'm not important any more!"

When I interviewed Code Pink cofounder Medea Benjamin, she told me she believed that both Holder and other members of the Justice Department want to have accountability. "I think Holder would like to do more but keeps getting slapped down by the White House. I think he should have a degree of autonomy." She and other Code Pink activists have had friendly encounters with DOJ officials, who tell her that they want to move ahead, but "they tell us how hard it is."[129]

On April 21, Obama reversed Rahm Emanuel's declaration, at least partly. The CIA operatives were safe, he assured reporters, while "leaving open the possibility" that the lawyers were not. "With respect to those who formulated those legal decisions, I would say that that is going to be a decision by the attorney general . . . and I don't want to prejudge that. I think that there are a host of very complicated issues involved here."[130]

By April 22, Code Pink was proudly proclaiming victory. "You did it!" its Web site announced. "Celebrate your power."

The following day, Obama's press secretary gave a White House briefing. Greenwald watched it carefully and found a "serious sea change in the political climate." Reporters were asking intelligent, well-informed questions about investigations and prosecutions. "There's still a very long way to go before any accountability is likely," he observed, "but it is clearly headed, however slowly, in the right direction."

The ACLU immediately swung into action, putting out a petition again calling for a special prosecutor. Within a week, it had collected an amazing two hundred fifty thousand signatures. On April 24, a coalition of accountability activists representing Code Pink, Veterans for Peace, and other groups, showed up at a hearing of the Senate Appropriations Subcommittee where Attorney General Holder was due to appear. They presented the petition to an assistant attorney general, then sat in on the hearing.

Toward the end, David Swanson, an activist and prolific blogger for Democrats.com and AfterDowningStreet.org, spoke out loudly from the third row. "We need a special prosecutor for torture, Mr. Attorney General," he said as Holder prepared to leave the room. "Americans like the rule of law. The rule of law is for everybody."

Holder never flinched, and as he walked by Swanson, bodyguards in tow, he turned to him and said, "You will be proud of your country."

Swanson immediately fired off a blog: "Eric Holder Made Me a Promise." But would he keep it? Swanson couldn't help but be skeptical.

The mainstreamers react

By now, *The New York Times*, the arguably preeminent opinion-molder of the country, began to give serious consideration to the culpability of Bush's lawyers. Its editorial board acknowledged the novelty of the situation. "There is little precedent for prosecuting government lawyers who provided arguably bad legal opinions," it opined. But what if these opinions were not just bad, but, rather, provided cover to lawbreakers? The issue debated at Velvel's Jackson conference had finally made its way into the *Times*. If Bush's lawyers "initially concluded that . . . the proposed [torture] program would be illegal, then reversed that conclusion at the request of policy makers, then prosecutors could make a case that the officials knowingly broke the law."[131]

The New York Times was clearly onto something. The one thing that could affect the whole dynamic, it reported, was an internal ethics investigation by the Office of Professional Responsibility (OPR), a division inside the Justice Department. Investigators had assembled DOJ emails indicating the lawyers' thinking at the time. According to *Newsweek*, OPR investigators "focused on whether the memos' authors deliberately slanted their legal advice to provide the White House with conclusions it wanted. . . . One of the lawyers said he was stunned to discover how much material the investigators had gathered, including internal emails and multiple drafts that allowed OPR to reconstruct how the memos were crafted."[132]

Tensions ran high on Capitol Hill as Democrats battled Republicans over the pros and cons of prosecution. Republicans like John McCain and Lindsey Graham and Independent Joseph Lieberman told Obama that prosecution was a distraction and a mistake. Senator Russ Feingold (D-Wisc.) cautioned Obama not to rule out prosecution until the findings in the Justice Department report were made public. Also in progress was an investigation by Dianne Feinstein of the Senate Intelligence Committee. Among the committee's reported objectives was to determine just how useful the torture had been (as Cheney had insisted it had been) in acquiring actionable intelligence. Her report, Feinstein indicated, would take another six months to complete.

Even Senator Leahy got back into action with his truth commission idea. On April 22, *The New York Times* reported that Obama had "sketched out the parameters" for a commission that would "look much like the one that investigated the September 11 attacks." What Obama wanted was some way for Congress to have an accounting be conducted "in a bipartisan fashion."

So, I thought, Obama *was* behind the truth commission after all, and Leahy may have been simply a stalking horse.

But the print was barely dry on the newspaper before Obama changed his mind again, prompting the *Times* to run yet another story, this one headlined "Obama Resisting Push for Interrogation Panel."

I wondered: Was it Obama resisting, or someone else? Obama's reported "shift in emphasis" apparently came after he spoke with Democratic congressional leaders on Wednesday night and after a bipartisan meeting with congressional leaders on Thursday. That meant the Republicans clearly had some kind of leverage over him. Something strong enough to make Obama think that even a truth commission "would steal time and energy from his policy agenda and could mushroom into a wider distraction looking back at the Bush years."[133]

Once again, the Democratic Party leadership was bending to the Republicans. According to Senate Majority Leader Harry Reid, naming a special panel would "exact retribution." It was "premature to act without the facts that will be provided by the intelligence committee [of Senator Dianne Feinstein] . . .

toward the end of this year." An intelligence committee, I might add, that did its investigations in secret.

And there was that awful word again: "retribution." What was so wrong with retribution? Isn't that what people want after someone has broken the law? The federal judge who imposed a 150-year prison sentence on fraudster Bernie Madoff spoke of the importance of symbolism and the need for "retribution, deterrence, and a measure of justice for the victims."[134] A crime is a crime, and the more serious the crime, the more deserving of retribution. Dictionary definition: "the infliction of punishment." Clearly, the Right—and no doubt the CIA—was pressuring the Democrats behind the scenes to cease and desist *any* kind of investigation.

I was beginning to think maybe Obama was once again stalling for time. And as if to drag it out even longer, who should appear on the Sunday talk show circuit three days later but Patrick Leahy on *Face the Nation.* He wanted a truth commission, he told CBS host Bob Schieffer on April 26, so the American public would learn "what happens when we lose our national honor."

What the hell is going on here? I'm thinking. Perhaps the Democratic Party is split. Right at the top. Would Leahy be going on national TV without Obama's blessing? I don't think so. Are we in for more trial balloons? Stalling tactics? Who knows?

I watched Leahy on TV to see if he had anything new to say.

"I want to know who it was who made the decision that we violate our own laws," he said, once again suggesting that he logically wanted to go all the way to the top. "We'll violate our treaties. We'll even violate our own Constitution," he said. "We don't know the chain of command," he added.

Schieffer moved right in. Would the senator subpoena Vice President Cheney if he refused to appear under oath?

"No I would not," Leahy said, once again dashing people's hopes that he was sincere about going after the top people.[135]

I pictured the Jersey Girls reacting in disgust. Once again, Leahy seemed to be throwing their and millions of others' concerns to the wind. *"The days of no fault government must end,"* they had written him back in February. *"And where there is clear criminal activity, people must be prosecuted. . . . "*

I thought again about Dan DeWalt's final comments to Leahy: "Senator, we have lost faith in Congress." And Leahy's indignant reply: "Then I've failed, haven't I?" Most Americans who watched the news on the mainstream media were probably bewildered and confused by the antics of their elected officials jockeying back and forth on the torture issue. But a small group of Americans, those who were active in the accountability movement, were not confused one bit. When Eric Holder released the torture memos, it was as if he released a genie from the bottle. Just as the CIA had no doubt feared, the "damage" incurred by the memos' release—to the CIA's reputation, the Republican Party, and Bush and his lawyers—was done. For all the Democratic Party's prevaricating, it was just a matter of time before justice would take its course.

CHAPTER EIGHT

Sovereign Impunity

While Senator Leahy was hedging his way through a Sunday talk show about how far up the chain of command he wanted to go in his quest for the truth, something very different was happening on the streets of Washington, D.C. April 30 marked the final day of the 100 Days Campaign to Close Guantánamo and End Torture, and activists began preparing for a final big demonstration in front of the White House.

They called themselves Witness Against Torture, and many of them had been protesting at the White House for the closure of Guantánamo for most of the first one hundred days of the Obama administration. They had talked to thousands of tourists, and what they had to say no doubt came as a shock. Contrary to widespread popular opinion, conditions at the prison were not better since Obama came into office. They were actually worse. Many of the prisoners had hoped things would change, and when they didn't, they despaired. Of the 230 remaining prisoners, 50 went on a hunger strike. According to witnesses, they were being strapped to their chairs and force-fed. Some were on the critical list. Many had been savagely beaten.[136] The press had pretty much ignored the story, but every tourist confronted with the facts was taking this news back home.

On this final day of the campaign, some 150 protesters, all clad in the signature orange jumpsuits and black hoods, walked quietly from the Capitol to Lafayette Park across from the White House. Sixty-one of them had the name of a detainee stenciled on the back of their jumpsuit—the names of the fifty-five detainees who had been cleared for release by the Bush administration but were still languishing in the Guantánamo prison, and the five others who had been cleared but died in prison.

When the protestors got to the White House gates, they unfurled a black banner with large words scripted in white: JUSTICE DELAYED IS JUSTICE DENIED. Then police moved in and arrested the sixty-one mock detainees.

Mathew Dalasio, one of the event's organizers and a former resident of the Catholic Worker House in New York, put on a brave face. He told the few reporters who had come to cover the event that the protesters had sent a strong message to Obama. And, indeed, since its founding in 2005, when twenty-five activists traveled all the way to Guantánamo to protest outside the prison, Witness Against Torture's visibility had increased and its call for closing Guantánamo had been heard by the incoming president. Dalasio could even point to the impact of their vigils on the Secret Service: When a passerby stopped to ask why he and others were still protesting when President Obama had already promised to close the prison, a Secret Service officer quietly intervened and explained that the prison was still open and would be for another year. The protesters, he told the tourists, were simply expressing their concern for the detainees.[137]

And yet, Dalasio could not hide his disappointment. "At the end of the 100 days," he told a reporter, "we had hoped that life for the people in Guantánamo would have been materially changed."

Vermont's Martha Hennessy was there on April 30. She had seen priests and nuns get arrested the day before, and she had endured walking in the cold, with a dark hood over her head and her hands tied behind her back. Not everyone among the passersby was sympathetic. "I heard a few people say things like, 'Kill them all [i.e., the detainees]' and 'You guys should be put in jail' and 'Go get a job.'" She brushed it off as a lack of understanding. "Hatred comes from ignorance," she reasoned. She had seen members of the European press covering the event, but that was it, and the lack of journalists concerned her. She was coming to the conclusion that the only way the voice of the people was going to be heard was through a mass protest, with mass arrests.[138] This event was a beginning, but because of poor media coverage, it was not enough to break through people's consciousness.

In the mainstream media and blogs, the first 100 days were presented as a success story and Obama as a master in getting his message across to an adoring public. Wrote John Woolley and Gerhard Peters of the American Presidency Project, Obama "has benefited from skillful oratory, personal charm and charisma. He has assembled an experienced group of policy planners and administrators to develop new programs. He has used the unilateral power of the presidency more vigorously than any of his predecessors. He has used new and old media strategies to sustain and build popular support. . . . Obama communicates to the Internet generation through YouTube. He has a YouTube channel and maintains a presence on MySpace." In other words, his communications team had succeeded in presenting the new president in a flattering light.

But not everyone was convinced. Debra Sweet, who had demonstrated outside the White House on April 30, had learned since the Vietnam era that presidents should not necessarily be trusted with what they say, particularly in a time of war. Ironically, her political activism began after she got an award from President Nixon for her work on raising money in high school for overseas development. Rather than bow and curtsy in grateful acceptance, she told Nixon to his face, at a White House ceremony, that she could not accept the award because "You have killed millions of people in Vietnam and you should stop." Her protest made the evening news and the front page of national and international newspapers the next morning. "It was a big story," she told me, something which no doubt gave her an inkling of how powerful the press could be if you won its sympathy.

The mainstream press wasn't so sympathetic now, something she was keenly aware of as the leader of an antiwar group called World Can't Wait. The tourists may have been moved by what they saw, but the American public was largely oblivious to the orange jumpsuit demonstrations. The movement was still active, but with many fewer people involved. World Can't Wait had seventy chapters when Bush was in power, Sweet told me. By July, when I caught up with her for an interview, it had eleven.[139] Sweet had been arguing for some months now that the election of Barack Obama may have been the worst thing to happen to the antiwar and accountability movement, rather than the best. "Very little has changed," she said. "The U.S. is now involved in two wars. The Obama administration has adopted many of the Bush policies toward detainees. But people just don't want to see it." As an eerie testament to this seemingly stalemated condition, the World Can't Wait's telephone answering machine still greets listeners with the message, "Drive out the Bush regime." She attributes it to a "gremlin in the system." No matter how hard her group has tried to change the message, "it won't go away."

Reality check

Remnants of the Bush regime were in fact still active both inside and outside of the Department of Justice, the CIA, and the Department of Defense, which may have explained why President Obama's administration kept putting out mixed signals regarding what he intended to do with the perpetrators of war crimes.

This became clear to me in early May. I had just began to think there was some forward movement on the prosecution front. And then, on May 6, *The New York Times* ran this headline: "Torture Memos: Inquiry Suggests No Prosecutions." Beneath this ran a slight hedge: "Draft By Justice Dept: Serious Lapses Cited—Disciplinary Actions Are Still in Play."

This seemed to be a sneak preview of the long-awaited internal ethics report by the Department of Justice's Office of Professional Responsibility. Bush's second attorney general, Michael Mukasey, had reacted strongly to it after it was finished in late 2008, insisting that the accused officials get a chance to respond before it was made public. *The New York Times*, in its May 6 story, reminded readers that Mukasey had been "upset over its scathing conclusions" and had "warned against second-guessing the legal work of the department's lawyers."

Now it looked like the draft report had been seriously watered down. According to the *Times,* it was likely to say that the lawyers had committed "serious lapses of judgment" in writing their secret memos but were unlikely to be prosecuted. Instead, "the report . . . [is] likely to ask state bar associations to consider possible disciplinary action, which could include reprimands or even disbarment. . . . "

Lapses of judgment? Possible disciplinary action?

I searched for an explanation and found it in a *Washington Post* article. It reported that "former Bush administration officials have launched a behind-the-scenes campaign to urge Justice Department leaders to soften an ethics report criticizing lawyers who blessed harsh detainee interrogation tactics, according to two sources familiar with the efforts."[140]

The ACLU was indignant. "Congress must intervene and assert its oversight role," exclaimed Caroline Fredrickson, director of the ACLU Washington Legislative Office.

Fredrickson referred to the ethics review as "only one piece of the puzzle," a puzzle that had gone strangely unsolved since the first disclosures of torture over five years earlier. "There is a 200-page draft government report on the role of three lawyers," she complained, "but absolutely no Justice Department investigation of their clients—those top White House and CIA officials who asked for the opinions and reportedly made decisions on what torture tactics to use on which detainees."

On reading this, I turned to Jerry, read it aloud to him, and said, "It's just unbelievable! These guys think they can get away with everything!"

"The powerful protect their own," Jerry responded dryly. He should know. He has written two huge books on two of the richest and most powerful families in America, the duPonts and the Rockefellers.[141]

A double standard in the law: The legacy of monarchy

I'd seen it before, in my own law practice, how the rich and the powerful enjoy built-in legal protections that shield them from civil liability and criminal prosecutions. One of the most insidious obstacles in civil litigation is the doctrine of sovereign immunity. It originated under the British monarchy, effectively meaning "the king shall do no wrong." It now has been extended to all government officials down to the lowest-level government functionaries.[142]

We're often told that government officials should be immune from suit because they shouldn't be distracted by frivolous and frequent lawsuits. But in reality, sovereign immunity is a vital tool for protecting the powerful from lawsuits by injured citizens. There are whole areas where the government is absolutely immune from suit. If you've been beaten up, or falsely arrested or imprisoned by a federal officer, for example, you can't sue. If you've been harmed by "fiscal operations of the Treasury," you are out of luck. If you've been slandered or deceived by a government official, forget it. Even in those areas where the government has waived its immunity, allowing private individuals to sue, you've got to be able to prove gross negligence and willful intent on the part of the wrongdoer.

Says James Bovard, author of *Lost Rights*, "Sovereign immunity creates a two-tiered society: those above the law and those below it." The very notion of sovereign immunity has become so untenable, in my opinion, that it's almost Orwellian. As Bovard cynically observes, "Sovereign immunity presumes that the more evils government officials are permitted to commit, the more good they will achieve. Sovereign immunity presumes that in order to protect people, government must be permitted to destroy them: to crash into their cars, to break into their homes and businesses, and to drug them at its convenience."

In this country, human-rights attorneys who have tried to sue top U.S. government officials for very serious offenses—including wrongful death—know that the chances of winning are almost nil. ACLU lawyer Laura Rótolo had her first of many brushes with sovereign immunity when she and a group of law students sued Henry Kissinger for his role in the death of a Chilean general opposed to the coup that overthrew President Salvador Allende. A federal court threw out the lawsuit, reasoning that the decisions Kissinger made as national security advisor were protected by sovereign immunity. But at least now, in Latin America former military officials responsible for human-rights abuses during the age of dictatorships are being put on trial. They may still end up being given amnesty by a new civilian government, but in the United States, Rótolo laments, "the situation is even worse. You don't even get to trial because of sovereign immunity." Remember, I'm talking here about civil lawsuits, not criminal prosecutions.

As noted earlier, George Bush and Dick Cheney have no immunity if they committed a crime in office. Still, thanks in part to the (civil) doctrine of sovereign immunity, government officials seem to think they can do whatever they want and they won't be held accountable. I've given this condition a name: sovereign impunity.

I witnessed it during my own campaign on what I considered a serious health-and-safety issue that brought me just short of accusing the incumbent attorney general of covering up for Vermont's Department of Health (VDH) in matters relating to Vermont's aging nuclear power plant. This story has parallels to what has been going on in Washington, D.C.

One day in late October, 2008, a group of irate legislators called in a top Vermont Department of Health official, Dr. Willliam Irwin, to ask him why he failed to notify them (as required by law) about changes in the way the department measured radiation emissions at the dangerously old Vermont

Yankee nuclear power plant. Had he notified them, they pointed out, there would have been mandatory public hearings about those changes, which many felt lessened safety at the plant.

I attended one of Irwin's questioning sessions, and what transpired shocked me. When one of the legislators asked Irwin who had advised him to avoid notifying the legislature about the rule changes on emissions, he answered "counsel." During the lunch break, I walked up to him and asked him if "counsel" meant the attorney general's office. He said yes. During the lunch break, I drew up a quick public-records request, asking for more information about the role of the AG's office in dispensing advice to the VDH[143] and any additional information on VDH's relationship with Entergy, the corporate owner of Vermont Yankee. Just as I suspected, it turned out that Entergy had actually paid the Department of Health to fund a study a) devised by one of the nuclear industry's top research centers to b) come up with a new formula for measuring radiation that c) would make Vermont Yankee's increased radiation levels appear to be in compliance with Vermont law when, in fact, they exceeded them.[144] Talk about collusion! And who was working behind the scenes, arguably counseling a state agency in how to break the law, avoid the legislature, and thereby avoid public hearings? The top law-enforcement agency of the state: the office of attorney general. An assistant attorney general, who was present at Irwin's hearing insisted to me that everything the AG's office had done was perfectly legal. But I've heard that before. Sounds like the same "perfectly legal" arguments used by the lawyers of the Office of Legal Counsel at the Department of Justice.

In short, whether at the state level or the national level, the office of attorney general can easily adopt an attitude of "sovereign impunity" if not carefully monitored. And this is not a mere fluke. The origin of the office of attorney general goes back to England, when in 1461 the monarchy appointed a chief law-enforcement officer to act as the crown's representative in legal proceedings. During the seventeenth century, the attorney general was "often accused of subservience to the monarch."[145] Over the centuries, the duties of the attorney general have gradually evolved so that it also serves the people's interests in matters of employment discrimination, the environment, protection against fraud, and in criminal prosecutions. But these duties sometimes run at cross-purposes, to the detriment of "the people," even in the People's Republic of Vermont. Even in the United States of America under President Barack Obama.

One of the first indications that Obama's Department of Justice had not yet broken free of its sovereign masters was when its attorneys wrote a brief for a federal judge in *Jewel v. NSA* this past spring arguing that lawsuits against the National Security Agency for warrantless eavesdropping on Americans should be *dismissed*. On what grounds? Sovereign immunity *and* protecting state secrets. In fact, the DOJ's sovereign-immunity arguments were even more outrageous than previous ones made by the Bush administration. Why? Because the Obama administration, commented Salon blogger Glenn Greenwald, "invented a brand new radical argument that not even the Bush administration had espoused that says that the government [when engaged in illegal eavesdropping on Americans' phone calls and emails] is completely immune . . . from lawsuits unless they willfully or deliberately disclose to the public what it is that they learned."[146]

In the past, as a result of government eavesdropping abuses that had come to light in the mid-1970s, Congress passed some laws making the government liable for illegal surveillance of Americans. Now, the Obama administration was effectively repealing those laws, claiming its authority under the USA Patriot Act. Not even the Bush administration had gone that far.[147]

Hail to the people's watchdogs

Glenn Greenwald was among the loudest to howl in protest and for good reason. He had become an expert on the subject of government surveillance as a freelance blogger, winning such widespread recognition for his original reporting that he eventually quit his full-time work as a lawyer (helping, as he told me, "the small guy taking on big institutions") to devote his time to monitoring the entire legal landscape of the Bush administration for Salon .com. For the past one hundred days, he had turned his attention with equal incisiveness on the Obama administration.

"Whatever else one might say, the rule of the law, the Constitution, and core civil liberties are the centerpiece of a healthy and well-functioning government," he insisted, and then reviewed for us [148] what other noted bloggers had said:

- The George Washington University Law School law professor Jonathan Turley (whose CV reads like a *Who's Who* of impressive clients, institutions, and media connections, most notably MSNBC, where he frequently appears as a legal commentator) couldn't resist praising Bush officials for a "mission accomplished," i.e., getting Barack Obama "to adopt the same extremist arguments and, in fact, exceed the extremist arguments made by Bush."
- Blogger Josh Marshall of Talking Points Memo, the man who made blogging history by single-handedly breaking the scandal of Bush's political firings of U.S. Attorneys, surveyed a panel of experts and found that they agreed that the Obama administration had in fact "set a broad and dangerous precedent for future cases by asserting that the government has the right to get lawsuits dismissed merely by claiming that state secrets are at stake, without giving judges any discretion whatsoever."

In a subsequent interview with Greenwald, I asked him if he thought there was a double standard of justice in this country, one that institutionally protected the big guys, the so-called sovereigns, against the rest of us. He agreed. In fact, the double standard now confronting us struck him as "unprecedented." If you look through our history, he said, "there have always been severe injustices, but there has always been the idea, promoted by the Founding Fathers, that everyone was equal under the law. As Thomas Paine once said," and he was paraphrasing here, "There is no King. Law is the King."[149]

Granted, the notion that no one is above the law is a lofty principle, one to be aspired to, like the saying I once pondered that's engraved on the pediment of the New York Supreme Court building: "The true administration of justice is the firmest pillar of good government." The doctrine of sovereign immunity in civil law put a huge dent into such noble ideas, but the higher-ups' expectation of complete and total immunity under all circumstances—including immunity from criminal liability—was pervasive under the Bush administration. "When the elites think they are no longer subject to the rule of law, it's a huge shift," Greenwald said. Then he offered a final thought, one that has driven the accountability movement and its calls for prosecutions:

"Once we remove the punishment aspect for their violations, we remove their incentive to abide by the law."[150]

In other words, if we don't do everything in our power to reverse this trend, we will be forever abandoning our democracy. We will be succumbing to a rule of, for, and by the elite. All the work begun by the valiant American revolutionaries, the Tom Paines of our history, will be undone. I remember what Sue Serpa, a descendant of Tom Paine, said to me: "I couldn't just sit idly by and silently witness the undoing of everything my ancestors strove to achieve."

The People v. Bush: Common sense for the twenty-first century

The thought of doing my own framework for prosecuting Bush and Cheney et al. had been brewing in me for some time, fueled by each new revelation of "sovereign impunity" on the part of Bush's torture team. Writers like Jane Mayer (author of *The Dark Side*), Michael Haas (*George W. Bush: War Criminal?*—a book that had identified 269 war crimes), and Chris Pyle (*Getting Away with Torture*) had already provided ample evidence to bring charges against the former president, vice president, secretary of defense, and their lawyers for conspiracy to commit war crimes.

Former federal prosecutor Elizabeth de la Vega, for her part, had been one of the first to advance the idea that the top officials in the Bush administration could be prosecuted—for conspiracy to defraud the United States in violation of Title 18 U.S. Code Section 371. Her imagined indictment of the president in her book, *United States v. George W. Bush et al.,* for tricking us into war was groundbreaking when it came out in 2006, and contains background information going as far back as the 1990s as she makes the case for "deceit, craft, trickery, dishonesty, and fraudulent representations . . . while knowing and intending that such fraudulent representations would influence Congress's decisions regarding authority to use military force."

As I said earlier, every effort is incremental. The case against Bush et al., however it is to be argued, becomes deeper and more damning with each new revelation and each new contribution to a growing body of evidence. I believe that Bugliosi's approach, that of prosecuting Bush for murder and conspiracy to commit murder, remains the boldest approach because the punishment is likely to be the harshest and it is precisely this level of seriousness that is most likely to deter a government official from committing a heinous crime while in office. The penalty could be life in prison—or even the death penalty, something I don't personally endorse but that nonetheless exists in some states. The message this sends to future administrations: Break the law, and you will regret it.

It did occur to me that by laying out the case against Bush's and Cheney's lawyers, patterns might emerge that would help in the murder prosecution. Velvel and Pyle made it clear: The lawyers were memoing up. But why? And what, exactly, were they covering up?

I was especially interested in what the lawyers did before Bush ordered troops into Iraq. Pyle had said that the torture was the work of Bush's lawyers. But the war in Iraq was also the work of Bush's lawyers. In fact, the first OLC memos were about devising a legal framework for going to war. The first use of torture came after the U.S. invasion of Afghanistan and before the invasion of Iraq. Detainees were tortured repeatedly until they made statements (since retracted) that Saddam Hussein was an imminent threat and involved in the 9/11 tragedy. After the release of the torture memos in April, I began to realize that torture in some cases was an effort to *strengthen the case* for the invasion of Iraq.

Suddenly it was all coming together. All I had to do was place the secret memos into a timeline (timelines, or chronologies, being something I swear by), then see what emerged. But something else was needed as well, something that rarely gets discussed, at least in the mainstream media: context. I would provide some missing context, the kind that gives us new insights into sovereign impunity as it plays out so blatantly in a time of war: the oil context. I'd written about it back in 2004: "The War on Terror and the Great Game for Oil: How the Media Missed the Context." It was time to put this missing context back into the picture.

From years of research on the subject, I knew the Great Game for Oil to be a high-stakes, high-level battle for power and world dominance that is carefully concealed from the public. Over the last two centuries it seldom played by any rules and today is more like a great, subterranean war, rarely mentioned and carefully veiled to most people except its victims. Now, I decided to combine what I knew about the Great Game and apply it to Bush's motive for going to war. With motive in place, his state of mind would follow and that, in turn, would lead to criminal intent.

The common sense I would employ would probably make its way into an opening statement in a courtroom, with the following facts going to motive:

> Ladies and Gentlemen of the Jury. We have undisputed evidence that the president of the United States, the vice president, and the secretary of defense (among others) wanted to gain control over the oil of Iraq as soon as Bush became president. They figured the best way to do this was to declare war. Since they had no good reason to justify this, they used the tragedy of 9/11 to develop their pretext. They relied on their legal team to come up with the necessary justifications. They told the lawyers, "Find me a way." Their lawyers obliged, coming up with formulations that enhanced the powers of the war president while weakening the oversight powers of Congress and the dissenting rights of the citizenry. They did it all in secret because their operations were patently unconstitutional and illegal. And one day they would be caught. Now they should be punished for the damage they've done to our country, to our soldiers, to the Iraqi people, and now, it would appear, to the people of Afghanistan as well.

How could I say all that with such certainty? Like I said, the evidence (some of it based on years of my own research) is in. Besides, I have a rule of thumb for figuring out the *real* reasons wars are fought: Just look at the outcome. What was the prize?

One of the great prizes of World War I was the complete dismantling of the Turkish-based Muslim Ottoman Empire that previously controlled the oil-rich fields of the Middle East. The ultimate prize was the oil of Iraq, then known as Mesopotamia.

One of the great prizes (at least for the U.S.) of World War II was securing control over the newly developed oil fields of Saudi Arabia, the richest in the world.[151]

One of the great prizes of the second Iraq war, for the Americans and the British, was to secure and privatize the oil of modern Iraq.

Why is oil the main prize in all three cases? Because oil, more than anything else, is needed to fight wars! The president of the American Petroleum Institute said it all back in November, 1943: "Oil is ammunition. It is a secret behind the secret weapons in this war. . . . We are not floating to victory in this war—we are fighting literally every inch of the war with oil—on land, on and under the seven seas, and in the skies."[152] Without oil, you lose. The Germans discovered this fact too late in World War I when German lorries literally ran out of oil as they pressed to get to the oil fields of Russia. Hitler tried to correct that problem in World War II, even creating synthetic oil factories at IG Farben and filling them with slave labor from nearby Auschwitz. He failed again. His adversaries were simply too powerful.

When Britain's Lord Curzon rose to address a gathering of the Inter-Allied Petroleum Conference in London in 1918, he robustly declared: "The Allied cause floated to victory upon a wave of oil."[153] These words would resonate throughout the rest of the century and beyond, into the next.

The War on Terror and the Great Game for Oil: The ongoing battle for empire

Today, a great many thoughtful people accept the fact that the war in Iraq is all about oil.[154] Bush's invasion was not about bringing democracy to Iraq. There have been plenty of dictatorships in the world that enjoyed U.S. support; some still do. What made Iraq important was its strategic location at the heart of the Middle East's oil deposits. It took a while for Americans to acknowledge this, because the corporate-controlled press has studiously avoided making the link between oil and foreign policy, even though the two subjects are intimately related and have been for over a century.[155] Certainly the Bush administration went out of its way to downplay oil as a factor in the war in Iraq. I will never forget Bush spokesperson Ari Fleischer blithely insisting back in 2003 that "The only interest the United States has in the region is furthering the cause of peace and stability." In answer to a reporter's question, he embellished the lie even further, claiming he "wouldn't even try to start guessing what the military may or may not do" once Iraq's oil fields were liberated from Saddam Hussein.[156] Some people saw through him.

September 11 widows Mindy Kleinberg and Lorie Van Auken tried to raise questions about the role of oil in the War on Terror as they tried to get the 9/11 hearings off the ground. But the mere mention of oil made members of Congress exceedingly uncomfortable. "It was years before we could say the word," Lorie explained with apparent disgust. But, gradually, word got out, if only in fits and starts, and often in the foreign press before it ever reached the United States.

As early as May, 2003, Paul Wolfowitz, who worked under Secretary of Defense Donald Rumsfeld, was a mastermind of the war before leaving the Bush administration shortly after it began. He was quoted in the London *Guardian* as admitting at a Singapore conference that "economically, we just had no choice in Iraq. The country swims on a sea of oil."[157] As for the pretext given for invading Iraq, Wolfowitz told *Vanity Fair* magazine that same month, "We settled on the one issue that everyone could agree on: weapons of mass destruction."

Wolfowitz knew that Iraq had the largest oil reserves in the world next to Saudi Arabia. But there's something else Wolfowitz knew that, to this day, has rarely been reported in the U.S. media: Seizing Iraq's oilfields was only part of the challenge confronting Wolfowitz and his fellow neoconservatives in the Bush administration. Another major challenge was one that typically faces anyone in the oil business: Once you've got the oil, how and where do you ship it to market? And if you intend to rely on pipelines, which pipeline route is the most economical and *strategically secure*? During the 1990s, Wolfowitz and his fellow neoconservatives were scheming away in their think tanks way in advance of assuming power in 2000 under George W. Bush.[158] They knew the most logical pipeline route was the one that had been used before. It was the route followed by the British-controlled Iraq Petroleum Company pipeline built in the 1930s that connected the oil of Iraq to a major port and refinery on the eastern Mediterranean: Haifa (then part of Palestine, now part of Israel).

On April 4, 2003, only two weeks after the U.S. invasion of Iraq, *Asia Times* reported that "Iraqi consent [to building a new pipeline to Haifa] will be out of the question as long as the current [nationalist, anti-Israel] regime of Saddam Hussein is in power. As acknowledged by the Israeli minister [National Infrastructure Minister Yosef Paritzky] a prerequisite for the project is, therefore, a new regime in Baghdad with friendly ties with Israel." The new regime was to be headed up by Ahmad Chalabi, an exiled Iraqi leader, who openly supported the resurrected pipeline project.[159]

By March, 2003, everything and everyone seemed to be in place. The neocons now occupied top national security positions in the Bush administration. Key among them were Dick Cheney, Donald Rumsfeld, Paul Wolfowitz, Douglas Feith (undersecretary of defense for policy), and Richard Perle (past chairman and still member of the Pentagon's Defense Policy Board).

On April 20, 2003, *The Observer* quoted a former senior CIA official as saying that "it has long been a dream of a powerful section of the people now driving this administration (of President George W. Bush) and the war in Iraq to safeguard Israel's energy supply as well as that of the United States. The Haifa pipeline was something that existed [up until Israel's war of independence in 1948], was resurrected as a dream, and is now a viable project—albeit with a lot of building to do."

Just weeks into the war, Infrastructure Minister Paritzky was ordering his ministry to conduct a feasibility study on reopening the Iraq-Haifa pipeline, which, he said, could reduce Israel's energy prices by 15–20 percent and "transform Haifa into a new Rotterdam."[160] Another major cheerleader for the pipeline project was Israel's then-finance minister, Benjamin Netanyahu. "Soon you will see Iraqi oil flowing to Haifa," he exulted during the early part of the U.S. invasion. "It's just a matter of time until the pipeline is reconstituted and Iraqi oil will flow to the Mediterranean. It is not a pipe dream." Those comments, given to Reuters news service,[161] got Netanyahu in hot water because Israel wanted its plans kept secret. But the U.S. press did not pick up on them, and Netanyahu went on to become Israel's prime minister in 2009. Now, due to continuing instability in Iraq and quarreling between Kurds and Arabs over who will control northern Iraq's oil regions, Netanyahu's dream of reconstructing a pipeline to Haifa is still a pipe dream. But he's got other plans, like connecting Israel to oil and gas pipelines in Turkey through an energy corridor running up the entire eastern Mediterranean coast.[162] Recently, he's been talking about using Israel's strategic location on the Mediterranean to build pipelines to Europe and Africa.[163]

To this day, few Americans know this "pipeline" story, let alone the neocons' involvement in it. When Project Censored, sponsored by Sonoma State University in California, put out its annual report in 2003 on the twenty-five most censored stories of the year, it declared the "Neoconservative Plan for Global Dominance" as its most censored subject. The Project Censored report scored the media for missing the neocons' strategic oil concerns. But everyone (even the reporters who helped compile the Project Censored report) missed the pipeline angle. In other words, pipelines are even more invisible in our national discourse than oil itself, no doubt because of their strategic geopolitical significance. In any case, the hush-up about oil as a factor in the war was on, even inside the corridors of power.

In 2007, Alan Greenspan, the former head of the Federal Reserve, revealed in his new book, *The Age of Turbulence: Adventures in a New World*, "I am saddened that it is politically inconvenient to acknowledge what everyone knows: the Iraq war is largely about oil." Greenspan even wrote that the White House tried to steer clear of the subject when America's strategic needs came up in policy discussions. One lower-level White House official told him point blank: "Well, unfortunately, we can't talk about oil."

Even earlier, in 2004, former Treasury Secretary Paul O'Neill revealed in Ron Suskind's *The Price of Loyalty* that the Bush administration started planning for the invasion of Iraq as soon as he got into office—in January, 2001—nine months *before* the tragedy of September 11. Just days after the inauguration, O'Neill learned, Iraq was "Topic A" at the first meeting of Bush's National Security Council. "It was about finding a way to do it," the former treasury secretary told Ron Suskind. "That was the tone of the president, saying 'Go find me a way to do this.'"[164]

Why was Bush so anxious? For one reason, he and his advisors were worried about getting beaten out of Iraq's oil by foreign competition. Bush and Cheney, both formerly oil men, knew that more than forty companies from thirty countries had been negotiating oil deals with President Saddam Hussein in the expectation that UN sanctions against Iraq would soon be dropped. When Cheney set up a National Energy Policy Development Group in early 2001, his team drew up a map with an accompanying two-page list of "Foreign Suitors for Iraqi Oilfield Contracts."[165] Not one foreign subsidiary of an American company was on the list.

The whole Iraq-Haifa pipeline project could be threatened.

In addition, Afghanistan was (and is) considered a key transit route for running oil and gas pipelines between the resource-rich Caspian Sea and the vast markets of South Central Asia, most notably through Afghanistan to India and Pakistan. "Since the 1990s, Washington has promoted a natural gas pipeline south through Afghanistan," writes Canadian energy economist John Foster. "The route would pass through Kandahar province." (In 2007, he goes on to say, "Richard Boucher, U.S. assistant secretary of state said 'one of our goals is to stabilize Afghanistan' and to link South and Central Asia 'so that energy can flow to the south'.")[166]

Stabilization means pacification, and in Afghanistan the Taliban played a key role in pacifying the country's armed warlords in order to make Afghanistan safe for pipelines. But shortly before September 11, the U.S.-Taliban relationship soured.

The Great Game for Oil, with Bush at the helm, started to take a dangerous new turn, carefully navigated by secretive lawyers in the inner sanctums of the Department of Justice.

"Find me a way"

For Bush administration strategists, the way to get control of Iraq's oil and Afghanistan's territory was by creating a "war on terror." This would require Bush's lawyers to concoct bogus legal arguments to help pave the way for war while allowing Bush to assume extraordinary powers as a "war president." Cheney, who had been secretary of defense under George H. W. Bush, drew on the legal expertise of the lawyer who had loyally served under him while at the Pentagon and now served as his legal counsel, David Addington. A tall man, bespectacled and sporting a trim gray beard, Addington possessed an "I'm in command" aura whenever he entered a room. In the aftermath of September 11, he took immediate control over Bush's "war on terror."

Jack Goldsmith, a legal scholar and former Justice Department official who would repudiate many of the OLC's arguments once he took over the OLC in 2003, knew exactly what Cheney and Addington were up to. The two men, he later revealed, "viewed power as the absence of restraint, which is why they didn't go to Congress." After 9/11, they often spoke of wanting "maximum flexibility" to achieve their goals.[167] To the public, Cheney freely admitted that a certain amount of unconventional, if not illegal, behavior would occur: "We will have to work the dark side, if you will,"[168] he said shortly after 9/11. Back then, people were so traumatized by 9/11 that they apparently didn't think to question what he meant.

After Obama's Department of Justice released some of the OLC legal memos in early 2009, it began to dawn on some human-rights lawyers and reporters that Cheney and Addington were the chief architects of a secret *coup d'état* that not only got us into war but suppressed our civil liberties at home, including our right to dissent over the war. Bush's famous slogan, "You're either with us or against us," was a hint to everyone who opposed the war that they would be regarded as terrorists, too, if they chose the wrong side. As lawyer/author Chris Pyle would observe, "Fear of terrorism can be invoked to justify huge expansions of covert power to kill 'enemies' secretly, without accountability, while suppressing dissent at home."[169]

Each step on the way to war was carefully prepared by Bush's lawyers, although, as we shall see, events occasionally outpaced even *their* calculations, forcing them to paper over illegalities after the crimes had already been committed.

The legal timeline begins, of course, with September 11, 2001, that day of infamy that forever changed America and its place in the world. In previous attacks, like the 1993 attack on the World Trade Center and then the 1995 Oklahoma City bombing, such acts were regarded as crimes, not acts of war. Their perpetrators were hunted down, tried, and convicted in federal courts. But on the evening of September 11, President Bush declared in a meeting with his counterterrorism advisors that the attacks on the World Trade Center and the Pentagon were acts of war. "Everything is available for the pursuit of this war," Bush reportedly said to his advisors, including Richard Clarke. "Any barriers in your way, they are gone. . . . I don't care what the international lawyers say, we are going to kick some ass!"[170]

And kick ass they did. On September 14, just three days after 9/11, President Bush gave a somber speech to members of Congress about the need to rid the world of evil. The same day, Congress, understandably frightened and determined to show its patriotism, voted on giving the president the power to use "all necessary and appropriate force" to wage war against any "nations, organizations, or persons" that he believed had *"planned, authorized, committed, or aided the terrorist attacks that occurred on September 11, 2001* (emphasis added)." Actually, Bush had wanted this Congressional War Resolution to be much broader. The first draft of the joint war resolution, offered by White House Counsel Gonzales the day after 9/11 and rejected by congressional leaders, had an additional clause, one that called for the use of force "to deter and *preempt* any future acts of terrorism or aggression against the United States"[171] (emphasis added). This was the "elasticity" that Cheney wanted, a clause so broad it could justify any military action anywhere, including a *preemptive* war on Iraq.

So, congressional leaders prevented Bush and Cheney from getting the expansive authority they sought. But Bush and Cheney weren't about to give up; their legal team had only just begun. If Congress wouldn't grant them the broad wartime power they wanted, they would get it by acting in secret. They would draw up a series of secret memos in the two years leading up to the invasion of Iraq that gave Bush extraordinary war powers—indeed, the powers of a monarch to do whatever he pleased, to send troops wherever he wanted, and to terrorize detainees and extract false confessions in any way that he wanted.

I will not belabor what others have written before me, but I will highlight the key events that shaped Bush's mission, and ultimately proved his culpability for murder and war crimes. I will limit my timeline to what happened in the months leading up to the war in Iraq, because that's when some of the most devious and disturbing legal machinations took place, all to get us into a war with Iraq.

At each and every step on the way to war, Bush's lawyers in the Office of Legal Counsel had to figure a way to get around existing law to accomplish their goals. In other words, they had to devise new legal theories to advance their bosses' illegal policies.

It was not an accident that Bush chose John Yoo, who specialized in presidential power during war, to be in charge of drafting many of the secret legal memos that paved the way to war. Or that Cheney would rely on Addington, his lawyer from the days of Cheney's service as secretary of defense, to employ whatever legal stratagems were necessary to fulfill the ultimate object: send troops to invade Iraq.

In the following, I present my timeline in the context of Legal Hurdles (existing law) and "Ways Around the Hurdles" (what did Yoo do to defy existing law and come up with secret new laws?).

Legal Hurdle Number 1: The U.S. Constitution

Most legal scholars agree that the Framers, fresh from a war with the British monarchy, conceived of the separation of powers in our newly independent country. They wanted to restrain the power of the executive, which had the potential of getting out of hand during times of war. Article I Section 8 of the Constitution vests *in Congress* the power to declare war. Article II Section 2 of the Constitution states that "The President shall be Commander in Chief of the Army and Navy of the United States."

Even Justice Antonin Scalia, widely viewed as one of our more conservative Supreme Court justices, has stated that "for the actual command of military forces, all authorization for their maintenance and all explicit authorization for their use is placed in the control of Congress under Article I, rather than the President under Article II. As Alexander Hamilton explained, the President's military authority would be 'much inferior' to that of the British King."[172]

What did Yoo do?

On September 25, 2001, OLC's John Yoo (in collaboration with Cheney's legal advisor, David Addington) wrote a *secret* twenty-page "War Powers Memorandum." It gave the president unlimited war powers. Yoo titled it: "The President's Constitutional Authority to Conduct Military Operations Against Terrorists and Nations Supporting Them." He didn't limit this secret memo to waging war on suspected terrorists connected to 9/11 or, for that matter, tracking them down in Afghanistan, where Osama bin Laden held sway. He effectively gave the president, as commander in chief, free reign to conduct military operations *anywhere he pleased*, and that could just as easily mean Iraq as it did Afghanistan. He declared that Congress had no say in the "method, timing, or place" of the president's war on terror. "These decisions, under our Constitution, are for the President alone to make," Yoo wrote. This was just a blanket statement, with no legal precedent or authority backing it up.

It was an unconstitutional power grab designed for an imperial presidency, and it was kept secret from the United States Congress and from the American people for the obvious reason that it was patently illegal.

On October 7, 2001, American troops began their invasion of Afghanistan. This was, effectively, Phase I of Bush and Cheney's "war on terror." Bush ordered the invasion of Afghanistan after the Taliban refused to turn over Osama bin Laden, who everyone believed to be the mastermind of 9/11. (Less known is the fact that the Taliban had sought proof that linked bin Laden to 9/11, and that the Bush Administration refused to supply it.)

Given the recent national trauma following 9/11, there was virtually no opposition to the U.S. invasion of Afghanistan. It was, and continues to be, the "good war," the so-called war of necessity to go after Osama bin Laden and the Taliban who harbored him. Now, in hindsight, it seems that the good war was a stepping-stone to the "bad war," Bush's "war of choice" in Iraq. In fact, as will be shown, both wars helped propel the United States into some of the most strategically important real estate in the world—Iraq, with its huge reserves of oil, and Afghanistan, with its huge land mass, highly coveted as a transit route for oil and gas pipelines.* When we see what happened to the prisoners seized in Afghanistan, we even see how their torture and detention became useful for the war in Iraq.

Legal Hurdle Number 2: The Federal Judiciary System and the Uniform Code of Military Justice (Courts Martial)

In October and November, 2001, invading American forces began to take prisoners in Afghanistan. According to Rumsfeld, they "scooped up ten thousand people."[173]

Now the question was, what to do with the suspected terrorists among them? As one career prosecutor put it, "How can we prosecute them? What can we prosecute them for? And ultimately, where will they be detained?"[174]

---

*Ahmed Rashid in *Taliban: Militant Islam, Oil and Fundamentalism in Central Asia*, notes: "At the heart of this regional stand-off is the battle for the vast oil and gas riches of landlocked Central Asia . . . and the intense competition between the regional states and Western oil companies as to who would build the lucrative pipelines which are needed to transport the energy to markets in Europe and Asia." Afghanistan in 2001 was viewed as a major transit route for these pipelines. Today, progress on the Trans-Afghanistan pipeline has been stalled pending pacification of uncontrollable Afghan warlords by bombs, bullets, and drone attacks.

Debate commenced inside the president's War Council. One option was to treat them as criminals, in which case they would be tried in regular criminal courts inside the federal judiciary system. Military lawyers, on the other hand, favored trying them in military courts (courts martial) under the Uniform Code of Military Justice.[175] Cheney and his lawyer, David Addington, favored a third way: creating a military commission system that would operate separately and apart from the protections accorded the accused under both the U.S. court system and the military courts martial system. The advantage to the military commission system was this—it gave free reign to do anything the executive wanted done to the detainees, including forcing them to make false confessions through torture.

By early November, 2001, the thinking inside the White House was, according to Deputy White House Counsel Timothy Flanigan, "Are we going to go with a system that is really guaranteed to prevent us from getting information in every case—or are we going to go another route?"[176]

What did Yoo do?

On November 6, John Yoo, in a thirty-five-page secret OLC memo, gave the president as commander in chief the right to establish military commissions. Even though Article II of the U.S. Constitution does not grant this power to the president, the lawyers claimed that the creation of this new judicial system was an inherently executive function[177]—that is, one that derived from the president's "inherent power as Commander in Chief."

Part of Yoo's legal rationales was 10 U.S.C. Section 821, which allows for the *use* of military commissions as well as courts martial to try offenders or offenders of the law of war.[178] But it says nothing about the president's *authority* to create them. No matter. Yoo simply argued that "even if Congress *has not sanctioned* the use of military commissions to try all offenses against the laws of war, the President, *exercising his authority as Commander in Chief,* could order the use of military commissions to try such offenses"[179] (emphasis added). In June, 2006, in *Hamdan v. Rumsfeld,* 548, U.S. 557, 591–92, the U.S. Supreme Court would reject Yoo's interpretation of sweeping presidential powers, and asserted that the power to create alternative military tribunals rested with Congress, not with the president.

On November 13, 2001, the president, at the urging of Cheney, issued

Order No. 1, giving him the sole authority to establish military commissions and the right to detain, question, and prosecute any suspects of the president's choosing. The road to Abu Ghraib was just laid out.[180]

Bush's order for a military commission evoked immediate condemnation from the inside, both from experienced lawyers like William Howard Taft IV (Colin Powell's lawyer), and Rear Admiral Donald Guter, then the Navy's top lawyer and an expert in the laws of war. Guter and other military lawyers tried to amend sections of the military commission plan, but "we were marginalized," he said. "We were warning [the OLC lawyers] that we had this long tradition of military justice and we didn't want to tarnish it. The treatment of detainees was a huge issue. They didn't want to hear it."[181]

Colin Powell was furious over being bypassed. So, too, was John Ashcroft who, according to *The Washington Post*, was "enraged to discover that [John] Yoo, his subordinate, had recommended [against the DOJ having a say in the tribunal process] as part of a strategy to deny jurisdiction to U.S. courts."[182]

Conservative *New York Times* columnist William Safire immediately called out Bush's order for what it was: the creation of a kangaroo court:

> The Uniform Code of Military Justice demands a public trial, proof beyond reasonable doubt, an accused's voice in the selection of juries and right to choose counsel, unanimity in death sentencing and above all appellate review by civilians confirmed by the Senate. Not one of those fundamental rights can be found in Bush's military order setting up kangaroo courts for people he designates before "trial" to be terrorists. Bush's fiat turns back the clock on all advances in military justice, through three wars, in the past half-century.[183]

But why would Bush and Cheney want to set up a military commission system? As Chris Pyle would point out, "Courts without evidentiary standards could have only one purpose: to admit evidence that no constitutional courts would consider reliable, including hearsay, secret evidence, and statements made by torture."[184]

But this still begs the ultimate question: Why torture? And why use statements obtained by torture in secret trials?

Consider this. Bush, Cheney, and his crowd weren't always looking for actionable intelligence. FBI interrogators already knew how to get actionable intelligence—through persuasion. Rather, in typical Star Chamber fashion, straight out of the Spanish Inquisition, they were looking for answers that they wanted to hear, answers that would establish the detainees' connection to 9/11, Saddam Hussein, and Iraq. In short, answers that would help provide a pretext for an aggressive war against Iraq.

One of the first "enemy combatants" to be picked up in Afghanistan was an alleged al-Qaeda commander named Ibn al-Shaykh al-Libi. He was a great find. He knew Osama bin Laden. He had trained jihadists in one of bin Laden's camps. He gave the FBI details about the camps. Through simple conversation, he provided the FBI actionable intelligence. But then the CIA took over his questioning, ostensibly because of the urgency of the situation. They pressed him for information about ties between al-Qaeda and Saddam Hussein's regime in Iraq.[185] After failing to extract information, they warned him that he was going to be removed to Cairo. But first, one of his CIA torturers said, "I'm going to find your mother and I'm going to fuck her."

Once in Egypt, he was locked in a tiny cage for eighty hours.[186] Egypt's intelligence operatives, working very closely with the CIA,[187] worked over al-Libi until he finally started to confess. To what? Among other things, to *having visited Iraq* and getting training in chemical and biological weapons.[188]

He would later recant, in March, 2003, claiming that the information had been forced out of him through torture.[189] But by then, American troops were already headed to Iraq. In May, 2009, al-Libi was found dead in a Libyan prison.[190]

Another "high-level detainee" captured early on in Afghanistan was John Walker Lindh, the so-called American Taliban. In December, he was placed into U.S. custody. He immediately asked for a lawyer, and his family immediately found one for him. But for fifty-four days he was prevented from talking to his lawyer. Instead, he was repeatedly interrogated by soldiers, who threatened him with death, and by the FBI, without the presence of a lawyer. His wounds were left untreated; he was left in a cold, windowless shipping container for eight days. Government documents would reveal that William

Haynes, general counsel to Secretary of Defense Rumsfeld, had ordered Lindh's captors to "take the gloves off."[191]

John Walker Lindh was tortured, despite assurances from White House Press Secretary Ari Fleischer that he was being held as a prisoner of war under the Geneva Conventions. The Bush administration turned Lindh into a trophy find, describing him as a terrorist and a traitor who had conspired to kill a CIA agent who had died in a prison revolt where Lindh had been held captive by warlords loyal to the Northern Alliance.[192] In fact, Lindh had no intention of fighting the U.S. when he joined the then American-backed Taliban in 2000 to fight the Northern Alliance, who were even more fundamentalist Muslims than the Taliban. Most important, Lindh did not commit any acts of war against American soldiers.

The capture of such "high profile terrorists" as al-Libi and Lindh in the early months of the war in Afghanistan proved a boon to the Bush administration's PR about the "war on terror," but it also created a problem: Both had been tortured, and torture was illegal.

Legal Hurdle Number 3: Prohibitions Against Torture—The Geneva Conventions (1949) and the War Crimes Act (1996)

The Geneva Conventions of 1949, promulgated after World War II, prohibit the mistreatment of anyone picked up in the course of a war. Common Article 3 of the Geneva Conventions prohibits "murder, mutilation, cruel treatment, torture, outrages against personal dignity, particularly humiliating and degrading treatment."[193]

The War Crimes Act of 1996, 18 U.S.C. Section 2441, describes war crimes as "any conduct" prohibited in Common Article 3 of the Geneva Conventions, and holds anyone who commits a war crime, "whether inside or outside the United States," to be criminally liable—subject to fines, life imprisonment, or "if death results to the victim, shall also be subject to the penalty of death."

In October, 2001, U.S. General Tommy Franks gave the customary order to American troops in Afghanistan to obey the Geneva Conventions.[194]

But as we have seen, these orders were not obeyed—not by soldiers, not by the FBI, and not by the CIA—during the months of November and December, 2001.

What did Yoo do?

On January 9, 2002, John Yoo, with the stroke of a pen and no congressional oversight, removed al-Qaeda and the Taliban from the protection of the Geneva Conventions. Titling his memo "Application of Treaties and Laws to al-Qaeda and Taliban Detainees," Yoo argued that al-Qaeda was a "nongovernmental organization" and a "nonstate actor" and therefore did not fall under the protections of Common Article 3 of the Conventions. As for the Taliban, they too were not covered because Afghanistan was a "failed state" that "was without the attributes of statehood necessary to continue as a party to the Geneva Conventions" or was otherwise "functionally indistinguishable from al-Qaeda."[195]

On January 25, 2002, White House Counsel Alberto Gonzales prepared (with the help of Cheney's lawyer, David Addington) his now infamous legal opinion endorsing Yoo's memorandum. "As you have said," Gonzales wrote the president, "the war against terrorism is a new kind of war. . . . In my judgment, this new paradigm renders obsolete Geneva's strict limitations on questioning of enemy prisoners." Since the Geneva Conventions were "quaint" and "outmoded," they need not apply to members of al-Qaeda or the Taliban.[196]

Secretary of State Powell immediately challenged the memo, which was still in draft form, arguing (among other things) that circumventing the Geneva Conventions "will reverse over a century of U.S. policy . . . and undermines the protections of the law for our troops." William Howard Taft IV, legal advisor to the State Department, also objected, claiming on February 2 in a memorandum to Gonzales that his proposed rejection of the Geneva Conventions "deprives our troops [in Afghanistan] of any claim to the protection of the Conventions in the event *they* are captured"[197] (emphasis added). In short, Gonzales was putting American soldiers at greater risk.

What happened next may only come out through a long-awaited report from the OLC's Office of Professional Responsibility. While Gonzales and the OLC lawyers may argue that they had proposed a military commission system and denied detainees protections of the Geneva Conventions in good faith, they received heated objections from military and State Department lawyers that these orders were unlawful and dangerous. But they went ahead with them anyway. Why? If it can be shown, through emails obtained by the

OPR, that policy makers somehow intervened to be sure they hewed to the administration line, the case might be made that they knowingly broke the law.[198]

Gonzales may have slipped up in any event in his January 25 memo by actually acknowledging that *not* applying the Geneva Conventions "substantially reduces the *threat of domestic criminal prosecutions* [of administration officials] under the War Crimes Act (18 U.S.C. 2441)." If ever there were a smoking gun showing intent to break the law, this was it. OLC future-head Jack Goldsmith himself would go on describe the January 25 memo as a "conspiracy to commit a war crime."[199]

Picture this hypothetical exchange, on cross examination, in a courtroom:

> Q: Mr. Gonzales, why were you concerned about domestic criminal prosecutions?
>
> A: Ah, I don't recall.
>
> Q: Were you aware that the Geneva Conventions prohibited torture?
>
> A: I suppose. (Gonzales, incidentally, had no prior experience in international law.)
>
> Q: Isn't it true that you created military commissions as a legal means to get you off the hook if the question of torture ever came up, while allowing torture to happen?
>
> A: I woudn't say that.

Gonzales's hedging in this hypothetical is consistent with the conduct he actually displayed while being questioned on a broad range of issues by the Senate Judiciary Committee. It seemed like he could never give a straight answer.

The Bush administration had their own problem with Gonzales's memo: It came too late to protect any interrogators who had illegally tortured detainees (like al-Libi and Lindh) before it went into effect in January, 2002.

Whatever went on inside the Bush administration, it appears Bush listened enough to criticisms to sign a slightly reworded memorandum titled "Humane Treatment of Taliban and al Qaeda Detainees." The memorandum still maintained that the detainees would not be accorded the protection of the Geneva

Conventions but did call for their "humane treatment" in a "manner consistent with the principles of Geneva"—to the extent appropriate and consistent with military necessity.[200]

Despite its humanitarian gloss, however, this memo now cleared the way to send detainees to Guantánamo with no protections against cruel and inhuman punishment if "military necessity" so allegedly required.

The next question to arise was this: If "enhanced interrogations" were to occur because of military necessity, how far could they go without constituting torture?

Legal Hurdle Number 4: The definition of torture according to 18 U.S.C. Section 2340 (the U.S. antitorture statute)

The U.S. Criminal Code broadly defines torture as an act "specifically intended to inflict severe physical or mental pain or suffering . . . "

What may have brought the question of "what constitutes torture" to a head was the March 28, 2002, raid by the CIA, FBI, and Pakistani special forces on a compound in Pakistan near the border of Afghanistan and the capture of an alleged al-Qaeda logistics chief, Abu Zubaydah, by surprise—along with twenty-four other suspected al-Qaeda followers. Abu Zubaydah was well known to U.S. security forces. He had been involved in a Palestinian uprising against Israel, then purportedly joined bin Laden to fight the Soviets in Afghanistan. When he was captured, he left behind cell phones, notepads, computer disks, and a personal diary. He was one of the CIA's first "big fish" to be captured.

Bush was exultant. "The other day," he told a group of Republican supporters in Connecticut, "we hauled in a guy named Abu Zubaydah. He's one of the top operatives plotting and planning death and destruction on the United States. He's not plotting and planning anymore. He's where he belongs."[201]

It was later determined—in part, from reading his diaries—that Zubaydah was not such a valued prize as originally suspected. From being considered one of Osama bin Laden's top deputies, he was eventually downgraded to an operator of safe houses in Afghanistan and Pakistan. The downgrade had no impact on his treatment, however.

Bush, when told of the downgrade, did not want to change his stance after making such a big deal about Zubaydah's capture. "I said he was important," he told CIA director George Tenet at a daily briefing. "You're not going to let me lose face on this, are you?"[202]

During the spring of 2002, based on subsequent interviews with investigating members of the International Red Cross, Zubaydah, already injured with bullet wounds during his capture, endured torture, including being held in a small cage for hours at a time, an experience which he likened to being confined in a tiny coffin.[203]

Sometime during the summer of 2002, Zubaydah became the first detainee to be waterboarded. Waterboarding was known to be completely illegal because it was a form of mock execution. U.S. soldiers had been prosecuted for waterboarding detainees in the Philippines in 1900 and the Department of Justice had successfully prosecuted a sheriff in 1983 for waterboarding prisoners.[204] There was apparently enough uncertainty within the CIA about what they were doing with Zubaydah that summer that they sought an opinion by the OLC.

What did Yoo do?

After Zubaydah had already been waterboarded and severely tortured—to the point that the FBI called him "mentally unhinged"—John Yoo and Jay Bybee came up with what would become known as the "Torture Memo" of August 1, 2002. It provided a new definition of torture, one that effectively gave the green light to all forms of physical and emotional abuse except in cases where the activity was intended to cause organ failure and death.[205] Its apparent purpose was to reassure CIA interrogators that they would not be held "criminally liable for what they had done to Abu Zubaydah."[206]

With the necessity defense in mind, which allows an accused person to claim he or she was trying to avoid a greater crime by committing a lesser one, Yoo and Bybee argued that the torturer could claim that he was "acting on good faith" to protect the American people from greater harm. However, as constitutional lawyer Chris Pyle points out, "this advice directly contradicted both the federal and international law on torture, *which proves that torture is never justified or excused under any circumstances.*"[207]

Finally, the torture memo stated that the president's power as commander in chief during a time of war had to take precedence over any legal prohibitions against torture, including the UN Convention Against Torture.

When this memo was leaked to the public in 2004 in the aftermath of the Abu Ghraib scandal, it caused a sensation. It was this memo that caused *New York Times* columnist Anthony Lewis to refer to it as being more akin to the advice of a lawyer to his mafia don than evenhanded legal advice. And it was this memo that others called an "advance pardon" due to the belief that it was "almost impossible to convict anyone who chose to claim that he relied in good faith on an OLC opinion."[208] Yoo's own Yale Law School professor, Dean Harold Koh, called his student's memo "a stain upon our law and our national reputation."

In April, 2009, a second Yoo memo written the same day, August 1, 2002, was released to the ACLU describing in painstaking detail what the CIA could do to Zubaydah, including waterboarding him. As noted in the previous chapter, it caused an absolute uproar. The last time such an uproar occurred was in 2005, when the so-called Downing Street memo was leaked to the press. In the memo, dated July 2002, the head of Britain's foreign intelligence agency, MI-6, admitted after a visit to Washington that "the intelligence and facts were being fixed [by the U.S.] around the policy" of removing Saddam Hussein from power.

The ultimate evil

Moving into the fall of 2002, President Bush and his "torture team" were gearing up for the war in Iraq, which would begin in March, 2003. The CIA had been conducting research on false confessions[209] and looked to incessant waterboarding as a favored route to follow.

By October, 2002, Bush, Cheney, and their lawyers still hadn't found a suitable pretext for getting us into war. As Bugliosi reported in his book, *The Prosecution of George W. Bush for Murder*, Bush had received the infamous National Intelligence Estimate of October 1, 2002, with its deep reservations about Saddam Hussein being a threat to national security. You will recall, as Bugliosi has argued, that the president chose to ignore the findings of the National Intelligence Estimate and instead, in the White House's white paper (a summary of this classified report) *deleted this all-important position of U.S. intelligence*. The white paper was given to members of Congress and used to make Bush's case for war in front of the American people in his October 7 televised speech. It was then that he claimed Saddam Hussein actually *was* a threat, in fact "a great danger to our nation" who intended to use biological or chemical weapons to attack us, or give them to terrorists who would.

On October 10, Congress authorized President Bush to go to war against Iraq. While on the surface, everything was a "go" for the Bush administration, internally there was a problem: A sound pretext for going to war had yet to materialize. Bush could argue all he liked about Saddam Hussein posing an imminent threat with his WMDs, but the WMDs were yet to be found. In fact, they didn't exist. As Washington journalist Ron Suskind describes in his book *The Way of the World,* in the fall of 2002, Rob Richer, head of the CIA's Near East Division, admitted that the CIA did not have proof of WMDs.[210] This must have been a source of some consternation for the Bush administration, for over at the Office of Legal Council, Yoo and Bybee were working feverishly on yet another memo, this one trying to legally justify the invasion of Iraq. On October 23, 2002, they presented it to the president in all its forty-seven-page glory. They titled it "Authority of the President under Domestic and International Law to Use Military Force Against Iraq." This document, released to the public in January, 2009, has generated very little commentary. The mainstream press was absolutely silent about it.

The entire document was, for all intents and purposes, forty-seven pages of hypotheticals on how to convince the American people to go to war with a veneer of legality. It had nothing to say about our country being in imminent danger. The wording is provisional, as you can see from this quote under the section "Constitutional Authority" for "Use of Force Against Iraq": "For example, *were* the president to conclude that Iraq's development of WMD *might* endanger our national security because of the risk that such weapons either *would be targeted* against the United States, or *would be used* to destabilize the region, he *could* direct the use of military force against Iraq to destroy its WMD capability" (emphasis added). The rest of the document goes something like this: You could argue constitutional law, as in ordering the use of force to "protect our national interests," or you could argue international law, saying the UN Security Council gave authorization to use force because it did in the first Gulf War; or, if all else failed, you could claim *"anticipatory self-defense."* In light of what Bush said on October 7, this October 23, 2002, memo was particularly revealing in its sheer desperation to show Saddam Hussein as a threat. Bugliosi, remember, was fond of arguing that the only defense Bush would have in a murder charge was self-defense. If it could be shown that Saddam Hussein was not a threat to our nation, then his only defense evaporates.

So what does the Bybee memo do? It comes up with a new legal term: anticipatory self-defense. It provides strong circumstantial evidence that the Bush administration didn't have the proof of WMDs and now had to concoct some legal theory as if it did. Here's what Bybee says:

> We observe, therefore, that even if the probability that Iraq itself would attack the United States with WMD, or would transfer such a weapon to terrorists for their use against the United States, were relatively low, the exceptionally high degree of harm that would result, combined with a limited window of opportunity and the likelihood that if we do not use force, the threat will increase, could lead the President to conclude that military action is necessary to defend the United States.

It was a classic case of Jay Bybee "memoing up," of providing yet another *post-hoc rationalization for conduct that had already occurred*—in this case, the conduct of Bush delivering a speech over national TV designed to get us into a war in Iraq under false pretenses.

For me, it was like finding the mother lode of incriminating documents. When I first read the document, I muttered a private remonstrance to Bybee: "Why not just say the President can do whatever he damned well pleases, come up with phony theories about why we needed to go to war, and be done with it! Why even bother going through all this convoluted argument?"

But there was more.

In January, 2003, the CIA's Robert Richer had his British counterpart, Michael Shipster, meet secretly in Jordan with Saddam's head of intelligence, Tahir Jalil Habbush al-Takriti. At the meeting, Habbush declared point-blank that if the U.S. invaded, it would find no WMDs. When word of this got back to Washington, Bush reportedly muttered, "Why don't they [the British] ask him to give us something we can use to help us make our case?"[211] That "something" would eventually materialize in the fall of 2003. As Suskind describes it, "[in September, 2003] the White House orders the CIA to have a letter fabricated from Habbush to Saddam, backdated to July, 2001, which solves the White House's political problems."[212] The letter linked al-Qaeda's Mohamed Atta (one of the 9/11 highjackers) to Saddam Hussein. As the foreign correspondent for Britain's *Daily Telegraph* reported, "Now this is really concrete proof that al Qaeda was working with Saddam. . . . It basically says that Atta was in Baghdad being trained under Saddam's guidance prior to the 9/11 attack. It's a very explosive development." In fact, it was a forgery.[213]

Meanwhile, we now know (thanks to the DOJ's release of the torture memos in April, 2009) that during the month of March, 2003—in the days leading up to the war in Iraq—al-Qaeda operative Khalid Sheikh Mohammed (known as KSM) was waterboarded *183 times*. He was also beaten continuously, suspended from the ceiling by his arms for eight hours a day, and forced to crouch naked in his cell while chained to a metal ring—in short, subjected to hundreds of different torture techniques in the course of one month. At this point, according to one CIA officer, "brutalization became bureaucratized."[214]

Dick Cheney admitted on national TV on December 15, 2008, that he authorized the torture of Khalid Sheikh Mohammed. He claimed it produced great intelligence, but that has yet to be determined. As pointed out earlier, the real purpose for the brutalization was to get KSM to confess to something that was not true, namely al-Qaeda's link to Saddam Hussein and 9/11. The same had been done with al-Libi, who had been captured in Afghanistan in December, 2001, and subjected to particularly harsh torture in the months leading up to the war.

Meanwhile, author Jane Mayer has written in *The Dark Side*, al-Libi's captors tried to press him for information connecting Saddam Hussein to anthrax and other biological weapons:

> According to [a 2006] Senate report, al-Libi said he "knew nothing about the subject and didn't understand the term biological," so he couldn't even invent a confession. . . . Again he was beaten. . . . He subsequently fabricated additional details, which were piped into the Vice President's office, among other places, and used by the

Bush Administration to buttress its allegations that Iraq was on the verge of supplying Al Qaeda with potentially terrifying weapons of mass destruction. President Bush fanned these fears October 7, 2002, in a speech in Cincinnati, Ohio, announcing, "We've learned that Iraq has trained Al Qaeda members in bomb-making and poisons and deadly gasses."[215]

All this while, according to Mayer:

> Bush approved of White House meetings in which his top cabinet members were briefed by the CIA on its plans to use specific "enhanced" interrogation techniques on various high-value detainees. The meetings were chaired by Condoleezza Rice, who was then National Security Advisor, in the Situation Room. The participants were the members of the Principals Committee: the five Bush cabinet members who handled national security matters: Vice President Cheney, Secretary of State Powell, Secretary of Defense Rumsfeld, CIA Director Tenet, and Attorney General Ashcroft. . . . There is no indication that any Bush cabinet members objected to the policy. Cheney was described as "totally pushing it," and Rice, during the early period when [waterboarded detainee] Zubaydah was captured, was described by a knowledgeable source as "a total hard-ass." The source suggested, "She was probably reflecting what the President wanted."

The one person who admitted discomfort over discussing these highly sensitive and potentially incriminating conversations was John Ashcroft. "History," he reportedly said, "will not judge us kindly."[216]

He was right. Here's what the influential *New York Times* columnist Paul Krugman said in his column of April 24, 2009, about this newfound link between Bush's torture police and getting us to war in Iraq:

> The fact is that officials in the Bush administration instituted torture as a policy, misled the nation into a war they wanted to fight, and, probably, tortured people in the attempt to extract "confessions"

that would justify that war. And during the march to war, most of the political and media establishment looked the other way.

Krugman's blog the day before was even more unrelenting:

> Let's say this slowly: the Bush administration wanted to use 9/11 as a pretext to invade Iraq, even though Iraq had nothing to do with 9/11. So it tortured people to make them confess to the nonexistent link. There's a word for this: it's evil.

I could hear Bugliosi's impassioned cry before the House Judiciary Committee: *How dare they? How dare they do what they did?* I immediately put in a call to him.

"You're not going to believe this, Vince, but some of those recently released memos make a direct link between the torturing of detainees and Bush taking us into war in Iraq under false pretenses. Bush was *desperate* to find the right pretext, Vince. So he practically tortured these guys to death to get them to admit they were tied to Saddam Hussein and 9/11. It all ties together. And the fact is, Bush's lawyers *knew* they were breaking the law all along."

I faxed him the cover page of Bybee's October 23, 2002, memo that desperately tried to make the case for invading Iraq, arguing "anticipatory self-defense." When I got back to him the next day, he acknowledged that he had not seen this memo before. "That's right!" I replied. "Because it was only released in January. And no one is talking about it. Everyone continues to be focused solely on torture," I said.

I was beginning to think there was a reason for this: The torture brouhaha diverted people's attention away from two ongoing wars, one in Iraq, one in Afghanistan. It was as if the media had decided to truncate torture away from war, when the two were inextricably related.

As far as I was concerned, the case for prosecuting George W. Bush for murder (taking us to war on false pretexts, with no legitimate defense) had never been stronger. As for the truth, there is one piece of it that will probably never come out unless a journalist tells it. In the next chapter, I don my journalist's hat again and provide the ultimate missing context.

CHAPTER NINE

Making Sense of It All: What's Really Going On?

On May 28, at the height of the evening rush hour, New Yorkers swarmed into Grand Central Station as usual, only to stop suddenly to gaze upon something highly unusual: a procession of twenty-two people in black hoods and orange jumpsuits heading for one of the two ornate staircases in the Grand Concourse. As the procession moved toward the staircase, a protestor yelled to bystanders: "These detainees are being taken by the U.S. government to Guantánamo! We can hold them forever without charges! President Obama just proposed prolonged detention!" Once they reached the top of the steps, they unfurled a large black banner that read, in huge orange letters, "PROSECUTE WAR CRIMINALS. RELEASE THE TORTURE PHOTOS." The concourse erupted in applause.

Suddenly, hundreds of startled commuters whipped out their cell phones and began to take pictures. Others began to talk with people around them, and before you knew it, according to World Can't Wait protestor Debra Sweet, "There was this massive debate about torture on the floor of the Grand Central."[217]

On the same day, but on the other side of the country, demonstrators congregated outside the Ninth Circuit Court of Appeals in Pasadena, California, where former OLC lawyer Jay Bybee served as a judge. There, they set up a makeshift "torture museum" to mimic the staid official museum inside of the Ninth Circuit. And they held up enlarged copies of memos written by Bybee, rendering his opinion on torture. They wanted to let the public know that the court had a torturer among its judges.

Both demonstrations had been planned in anticipation of a court-imposed deadline for the Obama administration to release the torture photos. The plan had been to enlarge some of the photos so the general public could fully understand the horrors committed by our government and demand that the torturers be held to account.

But on May 14, President Obama reneged on his promise to release the photos. He was concerned, he said, that the photos would inflame sentiments where our soldiers were fighting. The activists, now angrier and more determined than ever, went ahead with their May 28 protest at both locations. Instead of showing just-released torture photos, they showed never-before-seen photos that had been released by the Australian press and circulated on the Internet. The photos showed dogs attacking a naked prisoner, a guard striking a group of detainees, and a detainee shackled in an extremely painful stress position.

These and other protestors I interviewed that spring and summer did not believe for a minute that Obama was concerned about protecting the safety of soldiers in Iraq and Afghanistan. "Everyone in the Middle East already knows about the torture," they would invariably tell me. "It's not the soldiers he's protecting by not releasing the photos, it's the CIA. They're worried about criminal investigations and prosecutions. They're worried that once the American people became fully aware of what they did, the American public would insist on accountability."

The protesters were heartened that their demonstrations had made an impact on those who had seen them, either personally or through some local TV coverage or local newspapers. The British Reuters news service was at Grand Central Station and a PBS crew was there to film the demonstration. But the vast majority of Americans who tuned in to the networks' nightly news knew nothing of these visually dramatic protests and so were left with Obama's unchallenged explanation about protecting the safety of the troops.

I myself had to turn to the Internet to find scenes of the orange jumpsuit demonstrations in various cities across the country.[218] They always took my breath away. The mere sight of hooded and handcuffed "detainees" being held captive on American soil struck me as so alien, so eerily un-American, that I had to wonder: What has our country come to? The last time I felt so uneasy was when I saw the U.S. military, armed with submachine guns, patrolling our nation's airports and railroad stations after 9/11. I was comforted to see them then, although somewhat disquieted by scenes of armed guards that reminded me more of a Latin-American banana republic than the United States. Little did I know then that while the U.S. military was guarding our transportation hubs, the police and FBI were doing massive sweeps of Muslim-American communities, picking up men who were not suspected of terrorism but who looked foreign and may have violated some immigration procedure. Michael Ratner of the Center for Constitutional Rights would later write that as many as three thousand had been arrested and detained during the first months after 9/11. "Many of these people effectively disappeared in U.S. jails," he wrote. "A number were beaten and ultimately deported. It was a real sign of times to come."[219]

Whenever discussions about torture *did* arise in the mainstream media, they invariably debunked the necessity of prosecutions. Glenn Greenwald boldly addressed this problem in a Salon piece titled "Meet the Press and the media's distortions of the prosecution debate."[220] The fact that a majority of Americans supported criminal investigations, he wrote, is "virtually always excluded from establishment media discussions, and those who advocate investigations and prosecutions—the view held by large percentages if not majorities of Americans—are virtually never heard from. That's because the belief that elites should be exempted from all consequences when they break the law is as close to a transpartisan religious tenet of Beltway culture as it gets. Beltway mavens love the idea that Beltway elites have exemption from legal consequences, but—for obvious reasons—that is not an idea embraced by many Americans."

Looking back to look forward

It had been a rough month for the accountability movement. By mid-May, everyone's fervent hopes that the new president would usher in a new era had come crashing down on a bedrock of cynical pragmatism. People were raising questions almost too difficult to even contemplate: Could Barack Obama actually be engaged in a cover-up? Even worse—by covering up, wasn't he enabling war crimes?

With the mainstream media doing its job to squelch debate on the subject, the only place to go was the blogosphere, and there the legal bloggers' opinions were raw.

They had all chronicled another side to Obama's first one hundred days, a series of decisions that signaled an abrupt reversal of his promises to close down military commissions, stop indefinite detentions, and restore transparency to government. In February alone, for instance, Eric Holder's Justice Department argued that it would continue the Bush policy of invoking "state secrets" in extraordinary-rendition cases. It also tried to dismiss or delay an ACLU challenge to the ongoing detention of Mohammed Jawad, who had already been held in Guatánamo for six years—since he was a teenager —based on his tortured confession that he had thrown a hand grenade at two U.S. service members in Afghanistan.* In April, the DOJ had come up with new sovereign immunity arguments for protecting Bush's illegal spying programs.

And then on May 16 Obama reversed himself and said he would not release the torture photos.

It was as if the "war community"—the CIA, the military, and the pliant corporate media—had hijacked the president and delivered his marching orders.

Those in the human- and civil-rights communities were beside themselves. Obama, to many of them, was looking more and more like Bush.

A chorus of outrage erupted on the Internet.

Jonathan Turley, the George Washington law professor and frequent guest on MSNBC, was unsparing in his criticism. "The Obama Administration has become the greatest bait and switch in history. No torture prosecution. No abuse photos. No citizen lawsuit on privacy. Absolute executive privilege claims."[221]

The ACLU, which had sued for the release of the photos, called Obama's decision not to release them "a mockery of [his] promise of transparency and accountability."

Andrew Sullivan of *The Atlantic* wrote with regret, "Slowly but surely, Obama is owning the cover-up of his predecessors' war crimes. But cover-

---

*The Bush administration had wanted to try him in a military commission, but even the former military prosecutor objected, noting that the commission system made it impossible "to harbor the remotest hope that justice is an achievable goal." The ACLU argued that Jawad was tortured, thus the evidence of his "guilt" obtained from torture was inadmissable and his detention was unlawful. On July 30, a federal judge ruled against the Obama administration.

ing up war crimes, refusing to prosecute them, promoting those associated with them, and suppressing evidence of them are themselves violations of Geneva and the UN Convention. So Cheney begins to successfully co-opt his successor."[222]

Glenn Greenwald unflinchingly documented "Obama's embrace of Bush terrorism policies,"[223] quoting none other than the former OLC director (and subsequent critic of the Bush administration) Jack Goldsmith: "Obama has copied most of the Bush program, has expanded some of it, and has narrowed only a bit. Almost all of the Obama changes have been at the level of packaging, argumentation, symbol and rhetoric."

To many who had counted on the new president to ensure justice, Obama's record was looking hypocritical—possibly even scandalous.

Others still held out hope that his seeming reversals were part of a grander strategy, one aimed ultimately at fulfilling his promise to restore account-ability. He was new on the job, after all. He was having to confront some monumental issues, like saving the economy while trying to negotiate some meaningful reforms in the nation's health care. Reforms take time.

On May 20, Obama hosted a meeting of human-rights lawyers and advo-cates at the White House. It was one day before he was to give a major speech on national security and civil liberties.

He clearly wanted to show these lawyers that he took them—a significant part of his electoral base—seriously. Sitting in the room with him were his chief of staff, Rahm Emanuel, his White House advisor, David Axelrod, his attorney general, Eric Holder, and his White House counsel, Greg Craig.

The conversation was reportedly blunt. According to *Newsweek* reporter Michael Isikoff (whose information came from someone present at the meeting), the lawyers and advocates accused Obama of basing his decisions on some of the same premises that Bush had accepted in his handling of detainees.[224] President Obama had reportedly bristled over their criticism, telling the lawyers it was "not helpful" to equate him with Bush.

Not helpful? What were they to think at this point?

The following day, he delivered his speech on national security at the National Archives building in downtown Washington, D.C. There was a certain irony to his choice of locale. The National Archives, a stately neoclas-sical monument whose pillars and pediments evoke the days of the Roman

Republic, houses the Constitution, the Bill of Rights, and the Declaration of Independence. Months earlier, when the Bush administration was still in power, a group of protestors from Veterans for Peace had climbed over a nine-foot fence and draped a huge twenty-two-foot by eight-foot banner over the Constitution Avenue entrance to the building. "Defend Our Constitution," the banner proclaimed. "Arrest Bush-Cheney. War Criminals." Some had distributed "citizen arrest warrants" to tourists while others spoke to the press. "We are not trespassing," they said. "We have come to the home of the Constitution to honor our oath to defend it."

One of the vets explained that the Bush administration, by thumbing its nose at the Constitution, had set a "terrible precedent for any future administration. If there's no justice and no accountability," he said, "you might as well have a king."[225]

Now, four months into his term, President Obama was delivering his speech on national security at the home of the Constitution as if to reiterate his promise during his inaugural address: "We reject as false the choice between our safety and our ideals. . . . Our Founding Fathers . . . drafted a charter to assure the rule of law and the rights of man, a charter expanded by the blood of generations. Those ideals still light the world, and we will not give them up for expediency's sake."

What would he say now?

Obama's National Security Speech

I was driving around Manhattan in my usual hunt for a parking space while I listened to Obama's speech on the radio. For almost an hour, he addressed the very same issues I had been writing about in this book. I was stunned: Here I was, writing on issues that seemed to me decidedly unresolved, and here he was, sounding like someone who had finally resolved them. No more flip-flops from President Obama. He sounded strong, assertive, like a president and commander in chief rolled into one.

In the previous week, he had been pummeled from the right—and especially from now private citizen Dick Cheney—for criticizing the Bush administration on its torture policy. He was getting attacked from the left for authorizing military commissions and indefinite detentions when he had earlier said such commissions "were incapable of administering anything worthy of the word justice."²²⁶ He was even challenged by members of his own party, who joined Republicans in rejecting funds for the closure of Guantánamo unless he could come up with a clear plan for where to put the prisoners. In short, he was besieged. But he didn't act that way.

He made it clear he wasn't going to take any more fear-mongering from Dick Cheney, who in recent weeks had gone on every talk show imaginable trying to defend his and Bush's endorsement of torture. "All too often," President Obama said, "our government made decisions based on fear rather than foresight; all too often, our government trimmed facts and evidence to fit ideological predispositions. Instead of strategically applying our power and our principles, too often we set those principles aside as luxuries that we could no longer afford. And during this season of fear, too many of us— Democrats and Republicans, politicians, journalists, and citizens—fell silent. In other words, we went off course."

Well done, I thought to myself. What next?

He defended his position on calling waterboarding torture. "I categorically reject the assertion that these [brutal methods] are the most effective means of interrogation. [applause] What's more, they undermine the rule of law. They alienate us in the world. They serve as a recruitment tool for terrorists, and increase the will of our enemies to fight us, while decreasing the will of others to work with America."

He was right. Our country's more sophisticated elites—and I would put the powerful, oil-based Rockefeller family into this category—had learned over a century of rule that alienating people at home and abroad can be very harmful to their interests.

He defended his position on closing Guantánamo, "which has weakened American national security. It is a rallying cry for our enemies."

I agreed wholeheartedly.

He explained why he had released the so-called torture memos: "The existence of that approach to interrogation was already widely known, the Bush administration had acknowledged its existence, and I had already banned those methods."

This was sound tactical and legal thinking.

He explained why he opposed the release of the torture photos: "It was my judgment—informed by my national security team—that releasing these photos would inflame anti-American opinion and [cause harm to] our troops . . . endangering them in theaters of war." In other words, he said, he had to "strike the right balance between transparency and national security."

Well, at least he *sounded* reasonable, although I suspected he was also protecting the torturers.

But then he got into specifics, specifics that startled me. He said he would keep military commissions for those who had "violated the rules of war." He did not elaborate on the rules, nor explain why such commissions were preferable to a federal criminal court. I knew he would get in trouble on this one. Even conservative pundits like William Safire objected strongly to the creation of a military commission system. He said he would continue to detain prisoners at Guantánamo who "cannot be transferred." That sounded like indefinite detention, sure to get a rise out of the human-rights community.

There would be no independent investigating commissions, he said, "because I believe that our existing democratic institutions are strong enough to deliver accountability." The Congress, he said, "can review abuses of our values, and there are ongoing inquiries by Congress into matters like enhanced interrogation techniques."

If he stops there, I was thinking, then months of "accountability work" by thousands of people, including myself, were going down the tubes. Congress had held plenty of hearings, but with no teeth in them.

But then he added another sentence.

"The Department of Justice and the courts can work through and punish any violations of our laws or miscarriages of justice."

This was significant. It was a "no" to Leahy's truth commission and appeared to be a "yes" to the Department of Justice appointing a special prosecutor. Was this the trade-off for all the negative things in his speech?

In the excited commentary that followed, both the ACLU and the Center for Constitutional Rights were rightfully dismayed over his stated intention to keep the military commissions. Said ACLU director Anthony Romero, "Any [military commission] system designed to produce a preordained outcome, rather than a free and fair trial, is irreparably unjust. Creating a system of indefinite detention—holding detainees for years without facing charges—is a fundamental violation of the Constitution."

The day after his speech, I asked Ramona Allen, a smart young African American woman I knew, what she thought about Obama's speech. She hadn't heard it, so we turned on her computer and she watched it online. She watched Obama at the National Archives referring to the historic setting for his speech. "The documents that we hold in this very hall—the Declaration of Independence, the Constitution, the Bill of Rights—these are not simply words written into aging parchment. They are the foundation of liberty and justice in this country, and a light that shines for all who seek freedom, fairness, equality, and dignity around the world."

Whereupon Ramona started to laugh. I was a bit taken aback. Granted, Ramona is getting a degree in education psychology, and it's not easy to put one over on her. "I don't like to be bullshitted," she told me after watching the speech in its entirety, and apparently she felt like she was getting a heavy dose, especially toward the end of the speech, when the president started talking about staying tough on terrorism.

Ramona is not "political" in the activist sense of the word. But she has developed some opinions since becoming an adult in the post-9/11 era. "Listen, I really don't understand the war on terrorism," she said to me. "The way I see it, we're going in there and doing our thing and then we walk away and we leave the chaos behind. I think there's a reason these people are fighting back. Why don't we ever hear that? America is the [one] stirring the pot. We started mixing things up over there and then we say we have to go after the terrorists. But who is going after us? Who is holding us accountable? I don't know, Charlotte, but I'm seeing a Bush flavor to what he's saying."

I asked her why she felt that way. "Growing up black in America, I guess. I've seen it all before. And not just with blacks. Look what happened to the Native Americans."

I searched the Internet for other reactions and eventually landed on the World Can't Wait's Web site. The group's founder, Debra Sweet, was fuming. As someone who read other blogs (her Web page provides some thirty-three links, including David Swanson's After Downing Street; Convict Bush and Cheney; Defend Critical Thinking; Free Detainees; Glenn Greenwald; Iraq Veterans Against the War; and War Criminals Watch), she knew she was not alone. "This is truly a moment I must say, 'If you're not outraged, you're not paying attention,'" she wrote.[227]

The president, she announced, had just slipped a plan of prolonged military detention into his speech. "Preventive detention allows indefinite imprisonment not based on proven crimes or past violations of law, but of those deemed generally 'dangerous by the government for various reasons.' . . . That's what 'preventive' means: Imprisoning people because the government claims they are likely to engage in violence in the future because they are alleged to be 'combatants.'" She put out a call to action. There were only a "small number of us" who were outraged, she admitted. Yet the time to take a stand, to act visibly, was now. "We need to bring more people with us, and not stop, given the stakes."

And so, on May 28, those two imaginative and very public demonstrations took place in Grand Central Station and outside Bybee's courthouse in California. Both were powerful protests, but they did not make waves. As usual, the mainstream media wasn't there to cover either one of them.

By now I knew that everything about the accountability movement, as in other movements before it, was incremental. Every action has an effect, even if on just a small number of people—at first.

The Exigencies of Empire

When President Barack Obama emerged into the bright sunlight one spring day after delivering a speech at Georgetown University on the economy, he had to make his way past a group of women carrying huge pink signs with black lettering that read: "Human Need, Not Corporate Greed" and "Stop Funding Wars and Wall Street." They were members of the woman's peace group Code Pink. Their leader, Medea Benjamin, was still indoors. She had managed to get inside by flashing her press pass. She sat through his speech, and when it ended, she pushed her way up to the front of the room. Suddenly, she found herself shaking hands with the president and telling him to his face, in typical Code Pink bluntness: "We have to get out of Afghanistan and Iraq. With this economic crisis, we can't afford these wars."

Obama responded, "Give us time. Believe me, I want to get out as well."

She pressed on, "We also have to make deeper cuts in the military budget, like all those bases we have overseas where the local people don't want us."

His bodyguards were by now moving him along toward the door, but he managed to turn around and say to Benjamin, "Yes. We're taking a look at all the places in the budget where we can make cuts."

Nice words, Benjamin thought. "But in the meantime," she would later report, "Obama is widening the war in Afghanistan and Pakistan and committing more and more of our tax dollars to an unwinnable military folly. The only way we will force Obama and the Congress to change course in Afghanistan is if we are able to turn public opinion against the war, as we did in the case of the Iraq war."[228]

When I asked her later about her impressions of the president that day, she said, "He tells you what you want to hear. But I do think he genuinely doesn't want to be at war. He's not a war-monger like George W. Bush."

Still, she was troubled like so many other activists about the surge of troops in Afghanistan just after his election. She had hoped that all his talk during the campaign about sending more troops to Afghanistan was more of an effort to look tough and presidential. She understood that in a high-stakes presidential campaign, one did not win easily by going up against the military. But when President Obama made good on the surge, "We were really disappointed."[229]

Like Debra Sweet of World Can't Wait, she felt her group's message, of trying to stop the war in Afghanistan, just wasn't resonating the way resisting the war in Iraq had during the Bush era. With the bad guys gone and the purported good guys in, it was harder to mobilize the public into action.

Still, when I paid a visit to the "Pink House" in downtown Washington, D.C., during a trip to the nation's capitol in June, 2009, I found it packed with people—mostly young people, although there were people of all ages there. Every Wednesday night Code Pink hosts a potluck supper where activists gather at the group's 5th Street townhouse and share stories from the front lines. As I made my way to a back room—past pink scarves draped over a stairway, pink peace signs on the wall, pink dishes and pink artwork everywhere, and pink papier-mâché heads pinned to the wall of Bush, Rove, and Condoleezza Rice—I was struck by the bawdy creativity of these activists. On a more sobering note, it occurred to me that their leaders probably had been labeled "terrorists" by the Bush administration. I had just learned of the labeling while attending a "FOIA party" earlier that evening where a group of activists were getting trained in how to file their own Freedom of Information Act requests after learning that the Maryland State Police cooperated with the Department of Homeland Security (DHS) in getting "terrorist" dossiers on them.

How sad, I thought, that antiwar protestors should be labeled this way for simply exercising their right of free speech. Once again, I couldn't help wondering: What had this country come to?

But of course I knew. I had spent eighteen years with my husband researching and writing a book about empire, a book about America's "conquest of the Amazon," the lessons of which could be applied to any part of the world, including the Middle East and Central Asia.

I discovered that night at the Pink House that most of the people there understood that we are all witnessing the exigencies of empire on a global scale: expanded wars abroad, more than seven hundred military bases to support these wars, a debilitated economy, and suppression of dissent at home. Medea Benjamin had covered most of it in her one-minute exchange with President Obama.

What I did not expect that evening was a comment from one of the older women seated with others around a table in the back room of the Pink House. "Charlotte Dennett is here? The author of *Thy Will Be Done?*" She started telling everyone about Jerry's and my book about empire, whose full title has the word "Rockefeller" in it. "It's my bible," she said—a comment that I confess I've heard from a few others who have read the 900-page book from cover to cover. Suddenly, activists were asking me to talk about the book and what it meant for our times.

Lifting the veil—at the highest level

Where to begin? *Thy Will Be Done* traced the Rockefellers' role in shaping U.S. foreign policy around the world, but with a primary focus on Latin America. The book had been praised as a sort of "methodology of conquest," describing how America's corporate elite used the same tried-and-true methods in whatever country they coveted to gain access to ranching, mining, oil, and other industrial and financial resources there. It also explored the way Rockefeller-funded institutions had created the training grounds that groom up-and-coming leaders for foreign policy that favors an expansion of U.S. capitalism around the globe—setting the stage for eventual oil wars in the Middle East. And it made the point that America's elite families—those like the Rockefellers, Morgans, Mellons, duPonts, Fords, and Pews—formed the roots of an unelected empire that still holds broad sway over who gets elected, how we conduct much of our domestic and foreign policy, where we fight wars, and why we fight wars.

What these activists wanted to know was this: Had Obama, the leader they elected to get us off of this dangerous treadmill, fallen into the service of the elite, versus the people? Had he, too, fallen prey to the powers that be? Was he going to thwart empire, or support it?

Mere months into Obama's presidency, those questions were impossible for me to answer with certainty. Obama's rhetoric about ending war and denouncing torture remained cause for hope. But there were some discomforting signs, too. He was willingly escalating the war in Afghanistan. In oil-rich Iraq, Obama had appointed commanders who said that troops were likely to be there for years to come—despite his promise to remove American troops.

Had Obama knuckled under to oil interests? I knew the Rockefellers to be masters in the Great Game for Oil, and some of the most liberal members of the family, including Senator Jay Rockefeller, had come in big behind Obama.

"If you look at a videotape of Obama taking the oath of office," I said to these Pink House activists, "you will see Senator Jay Rockefeller smiling several rows behind him." Senator John D. Rockefeller IV (D-W.Va.) has been forthright, indeed proud of his role and that of his influential Chicago-born wife, Sharon Percy, in backing Obama. At a July, 2008, fundraiser at Rockefeller's mansion in Washington, D.C., Jay Rockefeller introduced Obama as a man of "profound intelligence" and confessed to his well-heeled audience that: "I've met the man, the only person I've really wanted to see as president."[230]

Endorsements like this alone do not indict Barack Obama as complicit with forces keen on securing Middle East oil. They do not mean that Obama is not a brilliant, charismatic man, a man who sincerely believes that he can be a force for change in the world, change we can all believe in. Perhaps (all things considered, including the extraordinary power of corporations) he is the best our nation has to offer to recover from the excesses and outrages of the Bush administration. I couldn't help but be reminded of the ringing endorsement of Obama that came from Senator Ted Kennedy, the "lion of liberalism" in the Senate. After eight years of rule by a renegade group of neoconservatives who quite simply went too far in their quest for power (not just for Iraq's oil, but for power over the hated Eastern elites headed by the Rockefellers, of which much has been written),[231] perhaps anything was better than what we just endured. And from the Rockefeller point of view, what better way to regain the trust of the volatile dark-skinned people of the "developing world" (and especially the oil-rich Middle East) than to help elect one of the most liberal members of the U.S. Senate, America's first black president, Barack Hussein Obama?

Unlike his predecessor, Obama is well read, thoughtful, and (as a law professor) he knows the law. And yet, for all his awareness of the forces that can impinge on any well-meaning politician—including "big money contributors" and "interest-group pressure"—he has shown in his short time in office that he is not immune to these pressures, especially when foreign policy is concerned.

I find many parallels between Barack Obama and John F. Kennedy when it comes to their first days in the White House. Both of them were out of their league, with little foreign-policy experience. Kennedy's solution was to turn to the Rockefeller Brothers Fund and its Special Studies Project on National Security, set up by Nelson Rockefeller with Henry Kissinger as executive director, as a key source of knowledge and expertise in foreign policy. When a foreign-policy issue would come up during the 1960 presidential campaign, Kennedy would yell to his press secretary, Pierre Salinger, and say, "Hey Pierre, get the Rockefeller Brothers Studies. It's all there."[232]

John F. Kennedy did not have the Rockefeller-funded and -founded Trilateral Commission to train him. It was not yet in existence. (Founded in 1972 at the Pocantico estate of banker David Rockefeller, then chairman of the Council on Foreign Relations, the Trilateral Commission has tried to chart out a neoliberal world economic order run by advanced capitalist nations: the U.S. and Canada; Europe; and Japan. Individuals considered worthy of higher office with the requisite credentials and world outlook—including, of course, support for corporate capitalism—are invited into this elite club and exposed to such vexing problems as world hunger, trade wars, and the "challenges confronting democratic government"—including the "excesses of democracy" that arose during the rebellious 1960s and 1970s.)[233] Obama, on the other hand, was, like presidents Jimmy Carter and Bill Clinton before him, literally groomed for world power by members of the Trilateral Commission.

Henry Kissinger, a longtime protégé of Nelson Rockefeller, is as much imbued with the concept of a new world order now as he was then. In January, 2009, Kissinger was quick to extol the virtues of President Elect Obama on MSNBC. Obama, Kissinger enthused, could "give new impetus to American foreign policy, partly because the reception of him is so extraordinary around the world. His task will be to develop an overall strategy for America in this period when, really, a new world order can be created. It's a great opportunity. It isn't just a crisis."[234]

At issue here is the long arm of globalization. How far does it extend in the Obama administration? Obama has chosen several cabinet members with links to the commission and other institutions that influence U.S. foreign policy in favor of the corporate world.

For political stability abroad, President Barack Obama chose as his secretary of state Hillary Clinton, whose husband, Bill, was groomed for the presidency by the Trilateral Commission before his successful campaign. For behind-the-scenes foreign-policy advice, Obama relies on Zbigniew Brzezinski, an original founder and former director of the Trilateral Commission. For economic stability at home and abroad, Obama chose as his treasury secretary Timothy Geithner, whose curriculum vitae includes a partnership in Kissinger Associates and positions at the International Monetary Fund and the Council on Foreign Relations (CFR), a group that holds much influence on the intersection between U.S. foreign policy and the corporate world.

For national security advisor, Obama chose four-star Marine Corps General James L. Jones, bringing him out of retirement from his leadership of the Institute for 21st Century Energy and his board membership of Chevron (formally Standard Oil of California, a Rockefeller firm). In a speech at the 45th Munich Conference on Security Policy on February 8, 2009, General Jones said, "As the most recent national security advisor of the United States,

I take my daily orders from Dr. Kissinger, filtered down through [Lieutenant] General Brent Scowcroft and Sandy Berger, who is also here. We have a chain of command in the National Security Council that exists today." Jones has already been dubbed Washington's "New Kissinger."

For director of national intelligence—the top intelligence position in the country—Obama chose retired naval flag officer Admiral Dennis Blair, who worked closely with fellow Trilateralist James Jones as a "guiding coalition member" of the Project on National Security Reform. PNSR, which studies modern challenges to national security and makes recommendations, hailed Obama in a press release for adding "two highly capable, experienced leaders to his national security team. . . . They bring the right mixture of leadership, experience and knowledge to confront the complex threats of the twenty-first century."[235]

Put this team together and what does it tell us? We are all living inside an empire, an empire that now sees the need to fight endless wars on endless terrains. All in the name of the war on terror. All, in reality, as part of the Great Game for Oil.

This is not some cockeyed conspiracy theory. This is a simple fact of life in twenty-first-century America.

Sometimes it takes someone living on the outside to point out to us what is going on in the inside. Acclaimed British journalist John Pilger had this to say when analyzing Obama's early acts in foreign policy:

> In Afghanistan, the U.S. "strategy" of killing Pashtun tribespeople (the "Taliban") has been extended by Obama to give the Pentagon time to build a series of permanent bases right across the devastated country where, says Secretary [of Defense] Gates, the U.S. military will remain indefinitely.

Pilger was equally dismissive about Obama's policy toward Iraq:

> According to unabashed U.S. army planners, as many as 70,000 troops will remain "for the next 15 to 20 years." On 25 April, his secretary of state, Hillary Clinton, alluded to this. It is not surprising that the polls are showing that a growing number of Americans

believe they have been suckered, especially as the nation's economy has been entrusted to the same fraudsters who destroyed it.[236]

Some say that Obama came into office with a loaded plate, and that it will take time for him to sort things out. This is true—up to a point.

But on matters of foreign policy and the world economy, Barack Obama is as much a prisoner of empire as the rest of us. Does he know this and accept it as his price for power?

Christopher Pyle, the Mount Holyoke professor, constitutional lawyer, and former defense intelligence analyst who exposed the Pentagon's spying in the 1970s, is never one to mince words. He came to believe, during the last administration, that we now live in an elected monarchy:

> Americans are reluctant to admit it, but the president is no longer a public servant. He is an elected warlord in charge of an unaccountable government with a secret army of CIA operatives and military commandos who can kidnap, detain, torture, and murder with impunity. . . . People say, "It can't happen here." But it has happened here.

If Pyle aims to shock us out of our complacency, I think he's done it here. He sees, as the only solution, a major shake-up in Congress and a change in the composition of America's most important federal courts. "This tall order is more, perhaps, than a docile Congress, a distracted president, and a fearful electorate are likely to accomplish. One more terrorist attack like 9/11 and the will to remain free may be extinguished for years to come."[237]

When I talk to groups about the lessons I've learned over the past year, I tell them that it doesn't matter what cause they espouse—health-care reform, environmental reform and an end to global warming, new rights for labor—their dreams will all come to naught if they don't take seriously the serious erosion of democracy in our country.

We, as citizens, are watching our president walk a tightrope between democracy and "national security," between meeting the needs of the people and meeting the imperial needs of corporate America.

President Obama apparently has accepted the argument that in foreign affairs there is sometimes a dichotomy between upholding the rule of law and protecting national security. While he often states his belief that national security is best achieved by acting within the rule of law, President Obama seems to find it difficult to put this belief into practice in the wars in Afghanistan and Pakistan.

I, for one, cannot predict how this tension will be resolved. The only thing I can do, as both lawyer and journalist, is to point out what I believe We the People are facing. We have the law on our side. Obama, a constitutional lawyer, knows this. And I believe he sincerely wants to abide by the rule of law.

We also have numbers on our side. The bigger question is this: Now that we have a better idea of who is running our government, what are we going to do about it?

It all depends on how much we care about our democracy. If we don't act now, we will simply go down in history as the People Who Gave Up. Do we want this? I don't think so. We don't want this for our children, nor for the rest of the world. We have only one option: We must fight back. The elites are powerful. But as our own history has shown, they are not *all*-powerful.

That's why holding leaders accountable for acting above the law—particularly in relation to wars motivated by oil—is crucial if we are to save this country from the abyss. We have to be proactive. We have to stand up to the president and to members of Congress, and say, "no more in our name!" We have to get out and talk to our neighbors and our friends and explain what is at stake. We have to get more people joining us in the accountability movement.

The fact is, there are a lot of great people out there who are taking action. They are, like Lawrence Velvel describes them, those people who, despite adversity, "hang on in the hope of making a better life for themselves and a better world. . . . They know that it will be a long, hard slog. . . . Their fate is to try." And by trying, they make history. And the world a better place.

In the final chapter, you will see why and how we can hold on to our hope.

CHAPTER TEN

More Tales from the Front
Lines and Lessons for the Future

It's amazing how perseverance and a little faith in the common decency of people can sustain you even during the darkest times. September 18, 2009, was the one-year anniversary of my press conference with Vincent Bugliosi, where we jointly announced that we were going to prosecute George W. Bush for murder if I got elected.

We had no idea how much this campaign would catch on, or what would happen if I lost. Sitting in front of the press that day was simply an act of faith. I don't think either of us anticipated that the prosecution of George Bush and other high-level government officials for war crimes would become, in the space of a year, a supercharged national and international issue, or that the torture policies that Bush, Cheney, and Rumsfeld authorized would become part of the evidence in the murder prosecution we envisioned.

I certainly had no idea that a movement for accountability was about to burst onto the national and international stage, or that lawyers and activists would keep up the pressure on their elected leaders not only in the U.S. but in Canada, England, and Spain (among other countries) for redress over the injustices visited on millions of people during the eight years of the Bush administration.

Or that the attorney general of the United States would announce in late August, 2009, the appointment of a special prosecutor to investigate possible crimes by the CIA.

Momentum for accountability is building, but there were times during the year when it hardly felt that way.

Beyond a lawless world

One day in early May, after I had learned that Bush's lawyers were likely to get away with torture, I fell into a funk. Everyone around me was gleefully shedding coats and hats to enjoy a warm spring day, and here I was glumly walking down 12th Street in Manhattan's Greenwich Village feeling cold, depressed, and politically betrayed.

I needed some kind of consolation, some kind of hope that the people responsible for these crimes would be held to account. I decided to buy *Lawless World* and *Torture Team*, two books by Philippe Sands, the internationally known human-rights lawyer. I had heard him speak at the Andover conference and kept reminding myself of his parting message that September, 2008, weekend: *Holding dictators to account takes time. Remember: It all caught up with Pinochet.*

I entered the Strand Bookstore (famous for its eighteen miles of books crammed into one building on Broadway and 12th Street), made my way through the crowds of browsers and went up to the "Help" section. I asked a clerk if they carried Sands's books. "No," the clerk answered. They were out of stock.

Doubly discouraged, I left and started walking back to the National Writers Union office on University Place and 13th Street when the most remarkable thing happened. A slim, bespectacled man carrying a small suitcase rushed across the street just to the right of me, and I caught a glimpse of his face, and it looked oddly familiar.

As he dashed past me, I called out, "Philippe?"

He turned around. I looked at his face. *By God, it's him!*

"Yes?" He seemed perplexed, with a faint look of recognition as he tried to place me.

"I can't believe it's you. I was just trying to buy your books. I'm Charlotte Dennett, the person who ran for attorney general in Vermont."

"Yes, of course! What an incredible coincidence! How did your campaign go?"

"Oh, I lost, but . . . "

"That's OK," he said, sparing me the embarrassment of announcing my percentage points. He made a thumbs-up gesture, as if to say, "You fought the good fight. That's what matters."

"But I'm writing a book about it."

"That's great!" He was clearly in a hurry, but had time to say, "Haven't the past three weeks been incredible?"

"Well, I don't know. Did you read *The New York Times* today—no prosecutions expected? . . . "

For some reason, he was not miffed at all.

"Don't worry," he said. "It will happen. Did you hear what the Spanish judge did yesterday?"

I had not. Sands told me a Spanish judge had sent a letter to the Department of Justice asking, "Are you going to prosecute or not?" That sounded like a hint and a courteous threat. Either the Americans were going to go after their war criminals or the Spanish would do it themselves, naming Spanish victims and claiming universal jurisdiction.

When I got back to my computer, I discovered that not one, but *two* Spanish judges had declared their intention to prosecute Bush administration officials. This was indeed a significant development—a complete reversal of the news last month that Spain's attorney general had pressured Judge Baltasar Garzón of Pinochet indictment fame to drop his investigation of the six Office of Legal Counsel lawyers. Garzón had complied, turning his case over to another judge for final disposition. But what the attorney general apparently didn't expect was the second judge's decision to *proceed* with the case, and with the same vigor as Garzón! And it was this second judge, Judge Eloy Velasco, who promptly notified the Department of Justice in a letter asking its intentions on prosecutions. If they didn't prosecute, he would.

But it got better. Garzón had plans of his own. The release of the torture memos in late April convinced him he had enough evidence to launch an independent criminal investigation. He had already assembled evidence gathered from four detainees who had been subsequently sent to Spain for trial. All four were accused of being al-Qaeda members, but two of them were later acquitted by Spain's High Court, and the other two had their warrants for arrest in the UK canceled. All four had been brutally tortured.[238]

Tortured, I wondered, to get false confessions of links to al-Qaeda? How big would the list get?

According to Garzón's own court filings, his targets were at the highest level: "any of those that executed and/or designed a systematic plan of torture or cruel, inhuman, and degrading treatment of the prisoners [at Guantánamo] that were under their custody." That meant Bush administration officials at the level of Condoleezza Rice and Dick Cheney. Maybe even George W. Bush.

Suddenly lessons from my own campaign leapt out at me. Just as Attorney General William Sorrell had told Vince Bugliosi and me that Vermont did not have jurisdiction to try Bush for murder (and he was wrong, as I explained in earlier chapters), this Spanish attorney general had told Garzón he could not and must not try Bush officials in Spain. But Garzón wouldn't bend this time. He had the doctrine of universal jurisdiction on his side, and more than enough evidence now that the lawyers had engaged in a conspiracy with the highest Bush administration authorities to commit the crime of torture against Spanish citizens at Guantánamo. Their systematic plan of torture, his brief explained, took on "almost an official nature and therefore entails criminal liability in the different structures of execution, command, design and authorization. . . ."[239]

No wonder Dick Cheney had begun to go on every TV show he could defending his torture policy. For all his bluster and bravado, he was probably running scared. And behind the scenes, his defenders in the Republican Party were working overtime on President Obama and Attorney General Holder to back off and tell the Spaniards to get lost. *The Christian Science Monitor* confirmed my hunch. "Pressures by the Spanish government to slow or stop Garzón are intense," it stated.[240] But so far, nothing had been stalled or stopped.

So the onus was back on the Department of Justice. That's why Sands was optimistic. Human-rights law was now, literally and truly, going global thanks to the doctrine of universal jurisdiction.

Eric Holder was touring Europe when news of the intended Spanish prosecutions caught up with him. It seems he had no choice but to sound reasonable. After all, he was on a mission to assure America's allies that his department wanted to "set a new tone" on detainee policies. The United

States, he told the press, wanted to show the world "a different face . . . in the area of rule of law [and] moral authority."

So when reporters asked him if he would cooperate with a Spanish investigation, he said yes. In so many words "Obviously, we would look at any request that would come from a court in any country and see how and whether we should comply with it, " Holder said. "This is an administration that is determined to conduct itself by the rule of law and to the extent that we receive lawful requests from an appropriately created court, we would obviously respond to it."[241]

And how could he do otherwise? The doctrine of universal jurisdiction, when adopted by countries around the world, was not supposed to be selectively applied. In January, 2009, an *American* court exercised universal jurisdiction in a torture case involving Roy Belfast, Jr., the son of Charles Taylor, the former Liberian dictator. If the Americans could do it, so could the Spanish.

Every time Holder considered saying no to prosecutions, he knew the Spaniards would be right behind him, hot on the prosecution trail. How would he look if he dropped the ball and they carried on? Wimpish, perhaps?

The Spanish criminal investigations have been turning up more and more evidence that conditions of abuse in the Guantánamo prison have continued, and in some cases even worsened, since Obama was elected. Since the Spaniards have no reason to cover up for anyone, we can anticipate some pretty shocking evidence to emerge. So far, we have learned that armed guards routinely drag men from their cells, beat them, step on their fingers, twist their arms, and force tubes down their noses in a reign of terror that one prisoner called "torture, torture, torture."

According to journalist Jeremy Scahill, "In April, Mohammad al-Qurani, a twenty-one-year-old Guantánamo prisoner from Chad, managed to call *Al-Jazeera* and described a recent beating: 'This treatment started about twenty days before Obama came into power, and since then I've been subjected to it almost every day,' he said. 'Since Obama took charge, he has not shown us that anything will change.'"[242] Vince Warren, executive director of the Center for Constitutional Rights, has been monitoring the situation. "The Obama administration should not need pressure from abroad to uphold our own laws and initiate a criminal investigation in the U.S.," he said. "I hope the Spanish cases will impress on the president and Attorney General

Eric Holder how seriously the rest of the world takes these crimes and show them the issue will not go away."

That was in May, 2009. And as of this writing five months later, the issue is not going away. Scott Horton, one of the accountability movement's most reliable legal watchdogs, spent some time in Spain interviewing people involved in the two criminal investigations launched by Judges Garzón and Velasco. "I learned that the two judges were closely monitoring developments in the United States," Horton wrote on September 11, 2009, "and particularly Holder's decision to appoint career prosecutor John Durham to conduct a preliminary inquiry into a group of ten or more incidents in which the CIA's inspector general concluded that the conduct of CIA interrogators exceeded the guidelines they were given by the Justice Department." Both judges wanted to know—how far up the chain of command would Holder's special prosecutor go? Would his investigation confine itself to CIA officers, or would it cover what Horton calls the "Gonzales Six"—Alberto Gonzales, John Yoo, Jay Bybee, David Addington, former Undersecretary of Defense for Policy Douglas Feith, and former Defense Department General Counsel William J. Haynes II (now a lawyer with Chevron).

The Spanish judges gave Holder's Justice Department until October to decide. If the inquiry limited itself to the CIA interrogators without going to the top, the Spaniards made it clear they would continue with their criminal investigation.

It's quite amazing to think that the United States, even if it were to try to engage in some kind of cover-up (and I don't think that would be Holder's desire), would still have to countenance an ongoing investigation by a European power.

And not just one, but two. For while the Spaniards are engaged in their own inquiry, so too are the British—of their own leaders' involvement in the war in Iraq and subsequent interrogation policies. In late July, a formal British inquiry began with the announcement by the inquiry's chief, seventy-year-old Sir John Chilcot, that it would be "thorough, rigorous, fair and frank." Most of it, he said, would be conducted in public. Documents would be subpoenaed and witnesses would testify. "The inquiry is not a court of law, and nobody is on trial," Chilcot added. "But I want to make something absolutely clear: This committee will not shy away from making criticism."[243]

And who will be one of the witnesses to testify? Why, that pesky Briton himself, Philippe Sands. Quoted in *The National Observer,* Sands commented on a document that reveals President Bush and Tony Blair desperately searching for additional pretexts to go to war after the failure to find WMDs. In a memo dated January 31, 2003 (two months before the invasion), Bush suggested flying a U-2 reconnaissance plane painted in UN colors over Iraq to trigger a retaliatory strike by Saddam Hussein, thus putting Hussein in breach of UN resolutions.

Noted Sands: "Documents like that raise issues of national embarrassment, not national security. The restoration of public confidence requires the new inquiry to be transparent. Contentious matters should not be kept out of the public domain." Indeed, the *Observer* article continued, it was precisely because bereaved families and antiwar protestors "expressed outrage" that the British prime minister decided to change his mind and make the inquiry public.[244]

There are several important lessons to be gleaned from this tale of two countries, lessons that have universal themes:

Lesson 1: Don't give up.

Lesson 2: See what a little public outrage can do?

Lesson 3: Getting bereaved families involved adds weight and credibility to your demands.

The ACLU: What would we do without you?

The American Civil Liberties Union has been fearless in challenging President Obama and Attorney General Holder to live up to their promise of transparency while upholding the rule of law. On July 2, 2009, for instance, when the government announced that it was delaying (for a fourth time) the release of a report by the CIA's Office of the Inspector General until August 31, the ACLU piped up: "We're increasingly troubled that the Obama administration is suppressing documents that would provide more evidence that the CIA's interrogation program was both ineffective and illegal. . . . The public has a right to know what took place in the CIA's secret prisons and on whose authority."

The fact is, much of the information about torture would never have seen the light of day had it not been for the hard work of lawyers for the American Civil Liberties Union. Remember Laura Rótolo, the Boston-based ACLU lawyer who had fled from Argentina as a young child? Her story shows how patience and perseverance can eventually bring justice, even if in unexpected ways.

Laura began to get involved in controversial human rights cases when she was still in law school. As part of her legal clinic work at the American University Washington College of Law, she got started on a human-rights lawsuit against, of all people, Henry Kissinger, then Nixon's former national security advisor. In *Schneider v. Kissinger,* Rótolo and her fellow law students, supervised by litigator Michael Tigar, obtained declassified documents proving that Henry Kissinger had sent $100,000 to a group of assassins with the idea of silencing René Schneider, a top Chilean general who wanted nothing to do with a coup plot against the democratically elected government of Salvador Allende. Schneider was shot and killed. The lawyers found his family, took them on as clients, and sued Kissinger on nine counts, including arbitrary detention, torture, and summary execution. Among other things, they relied on a federal law called the Alien Tort Claims Act (ATCA, 18 U.S.C. § 1350), which allows U.S. federal courts to have jurisdiction over cases involving unlawful acts committed by government actors against aliens.

Rótolo knew it was an uphill battle, that the courts would probably knock it down by claiming that Kissinger was acting within the scope of his (governmental) authority and was therefore shielded from lawsuits by the doctrine of qualified immunity. But Rótolo and her group of student-lawyers pressed ahead anyway, having obtained evidence that showed that Kissinger was in fact responsible for killing people in Chile. They claimed that Kissinger had violated international law and that his involvement in killing a foreign leader was not part of his job. (In fact, according to Rótolo, he even shielded his involvement in the assassination from Congress, and possibly the president.)

They lost, but the loss did not deter Laura and her colleagues from seeking accountability. Laura's trips to Chile to meet with members of the Schneider family stayed with her for the rest of her life. She particularly remembers the comments of one of the Chilean lawyers helping out in the case: "I've been doing this kind of work for decades. You just have to stay in there. One day there will be justice."

More recently, ACLU lawyers brought a lawsuit in 2006 against former Defense Secretary Donald Rumsfeld. Suing on behalf of eight detainees in U.S. military prisons in Abu Ghraib, Iraq, and Bagram, Afghanistan, the ACLU charged him with authorizing the torture they had endured. That torture reportedly included being suspended from the ceiling by chains, being urinated upon and sexually humiliated, being locked inside boxes, and being confronted by fake executioners. The attitude of the judge gave reason for hope. "What you are asking has never been done before," he said. And he acknowledged his discomfort in trying a case of torture. Ultimately, he accepted the government's argument: that Rumsfeld could not be sued because of sovereign immunity and his acting within the scope of his authority by trying to combat terrorists and prevent future attacks. Once again, a high-level government official got off on an immunity defense. But the judge could not restrain himself from saying the facts in this case were appalling and lamentable.

Rótolo and her fellow lawyers at ACLU knew the one area where they were likely to get a more successful outcome was by using the Freedom of Information Act to sue the Department of Defense, the CIA, and the Department of Justice to recover documents about interrogation techniques. From *more than one hundred thousand* heavily redacted pages they got back, they have yet to find convincing evidence that the use of torture produced, as Dick Cheney insisted, information that was "absolutely crucial to getting us through the last seven-plus years without a major casualty attack on the U.S."[245]

When the time came to challenge the government on extraordinary rendition, ACLU lawyers knew that they had to find a way of getting around the sovereign immunity defense. They decided to sue a private contractor that the CIA used to fly five detainees to various secret torture sites around the world. That contractor was Jeppesen, an aviation company and a subsidiary of Boeing. In April, 2009, right in the midst of all the hullabaloo over the release of the latest torture memos, the Ninth Circuit Court of Appeals in California came down with a historic decision. It rejected a lower court's dismissal of the case on the basis of protecting state secrets and instead ruled that state secrets could be argued only on a case-by-case, document-by-document basis. This was a repudiation of both the Bush and Obama administrations' prosecution strategy. The case was remanded back to the lower court and is now pending.

What the ACLU has achieved in the space of a few years is nothing short of sensational. "We are trying to use the law to make changes," Rótolo explained to me. And the ACLU has done that and more.

Today, if you go to the ACLU Web site (aclu.org), you will find a chronology of all the documents released under FOIA since the ACLU first began filing its FOIA requests on U.S. detention policies and practices. Each entry has a statement describing the document and a copy of the document.

As a clear indicator of the growing importance of blogs in the accountability debate, the ACLU recently set up a "Blog of Rights." On its Web site, it has set up an entire page devoted to "Accountability Now." The site makes this appeal: "We've uncovered more than one hundred thousand pages that show both that hundreds of prisoners were tortured in U.S. custody, and that the torture polices were devised and developed at the highest levels of the Bush administration—yet there remains debate on whether or not the government will hold those who authorized torture accountable."

For example, the ACLU urged its members and Web visitors to sign a petition calling on Attorney General Holder to appoint a special prosecutor. And when Holder did in fact appoint a special prosecutor, the ACLU did not rest on its laurels. Instead, it stepped up the pressure to make sure that the special prosecutor's investigation did not limit itself to a dozen cases where CIA interrogators may have violated U.S. torture laws. "Justice demands an investigation without such limits," the ACLU replied in a press release. What was needed was "a comprehensive investigation that doesn't exempt high-ranking officials."

Out went the call to the ACLU's supporters to "Urge Attorney General Holder to conduct a thorough examination of the Bush torture program." With it came words of praise for "the persistence of ALCU supporters like you and of our amazing lawyers and advocates." Thanks to them, "accountability for torture [is now] at the forefront of the national debate. Now, we must insist that the investigation started today is only the beginning."

Lesson: Give the ACLU your support. They have done amazing work and even though the sought-for results take time, they have the clout to make things happen.

The FOIA party

Do you know what fusion centers are? I'd never heard of them until June, 2009, when I was invited to a "FOIA party" in Washington, D.C.

The "party" was being held above a local Ethiopian restaurant. I climbed a flight of stairs and found a roomful of activists sharing light food and talking strategy. Most of them had been involved in the National Campaign for Nonviolent Resistance (NCNR), a coalition of peace groups that had been protesting the illegal invasion of Iraq and calling on Congress to end the occupation.

One of the activists, Malachy Kilbride, handed me a letter written by members of the NCNR on May 11 to Eric Holder. I was pleased to see some of the arguments mentioned in Bugliosi's book cited in the letter. "Hussein was not an imminent threat to the security of this country," the letter stated, referring to the National Intelligence Estimate of October, 2002. The letter chronicled "more than four thousand members of the U.S. military dead, thousands more wounded, hundreds of thousands of dead Iraqis, and the wholesale destruction of a country." It could be argued, the letter went on, "that the architects of this war had a criminal state of mind."

From the war in Iraq the letter turned to Bush's lawyers attempting to "justify and legalize torturous, cruel, and inhuman treatment," as revealed in the recently released torture memos. The letter described such acts as "banging heads into walls 30 times in a row, prolonged nudity, repeated facial and abdominal slapping, dietary manipulation, and dousing with water as cold as 41 degrees Fahrenheit. They allow shackling in a standing position for 180 hours, sleep deprivation for 11 days, confinement of people in small dark boxes with insects for hours, and waterboarding to create the perception they are drowning."

The letter was signed by representatives of NCNR, Peace Action (Maryland), Veterans for Peace, Military Families Speak Out, New Jersey Labor Against the War, The Shalom Center, and People for Peace. These groups wanted a meeting with the attorney general to discuss "several examples of what we perceive to be illegal behavior on the part of the Bush administration."

Sounds reasonable enough, right? But here's the disturbing part: Under secret rules set up by the Bush administration, these activists, probably all if not some of them, are being called "terrorists."

Are you shocked? I was.

Fifty-three activists, including some sitting in this room above the restaurant, had been notified by certified mail during the summer of 2008 by the Maryland State Police that their names were in a national database. Why the state police contacted them remains a mystery. But that was the least of their concerns.

Pat Elder, a fifty-four-year-old school teacher and member of the steering committee of the National Network Opposing the Militarization of Youth (NNOMY) told me he was "implicated in counterterrorism." *What?*

Elder, who is also the cofounder of D.C. Anti-War Network (DAWN), explained that in December, 2008, he had received more than one hundred pages of documents through a Freedom of Information Act request. The documents revealed, among other things, that the Maryland State Police had spied on his group during a peaceful demonstration in 2005 at a military recruiting center in Silver Springs, Maryland. Apparently, the police had been tipped off about this and other demonstrations by the Department of Homeland Security, which labeled DAWN a terrorist group.

Pete Perry, another activist at the FOIA party, told me he got notification that the Maryland State Police had a "database on terrorism," and his name was on the list. The information they got was wrong—he did not participate in a demonstration against the National Security Agency, as was alleged; he was at a rally protesting the confirmation of Alberto Gonzales as attorney general. Still, what he and others wanted to do was file their own, personal FOIA requests to government agencies. They wanted to learn more about how and why the government had been spying on them. This had happened during the Vietnam War as well, but now, some forty years later, there was one very big difference—the sheer scale of the operation.

Turns out the Bush administration had created a nationwide network of "fusion centers" that combined state and local police units with the U.S. military and even private corporations. Their purpose: to share intelligence and spy on Americans whose so-called terrorist activities involved exercising their First Amendment rights to peacefully protest government policies they considered unjust. If this wasn't disturbing enough, the activists discovered that not only was the Department of Homeland Security involved (or, as one of them told me, "it's the federal government wagging the states' tails"), but the DHS was also tracking the activists' emails, including Elder's.

They got in touch with Maryland's ACLU attorney David Rocah, who on their behalf contacted Senators Barbara Mikulski (D-Md.) and Russ Feingold (D-Wisc.). The two senators, sufficiently alarmed that the federal government was spying on peaceful protestors whose actions were protected under the First Amendment, proceeded to contact DHS for an explanation. DHS replied, saying an "exhaustive review" of the agency's records and databases had come up dry. Mikulski and Feingold were not satisfied, however, and sent another letter, this time to the new director of Homeland Security, Janet Napolitano, asking the agency to reexamine the files and report on how the activists' emails got into DHS's hands, and for what reason.

Elder believes that federal agents must have infiltrated his group in order to get ahold of the emails.

The ACLU first started investigating fusion centers in 2007, when ACLU lawyer Mike German wanted to know how and where the federal money was being used and what rules applied governing DHS's modus operandi. German, only two years out of federal law enforcement (he was in counter-terrorism with the FBI from 1988–2004), was shocked by what he found. He and another ACLU colleague tracked down forty-two fusion centers and so many instances of constitutional violations that they continued their investigation. In 2008 they reported on fifty-eight fusion centers. Today, there are seventy-two fusion centers.

As so often happens in the early days of a crusade for justice, German's initial warnings did not stir much concern. Today, they do. Today, whole teams of lawyers with the ACLU, the Center for Constitutional Rights, and the National Lawyers Guild are representing activists and filing more FOIA requests. In July, *Democracy Now* devoted two-hour-long programs on what they've found so far: infiltration of peace groups; intelligence sharing between (for example) the Air Force in New Jersey and the local police in Olympia, Washington, regarding peace activists; and all of this funded by the Department of Homeland Security. Minutes of meetings reveal, on the one hand, discussions about what Grannies Against the War were doing in a local mall and, on the other hand, what al-Qaeda was planning to do next—a shocking and apparently deliberate mixing of apples and pears of peace groups with terrorist organizations. Fortunately, members of Congress are beginning to take this issue seriously. Apparently Rush Holt, a New Jersey congressman, is calling for an investigation of the intelligence community similar to the Church Committee hearings in the 1970s that were prompted, in part, by the work of former defense intelligence agency lawyer (and now Mt. Holyoke professor) Christopher Pyle.

Interviewed in the July, 2009, two-day segment on *Democracy Now*, Pyle expressed his amazement over the sheer size of the fusion center networks that "bring together the services of the military, of police, and even private corporations to share information about alleged terrorist groups in cities throughout the country. . . . Police departments get a great deal of money to set up these intelligence units. And they monitor largely lawful political activity in violation of the First Amendment and, when the military is involved, in violation of the Posse Comitatus Act." Pyle's ultimate solution: "We need to prosecute the torturers. I think that's the biggest single message that we could give to the intelligence community, that it is not above the law. . . . There have been many other abuses of authority [in addition to domestic intelligence]. When you get into torture, kidnapping, secret illegal detention, and assassination, it seems to me you have gone over the hill to the most serious abuses any intelligence community can possibly commit, and that's the place to start."[246]

At the time of this writing, Eric Holder has hedged on prosecuting those who tried to legalize the torture or their superiors, who authorized the torture. He's also refused to characterize the warrantless surveillance of Americans under the Bush administration as a crime, instead telling Senator Russ Feingold at a June 17 hearing that he considered it "unwise."

He never met with the peace activists who had requested a meeting back in May, 2009.

Lesson: We must keep up the heat. There are attorneys who will help us fight for democracy and against government oppression. Be proud of them, and proud of yourself if you choose to join this movement for accountability, the sine quo non of democracy.

The school of assassins, the school of torture

After I left the "FOIA party" in Washington, D.C., I spent time with a man who had been arrested for protesting torture last November outside Fort Benning, Georgia. He was still serving a six-month sentence under house arrest. (He wanted to go to jail, he told me, but the judge would not allow it because he was an amputee.)

Every November, thousands of ordinary Americans journey to Fort Benning to protest outside the School of the Americas (now called WHINSEC, the Western Hemisphere Institute for Security Cooperation). The United States military has been running this school for decades, teaching Latin-American military officers methods of counterinsurgency, psychological warfare, and torture. The school has trained some of the most brutal dictators in Latin America, including members of Pinochet's junta in Chile; two Argentinian dictators who had been involved in Argentina's dirty war of coups, torture, and disappearances between 1976–1983; and nineteen of the twenty-six Salvadoran officers who in 1989 massacred six Jesuit priests.

Lou Wolf, a pleasant-faced gray-bearded man who lost one of his legs to a bizarre circulatory condition acquired during a long plane flight back from Southeast Asia, delivered a twenty-four-page, carefully documented summary of these and other shocking statistics during his sentencing hearing before Judge Mallon Faircloth in January, 2009.

When I asked him how he had come to this point, I found his story to be typical of so many people's stories I had encountered on the accountability trail. He had started out his young adult life as an idealistic American who wanted to serve his country. As a conscientious objector during the Vietnam War, he signed up with the International Voluntary Services (a precursor to the Peace Corps) to teach English in a remote village in Laos. Within days of arriving, he saw a two-engine Air America airplane land and unload stretchers of battle-wounded Hmong tribespeople. That was the first of many awakenings for him. As he took up various assignments in Laos, he learned that Air America was run by an agency called the Central Intelligence Agency, that the CIA had contracted with local Hmong tribespeople to fight "the communists," i.e., the Pathet Lao tribespeople and their North Vietnamese allies, and that large B-52 aircraft returning from bombing missions in North

Vietnam were routinely dumping leftover ordnance over Laos. The ultimate turning point in his life occurred the day a U.S. bomber struck the village he was working in, killing and maiming his friends. When he learned that the CIA had been responsible for the bombing, "I decided that I would spend my life investigating this secret instrument of American foreign policy."

For years, he published the *CovertAction Quarterly*, documenting abuses by the Central Intelligence Agency and other intelligence organizations. Currently, he contributes to a gutsy, locally produced paper called the *Rock Creek Free Press*, which is dedicated to exposing, among other things, some of the inaccuracies and distortions in the official story of 9/11. (Let's not forget that much of the information that went into the 9/11 Commission Report was obtained through torture, and is therefore highly unreliable.)

Before I left him that evening, he told me I could find a full report on America's fusion centers by simply going to the Web site of the Congressional Research Service (www.fas.org/sgp/crs/index.html)—"it will make your hair stand on end." He was right—fifty-five pages described a myriad of spy set-ups. Between all the mind-boggling acronyms like TTC (Terrorist Training Center), NTAC (National Threat Assessment Center), and CAPPS (Computer Assisted Passenger Pre-sceening Systems) are occasional juicy sentences like this one on page 39, under the heading "No-Fly and Selectee Lists": "The American Civil Liberties Union (ACLU) claimed in 2008 that the no-fly list contained over one million names."

When I got back to Vermont and read through Wolf's twenty-four pages of testimony about the School of the Americas, which he delivered at his sentencing hearing in Georgia, one sentence particularly caught my eye. Referring to himself and his five co-defendants, he said: "We state our profound insistence that the untold thousands of innocent men, women, and children who have been defiled, tortured, massacred, disappeared, and executed by graduates of this institution must neither be forgotten, nor swept under the rug of history."

I thought about how my friend Robin Lloyd had bravely served a six-month sentence in federal prison back in 2006 for protesting outside the School of the Americas and "crossing the line" (i.e., trespassing) onto SOA territory. And I silently sang the praises of Father Roy Bourgeois, the Maryknoll priest whom Jerry and I first met in 1976 when he was serving the poor in Bolivia and who has since 1990 headed up the campaign to close the School of the Americas. At a recent appearance in Burlington, Vermont, Father Bourgeois reminded his audience that torture had been an integral part of American foreign policy for a long time. When he was serving in Vietnam as a Navy officer, prisoners were thrown out of helicopters when they didn't cooperate with their torturers.

I spoke up. "Isn't this the time we should be reminding President Obama of his pledge that there would not be torture under his administration? And how can the accountability movement connect with what you are doing to close the School of the Americas?"

A woman came up to me and introduced herself as being with Amnesty International. "We are actively involved with trying to close the school," she told me. "The movements are connected."

Indeed, only recently did I learn that there is a "National Religious Campaign Against Torture," which represents tens of thousands of people in more than 250 religious groups, including representatives from the Roman Catholic, evangelical Christian, mainline Protestant, orthodox Christian, and Unitarian churches—as well as from the Quaker, Jewish, Muslim, Bahá'í, Buddhist, Hindu, and Sikh communities.[247]

People from all walks of life are willing to stick their necks out so that tragic history is not repeated.

Lesson 1: We must rally as many people as possible to protest the culture of torture in our country. Every November, thousands of protestors converge outside the gates of Fort Benning to urge its closing, many willing to get arrested and serve time to further the cause. Every year, the size of the protest grows.[248] Every year, members of Congress are asked to sign on to a bill to withhold federal funds from the school. This is the year to close the school, whose latest claim to fame is its role in having trained the leaders of the recent coup in Honduras. Notwithstanding President Obama's and Secretary of State Clinton's denunciation of the coup, the fact remains, according to SOA Watch, that the coup was carried out by SOA graduates General Romeo Vasquez Velasquez, the head of the Joint Chiefs of Staff of the Honduran military, and General Luis Prince Suazo, head of the Honduran Air Force.[249]

Lesson 2: Different groups are calling for different ways to achieve accountability. The National Religious Campaign Against Torture, for instance, is calling for a commission of inquiry. All types of pressure can be brought to bear on our elected officials. I, for one, agree with Chris Pyle. We must prosecute the torturers, because if we don't, they will continue to act with impunity—and before you know it, we will have a Latin-American–type dictatorship right here in the United States.

Inside the DOJ: An unlikely "whistleblower"

I can't recall which person in the accountability movement told me about attorney Jesselyn Radack, but when I found her and talked with her, I soon realized that I had finally found an attorney who could tell me what happened when a Justice Department attorney took the American Bar Association's Rules of Professional Conduct to heart.

She never really thought of herself as a whistleblower, she told me. She was simply an honest lawyer who did the right thing. In fact, she was just doing her job. But her superiors didn't see it that way.

A graduate of Yale Law School, she had everything going for her: pretty blonde good looks, an Ivy League education, and a supportive husband. She landed a plum job with the Department of Justice through the prestigious Attorney General's Honors Program. After four years working in civil litigation, she accepted a position in 2000 in the DOJ's newly created Professional Responsibility Advisory Office (PRAO). It was, she thought, the perfect job for someone who now had young children as well as multiple sclerosis. It was less stressful and required less travel and time away from home. Her job was to advise attorneys on ethical issues that arose in their practice, not only in D.C. but nationwide. She was given a top-secret clearance. She became an expert on legal ethics. She published with the *Georgetown Journal of Legal Ethics,* the most prestigious law journal of its kind. Everything was fine until September 11. Then everything changed.

Suddenly, the detached and sedate attorney general, John Ashcroft, became a polarizing force inside the DOJ, diving into the war on terror with such zeal he seemed to be on a religious crusade. His attitude affected the entire climate inside the department. Suddenly, careful attorneys who would have normally double-checked themselves for possible ethics violations felt that anything and everything was possible if it involved fighting terrorism.

On December 7, 2001, what had begun as a normal, laid-back Friday for Radack quickly turned into its opposite when she received a call from a counterterrorism prosecutor named John De Pue in the DOJ's criminal division. He informed Radack that an American by the name of John Walker Lindh had been captured in Afghanistan and turned over to the custody of the U.S. The FBI wanted to interview him. According to Radack, De Pue explained that Walker's father had retained counsel for Lindh and the FBI wanted to question Walker "about taking up arms against the United States." The man De Pue was talking about was soon dubbed by the media as "the American Taliban." The allegation that he was taking arms up against the United States, as pointed out previously, is totally false. He joined the Taliban in 2000 when the Taliban were still the allies of the United States, fighting the then-Russian-backed warlords of the Northern Alliance. Radack at this point knew very little about the facts of Lindh's capture, but she did know the ethics rule on this one inside out. Rule 4.2 of the American Bar Association's Rules for Professional Conduct forbade a lawyer from making contact with someone represented by counsel unless "the lawyer has the consent of the other lawyer or is authorized by law to do so."

She passed this on to De Pue, who passed it on to the deputy legal adviser of the FBI. Two days later, she got a call back from De Pue who told her that despite his advice not to question Lindh without counsel, an FBI agent had gone ahead and interrogated him over the weekend.

Now what?

She recommended that the interview be sealed. It could be used for national security, but not in a criminal prosecution.

She waited for a response. None came. Then her boss told her the case was closed.

During the next few weeks, the Office of Legal Counsel drafted its infamous memos saying the Geneva Conventions did not apply to detainees from the war in Afghanistan, i.e., the Taliban and al-Qaeda.

The "American Taliban," meanwhile, had already been blindfolded by American soldiers; handcuffed naked with the word "Shithead" scrawled on his blindfold; strapped to a stretcher for days in a cold, dark shipping container; interrogated; and threatened with death. When a CNN reporter interviewed him on camera, he was dehydrated, suffering from hypothermia, in pain from an untreated bullet wound to his leg, and close to death. Finally, on January 23, 2002, he was flown to the United States and taken to a prison facility in Virginia. Only then did he get to see a lawyer.

Meanwhile, John Ashcroft turned him into a freakish "terrorist," accusing him of having "knowingly and purposefully allied with terrorist organizations" and claiming that he had "embraced" those who "had murdered thousands of our countryman."[250] Ashcroft was out for blood. In answering a reporter's question, the attorney general said point-blank, "To our knowledge, he has not chosen a lawyer at this time." It was a blatant lie, in direct contradiction to what Radack had been told. She couldn't believe what she was hearing.

A few weeks later, her boss walked into her office and gave her a negative performance evaluation, accusing her of poor judgment and insubordination. It was so full of lies it reduced Radack, who prided herself on her work, to tears. She eventually decided to resign and find another job.

Meanwhile, in the following weeks she learned that her inch-thick file documenting what DOJ attorneys knew—that Lindh had been questioned without a lawyer—was suddenly reduced to three emails. She consulted a colleague who was about to retire. "Your file has been purged," he said, matter-of-factly. She was so stunned, she blurted out "We're prosecuting [the giant accounting firm] Arthur Andersen for obstruction of justice. How is this any different?"

"I suggest you cover your ass," her colleague told her. "Resurrect those missing emails."

She succeeded, and gave them to her boss, thinking they would be sent to the court. Apparently, they were not. Meanwhile, the Lindh case began to dominate the headlines. And worse, all the news reports were just repeating what she considered to be "false, misleading, and highly inflammatory information" emanating from the Justice Department. When she heard on National Public Radio the usual DOJ misinformation, that it never considered Lindh to be entitled to a lawyer, she had enough. She went to Kinko's and faxed her emails to Michael Isikoff of *Newsweek*.

The story finally got out. And on the eve of a suppression hearing for Lindh, his case magically settled. "The government didn't want it to come out that we had tortured him," Radack told me. "But it also didn't want it to come out that it knew Lindh had not been represented by counsel when they interrogated him." His defense lawyers argued that his confession had been coerced through torture and that it had occurred when he was not represented by counsel. It therefore could not be admitted into evidence.

A plea deal was struck. All the terrorist charges were dropped. Lindh was sentenced to twenty years for providing aid to the Taliban in violation of U.S. sanctions and carrying a rifle while serving as a volunteer soldier. Radack was relieved. She thought her nightmare was over. In fact, it had just begun.

Her release of emails to *Newsweek* apparently infuriated people inside the DOJ, and the next thing she knew, she was being visited by a representative of the DOJ's own watchdog group, the Office of the Inspector General (every federal agency has an OIG). He started to question her about the emails. A few weeks later, the same OIG agent called her new employer and told them that she was under a criminal investigation and was likely to steal clients' files.

She hired a criminal defense attorney. Then she learned that the Office of Professional Responsibility (that internal ethics division of the DOJ) had referred her case for possible disciplinary action to the state bar of Maryland and the District of Columbia. She knew that would hurt her chances of finding another job because a lawyer's malpractice insurance rates skyrocket when a referral to bar counsel occurs.

The Office of Professional Responsibility, she learned, was "totally tainted. They created a cloud that still hangs over my head." She was not even allowed to read an explanation of the charges against her. She is incensed that the OPR kept her from seeing her own file, but has allowed the CIA and Bush's OLC lawyers (Yoo, Bybee, et al.) to review its own internal report on their *known* misconduct.

She eventually saw the explanation. "It was so weak, the Maryland bar dismissed my case. But why does it stay with bar council in D.C.?"

For all she endured—hurt, humiliation, betrayal, and shunning by neighbors and even some friends—Jess Radack has emerged stronger from her ordeal. She found a wealthy individual who hired her to do legal work representing whistleblowers on reconstruction fraud in Iraq. And since 2007 she's worked at the Government Accountability Project, a group that represents whistleblowers. She is now an expert in what *not* to do as a whistleblower

("Forget going to the newspapers; go directly to Congress. Never use your home or office phone. Speak only on pay phones or throw-away cell phones. Document conversations in writing").

Like Candace Gorman, the dedicated "Guantánamo lawyer" described in Chapter Seven, Radack stays in touch with the accountability movement and follows the Department of Justice closely. She writes blogs for Daily Kos. She has self-published a book about her ordeal, calling it *The Canary in the Coalmine: Blowing the Whistle in the Case of "American Taliban" John Walker Lindh*,[251] and is hoping that it will eventually be picked up by a regular publisher so it can reach a wider audience. I promised to help her in that endeavor.

Lesson #1: Whistleblowers are vital to our democracy, and to our accountability movement. They need all the support we can give them.

Lesson #2: Become a whistleblower yourself. There's a support network out there for you.

Street heat, brazen blogs, and wonderful Web sites

One of the charming aspects of this movement is its originality. Take Code Pink, for instance. It took a certain amount of chutzpah to make fun of Bush's post-9/11, color-coded terror alerts. And pink is not an easy color to use for antiwar messaging, given its traditional association with all that is frilly and feminine. After some back and forth among the group's female founders, they decided nonetheless to go ahead with pink. Their plan, quite simply, was to "radicalize" the color pink.

"We tend to push the edges," Medea Benjamin told me, knowing that that's what captures attention and keeps the activists coming to the Pink House.

"We've had women literally just walk in off the street," veteran Code Pinker Diane Wilson told me. She recounts how a woman from Cincinnati, conservatively dressed and very well mannered, just showed up out of the blue. She had heard about the Pink House but never had participated in any action. Diane invited her to come along and sneak into a Washington press conference where Alberto Gonzales was holding forth. Their plan was to handcuff Gonzales as a war criminal. "So we snuck in, and this lady went right up to the front of the room and got really close to him and told him off and said he should resign." Needless to say, it got a lot of press coverage. "Afterwards, she was amazed at what she did."

Wilson, a shrimper whose battles against polluters of the Texas bay she lived and shrimped on turned her into an activist and author,[252] has participated in numerous vigils against the war in Iraq outside the White House. On one occasion, she started to climb the White House fence. When the police arrested her "and started to get tacky with me," she turned to one of them and said, with typical bluntness, "Does your mother know what you are saying and doing?" It threw them completely off guard.

She laughs when people accuse the group of being a bunch of bored upper-middle-class ladies with nothing better to do. "I'm as working class as you can get," she says. "My husband's a fisherman who pulls up gill nets, I was raised Pentecostal, and I've got five kids."

Code Pink's Web site has a picture of giant pink handcuffs that directs readers to "Arrest the War Criminals." Click on it and you'll find a whole page dedicated to the "Ten Most Wanted War Criminals." Under each name there is a statement of their alleged crimes—be it treason, revealing the identity of a CIA agent, misleading Congress into a war on false pretenses, illegal surveillance of Americans, or authorizing torture. (Cheney's list is the longest.) Under John Yoo's name (alias: Dr. Yes) Code Pink informs its readers that it has been keeping tabs on Yoo's whereabouts in California, where he teaches at Berkeley, and suggests staging a "Shame on Yoo" demonstration when possible.

Berkeley's Cynthia Papermaster, who tells me she was greatly influenced by studying political science at the University of California at Berkeley and being exposed to the "fundamental importance of the rule of law," has been organizing weekly protests outside John Yoo's house. On June 28, 2009, honoring Torture Accountability Day, she filed a judicial misconduct complaint against California's Ninth Circuit Judge Jay Bybee, noting that his actions have lowered the public trust in the legal profession.

Tobi Drabert, a now-unemployed legal assistant, works out of her California home sending out daily accountability alerts on an activist tree that includes some four hundred thousand people.

Meanwhile, Debra Sweet and World Can't Wait have set up a Web site called FireJohnYoo.org, which reports to Berkeley students and faculty about efforts to get Yoo dismissed and/or disbarred. It's becoming the go-to place for recent developments in torture accountability. So is its "sister Web site," warcriminalswatch.org, whose board includes some familiar names: H. Candace Gorman, David Swanson, and Lawrence Velvel.

Not everything that's been happening is "bicoastal." In North Carolina, Chuck Fager, the son of a WWII bomber pilot, has been monitoring rendition flights in and out of an airport near Fort Bragg, North Carolina. The director of Quaker House, he and his group of antitorture activists have been trying to get their airport and county commission to stop the torture flights, claiming that local authorities, by allowing them, are complicit in war crimes. Their protests have gotten some local press, but continue to be ignored by the mainstream media.

The organizer par excellence

David Swanson is a youthful-looking, high-energy guy with wavy hair and poster-boy good looks who seems to put his whole being into jump-starting activism. When I talked to him last May, I found out that he had had plenty of training: first as a community organizer, later as an organizer for labor organizations and as the press secretary for the 2004 presidential bid of Ohio's Dennis Kucinich. In 2005, Swanson, along with Robert Fertik, Tim Carpenter, Steve Cobble, and John C. Bonifaz, formed a nonpartisan coalition of some two hundred veteran and peace groups called "After Downing Street" to pressure Congress to investigate whether George W. Bush had committed impeachable offenses.[253] When a new presidential election season beckoned in 2006–07, the same group of people came up with the idea of "progressive democrats" as an antiwar pressure group on democratic members of Congress. "My role was to build the Web site and start writing a blog," Swanson told me in an interview. The idea was to mobilize the base and force the corporate media to pay attention and cover issues that mattered to them.

"At first, we were incredibly successful," Swanson said. "Back in 2005–06, the Democrats pretended to care. Our agenda lined up with theirs." Once the Democrats regained a majority in Congress, Swanson's hopes began to dim. War was still on the agenda, and impeachment was a nonstarter with all but two Democrats: Representative Dennis Kucinich of Ohio and Representative John Conyers of Michigan. Kucinich pressed ahead with his articles of impeachment, but the effort never got traction, no doubt because the party leadership was not interested.

By the summer of 2008, Swanson and other impeachment activists turned to supporting prosecution of high-level Bush administration officials. That's how he ended up on a panel at the Andover conference on prosecuting war criminals addressing the question of how prosecutions could be made into an issue for the fall 2008 electoral campaigns, prodded by a grassroots effort to engage the media and the Internet. One of Swanson's most active allies, Sue Serpa of Northeast Impeachment Coalition, would routinely fire off messages to an Internet list of over two hundred thousand people.

After the 2008 elections, both Swanson and Serpa admitted that interest in accountability began to wane. "When we weren't getting impeachment and prosecution," he told me in May, "our ability to get people charged up began to diminish. Interest in the war in Iraq and the crime of aggressive war had all but vanished."

Why? I asked.

"Because Republicans didn't want to touch it, and when Obama became president, it became the Democrats' war, and people loyal to the Democrats don't want to go near it."

But he was not about to give up. When not touring the country promoting his new book, *Daybreak: Undoing the Imperial Presidency and Forming a More Perfect Union*, he's still blogging and organizing events.

Swanson has no illusions about the link between torture and war. In a blog he wrote titled "Torture Is a Foreplay to War," Swanson dared to ask a question that rarely gets asked about any current big issue: Why? And specifically, "Why did we torture detainees?"[254]

> Why were Zubaydah and [Khalid Sheikh] Mohammed tortured so far beyond what even Dick Cheney could conceivably have fantasized? . . . Because the goal was false information, the overriding mission was to lie us into war, and the death and destruction wrought in that war would make even the murder of a small num-

ber of people through torture all but unnoticeable except to audiences kept miraculously ignorant of the horrors of the war.

In the next paragraph, he showed how war can often get rationalized, even justified, whereas torture has no excuse.

> Torture is cruel and criminal. It's morally reprehensible and it hurts people. War, on the other hand, is just part of our world, like air and water. A war can be wise or mistaken, efficient or mismanaged. But it's not criminal or sadistic or shocking. And even the worst war must be funded, fireworks lit, music played, and choruses of "support duh troops" sung.

Swanson probably hit on one of the most difficult obstacles that Vincent Bugliosi has faced—as have I—in trying to convince people that the president could be prosecuted for murder. War, in most people's minds, is a necessary evil. "But it's not criminal. . . . "

Actually, it certainly can be criminal. That's why we have the notion of war crimes. It's a legal category, after all. So is murder. People just haven't caught up to that yet. Maybe they will with this book.

The crime of aggressive war, I had learned from professor Amy Bartholomew at the Andover conference, is very hard to prosecute. Anyone who wanted to charge leaders with fighting an aggressive war would be, in effect, "litigating against the empire." Picking up on her insights, Swanson would later write:

> At Nuremberg, where we prosecuted from the top down, including the lawyers . . . we called aggressive war "the supreme international crime, differing only from other war crimes in that it contains within itself the accumulated evil of the whole."

Today, aggressive war is considered so all-encompassing that the International Criminal Court has yet to come up with a formal definition, making this overarching war crime out of bounds for prosecution until its elements are agreed upon. For now, we must use the crime of aggressive war as a way to provide horrifying context for all the accumulated evils that have developed in the war in Iraq. Swanson summarized them in his blog:

> Misleading Congress, defrauding Congress, misspending funds, use of illegal weapons that melt the skin off children or poison them in the womb, targeting of civilians and journalists and hospitals, murder, assassinations, warrantless spying, lawless detention, imprisonment of children, torture, domestic propaganda . . . selected exposure of classified information, retaliation against whistleblowers, domestic use of the military, and the hornswoggling of half a country into debating the wisdom of enforcing laws against torture, as if this were a political question to be decided by its likely impact on each of two sports teams.

He went on, even daring to mention the word spelled *o-i-l,* singling out "the secret establishment of government policy by closed-door meetings of oil barons, immunity for mercenaries, war profiteering without limit, secret laws, royal decrees, laws rewritten with signing statements, the undermining of preparedness for natural disasters, the exacerbation of climate change, the destruction of an economy through military waste and Wall Street theft and the transfer of wealth upward, and the complete politicization of the Justice Department."

Swanson's Web site (prosecuteBushCheney.org) and new book offer multiple ways to get involved—from signing petitions to helping choose a district attorney or attorney general on the state level to prosecute George W. Bush and his co-conspirators for murder.

How not to forget the original sin

Which, of course, brings us to Vince Bugliosi. He has not given up on his mission to prosecute George W. Bush for murder. "I'm not speaking loosely," he told me recently. "I'm making progress in finding a prosecutor at the local level to bring charges." He added that he had "no confidence" of anything happening under Holder or Obama on the federal level.

Bugliosi predicted months ago that "we're the only game in town" when it came to prosecuting Bush, precisely because he believed the atmosphere on the federal level was too politicized.

Meanwhile, Ben Davis, a law professor at the University of Toledo, has put together an ad hoc group of students to do a "Bugliosi research project." Their assignment: to work up additional arguments to assist Bugliosi in his case. "These are not exotic John Yoo theories," Davis told me. "This is just straight criminal law." And the ultimate goal is to go after the criminals on the top. "We don't need more information," he told me emphatically. "We need to *do* more."[255]

As Lawrence Velvel wrote at the beginning of my campaign: "For the first time, the need to use state murder statutes to punish presidential murder has now arisen, lest Bush and company get away with serious crimes. . . . Trial for murder in state courts, under the kind of jurisdiction states have possessed for scores of years, is the lawful and necessary counterweight to what has become the federal monster the framers desperately wanted to avoid."[256]

Those of us who were originally inspired by Bugliosi's strategies and/ or tried them out in Vermont are still reminding activists and lawyers alike that we should not forget the original sin that started this awful descent into madness, i.e., the war in Iraq.

Cindy Sheehan took time out from a book tour[257] to go to Dallas and stage a protest outside the ex-president's new home with banners saying "Mr. Bush, Turn Yourself In" and "War Is Not the Answer." In a brief speech, she said "We can't move forward until those criminals are in prison. There are still two wars raging. I'll never be able to get over the death of my son. It's important to call attention to what we believe are high crimes and misdemeanors against humanity."[258]

More recently, she and a group of supporters traveled to Martha's Vineyard while President Obama was there vacationing with his family. On August 19, she put out a message on the Internet explaining why. "I am going to Martha's Vineyard because someone has to speak for the babies of Iraq, Afghanistan, and Pakistan who do not deserve the horrible fate that has been handed to them by the U.S. Military Industrial Complex. The voiceless need a voice, and even if I am called every name in the book by all sides, I will speak up for them. I am going to Martha's Vineyard because so many people have been blinded to the fact that the system has momentum that rolls on and over and around no matter who is the titular head of the system."

It was a small group that showed up, and, as Sheehan would state later, the real story was not that she was protesting what have now become Obama's wars, but rather "that the leadership of the peace movement did not support her protest." She remains undeterred. My guess is that the loss of her son is what galvanizes her more than most people in the antiwar movement.

Now that the war in Afghanistan is starting to take an increasing toll on American lives, I'm certain it will become more of a focal point for debate and protest. My campaign manager, Ralph Lopez, made a trip to Afghanistan last spring to see for himself why our troops are now getting enmeshed there. His conclusion: The war makes no sense. The Afghan people need jobs and economic security, not war. If we helped them with money and social-service jobs, they wouldn't need to join forces with the Taliban. Ralph is hoping to get all his footage into a documentary.

We should be examining the roots of this war with the same precision as we did with the war in Iraq.[259] Meanwhile, we should be *clamoring* for a full-scale criminal investigation into possible U.S. complicity in the atrocities that occurred in the early war in Afghanistan.

Another My Lai?

When I first saw the video of mass graves in Afghanistan last July, I felt ill. The dead were not civilians, as they were in the scandalous My Lai massacres of Vietnam. They were Afghan prisoners believed to be members of the Taliban and al-Qaeda. Whatever people may think of them, they are entitled to one of the most fundamental tenets of the laws of war: protection against being killed while in captivity.

In 2001, some two thousand Afghans surrendered in what was then one of the biggest battles yet in Afghanistan. They were rounded up by forces commanded by a known CIA asset, Northern Alliance warlord General Abdul Rashid Dostum, and crammed into some twenty-five sealed containers with no ventilation. Then they were transported 120 kilometers through the hot desert to a prison in western Afghanistan. Half an hour into the trip, they began pounding on the sides of the containers. They were suffocating. Some of their captors shot into the containers, supposedly to give them relief. By the time the trucks arrived at the prison, bystanders saw blood oozing out of the bullet holes. When a soldier opened the backs of the containers, the stench was overpowering. The sight of human bodies stacked like cardboard was equally sickening. A few survivors were dragged from the containers and eventually taken to Guantánamo, others were shot at gunpoint, and then all of the dead were thrown into mass graves. U.S. soldiers were at the scene, guarding the prison and reportedly going through the effects of the dead Afghans. A number of them are said to have overseen the shootings at the mass grave site. Yet the Pentagon denied any knowledge of this incident. Small wonder. If it could be proven the U.S. was in charge of these prisoners and their ultimate fate, it could be charged with war crimes.

Why were we hearing about this now and not earlier? There was, in fact, a *Newsweek* report in 2002 as well as a documentary on the killings (*Afghan Massacre: Convoy of Death*) made by British journalist Jamie Doran and aired by *Democracy Now* back in May, 2003. But back then the country was caught up in the post-9/11 frenzy, followed by the "new" war in Iraq. The story did not get the kind of traction it should have. Now, nine years later, on July 10, *The New York Times'* James Risen broke a story showing satellite photos of the grave site and documenting the Bush administration's cover-up of the incident. The International Red Cross, the FBI, and the State Department all sought investigations, he reported, but they were rebuffed. Meanwhile, a forensic medical team with Physicians for Human Rights, which had found the mass grave at Dasht-i-Leili in 2002, kept getting cold-shouldered by the Department of Defense when they tried to get back to the grave site and do more forensic examinations. Now, PHR has called for protection of the mass grave site and a full investigation by the U.S. government about who was there when the massacres happened.

Here's the kicker. It turns out that the warlord who authorized the killings, General Abdul Rashid Dostum, was on the CIA's payroll. He has since been slated to join Afghan President Hamid Karzai's new cabinet.

When the Pentagon was first called by the Associated Press after Risen's story broke, it denied that U.S. forces had been present or in any way involved. It denied having any jurisdiction over Afghan warlords. President Obama, subsequently interviewed by CNN's Anderson Cooper, had to take a different tack. He said he would ask his "national security team" to investigate.

Now if this isn't the war crime to end all war crimes, what is? Images of soldiers being packed into sealed lories to suffocate and die on their way to prison, then unloaded, shot, and thrown into mass graves, evokes memories of Jews being sent off to death camps during the Holocaust. President Obama risks his entire reputation if he tries to forestall this investigation.

I spoke to Susannah Sirkin, the deputy director of Physicians for Human Rights. Her group's major frustration, she told me, was the lack of political will to do anything about these atrocities between 2003, when they were first reported, and 2007. This was arguably the biggest war crime post-9/11, but it was hard to get even the activist community moving on this. Part of the problem was that the dead were, in essence, "the enemy." And, of course, they could not speak out. Nor could the families they left behind, for fear of their lives. After PHR's team of forensic investigators discovered a mass grave in 2002 and exhumed fifteen remains, they called for the sight to be secured, protection of witnesses, and a full investigation. "Despite these appeals," according to PHR's Web site, "Afghan eyewitnesses were tortured, murdered, and disappeared, and sections of the mass grave site have been dug up and removed."[260]

Sirkin feels strongly that our current war in Afghanistan will not end well unless there is an "end to impunity." If the U.S. fails to investigate this atrocity and hold the perpetrators to account, "we will not rehabilitate our reputation in the world." PHR has long been in favor of accountability. It got its start years ago investigating the medical impact of torture on torture victims—in the Philippines, Argentina, South Korea, and Russia—but only after 9/11 did it begin to turn its attention to the U.S.'s role in torturing detainees. "When I started in human-rights work two decades ago," she said, "our task was to get people informed. Now we have to hold people accountable for what they did. We have to shout about this till we are blue in the face."

She's used to counting progress in decades, she admits. "The U.S had not even ratified the Convention Against Torture when I started. Now, when we bring up violations of human rights, we can talk about this treaty and others as well as the Constitution." Even so, this is not a time to rest on our laurels. "We have a unique moment in time when people have just left office and their crimes are fresh in people's minds. In the U.S. we have a legal system and the rule of law. We don't have to wait for decades for justice to be done, as happens in other countries. We already have a system of laws that should be followed."

Like the activists I spoke to, she is distressed that people who would otherwise get exercised about new revelations on human-rights abuses are not doing so now that Obama is president. "We need a loyal opposition," she insisted. "We have to get the public to see how vital this is!"

And don't think that Attorney General Eric Holder wasn't listening. Call it a coincidence, but right when this story was about to break in *The New York Times* he told *Newsweek* last July that he was considering appointing a special prosecutor to investigate Bush-era crimes.[261] He has since done so.

I will leave some final words to two journalists who have managed, through their own brilliance and sheer perseverance, to confound the mainstream media and keep us informed on breaking developments in the search for accountability. Last July, on Salon radio, Glenn Greenwald actually debated the political director of NBC news on the network's dismissive attitude toward prosecuting war criminals.

NBC's Chuck Todd asked, "What would happen—and is it good for our reputation around the world—if we're essentially putting on trial the previous administration?"

Greenwald replied, "I think what has destroyed our reputation is announcing to the world that we tolerated torture. If I go out and rob a bank tomorrow, what happens to me is that I get to prison. So, what do you think should happen when presidents get caught committing crimes in office?"

A rather lengthy exchange ended with Glenn pointing out that "powerful politicians know that they can break the law and get away with it."

Todd finally conceded, "I don't disagree with your conclusion here."[262]

Glenn Greenwald is not one to give up. He gets his inspiration from history. The past has shown him that people can overcome what seem at the time to be insurmountable problems. "With activism," he told me, " you can dramatically change things for the better. Any system set up by human beings can be torn down by other human beings. People should never lose sight of this."[263]

Amy Goodman gave a similar message of hope to Vermonters in July,

2009. She looked tiny as she spoke to an outdoor crowd from a giant sound stage flanked by six huge solar panels. But her message was grand and much broader than the theme of sustainable living and alternative energy being celebrated at SolarFest that day. The mainstream media, she said, today serves as a conveyor belt of lies. Part of its job is to denigrate activists. But she has found, in touring the country in support of independent media, that there are people of all walks of life who are willing to "stand up to the madness."[264] And they have often been successful. She spoke of three librarians who refused to turn over the names of their patrons and their reading habits and are now suing the government; of a presidential scholar who appeared at a White House reception and presented President Bush with a letter condemning torture; of the power of a YouTube video that covered the arrests of a *Democracy Now* cameraperson at the Republican Convention and got a million hits, prompting his immediate release from jail.

Now, she said, with Barack Obama in the White House, the brick wall of censorship had opened just a crack. "It's up to you to kick it open," she concluded, "or see it slam shut." She ended with only two words: "Democracy now!" Whereupon she quietly left the stage, and the crowd got up from the grass and cheered.

For me, the year since my candidacy for attorney general began has been a roller-coaster ride of uncertainty, and yet there is enough forward momentum in the accountability movement that it one day may be looked upon as a historic development in American democracy. Challenging a head of state for committing serious crimes in office is huge. We saw it with Watergate and the forced resignation of President Richard Nixon.[265] But there has never been a sustained accountability movement like the one I encountered during and after my race. I suspect that this will be going on for some time to come. Hopefully, for as long as it takes to get justice.

Vincent Bugliosi reminded me recently of a quote from Albert Einstein: "The world is a dangerous place to live, not because of the people who are evil, but because of the people who don't do anything about it."

It's time we, the people, wake up and take action to save ourselves and our fellow citizens from those who rule over us with impunity. As one of my Vermont neighbors told me recently, "we must be accountable to each other." That means exercising our sovereignty, something that my friend, now eighty-five-year-old "world citizen" and former war veteran Garry Davis has been arguing for over sixty years.[266] He points to Article 1 of the 1948 United Nations Declaration of Human Rights, which says "all humans are born free and equal in dignity and rights; they are endowed with reason and conscience and should act towards one another in a spirit of brotherhood."

Now, thanks to an earlier movement (the women's movement), that dream is easily extended to the spirit of sisterhood as well, and ultimately to the spirit of global personhood. Change does happen, and freedom does evolve, over time.

Mahatma Gandhi, the great nonviolent revolutionary of twentieth-century India, once said: "Even the most powerful cannot rule without the cooperation of the ruled."[267] Those words, uttered against the colonial rule of the British, are now taking on a new meaning and new urgency in our twenty-first-century world. They are showing up on Iranian Web sites, as citizens protest the stifling and repressive rule of the Iranian mullahs and imams.[268]

Shouldn't we be adopting these words for our own country? Our own communities? Our own democracy?

Our new movement is in its infancy. But in this age of globalization, it has the power to spread throughout the world and to join with other struggles for true democracy. We can restore, indeed improve, America's image in the world as a great beacon for freedom, so movingly portrayed by the Statue of Liberty. We can once again offer hope to the oppressed while showing respect to those in the global community who have decried our country's descent into the "dark side."

We should remember what our ancestors fought for: freedom from tyranny. And we must take strength from our forebearers and remember that with the power of the people behind us, we will succeed.

Accountability!

Now!

ACKNOWLEDGMENTS

First, my thanks to Vincent Bugliosi and everyone who has bravely created what is now called the accountability movement. I'm also very grateful to the hundreds of people who supported my campaign and my book writing. Every donation, every word of encouragement, meant the world to me and kept me going.

Special thanks go to some of my most loyal, long-term supporters: My friend Robin Lloyd, who has stood by me for years and then precipitated and supported my run for attorney general in Vermont; Kit Miller, who has carried on the tradition begun by her wonderful mother, the late Maya Miller, in supporting activists and writers like me; and William Preston, Jr., civil libertarian, professor, and author of the revitalized *Aliens and Dissenters: Federal Suppression of Radicals, 1903–1933*. Bill's support for my various writing endeavors has been a tremendous help to me, and is deeply appreciated.

Thanks go to Martha Abbott, chair of the Vermont Progressive Party, who urged me to run, and to Morgan Daybell, executive director, who graciously guided me through campaign intricacies. To Peggy Sapphire, fellow Prog and muse: Thanks for caring so much.

To my wonderful campaign staff, Kristina Borjesson and Ralph Lopez: Thanks for your professionalism, courage, and humor both during the campaign and afterward. Your continued dedication to justice and accountability is an inspiration. Sue Serpa, leader of the northeastern impeachment coalition, also has my greatest respect for her perseverance after impeachment efforts were throttled and prosecution efforts revved up. She continues to operate a large listserv for accountability activists.

To Kurt Daims, Dan DeWalt, Sue Harman, Tobi Dragert, Lee Madden, Birdie Emerson, Jeff and Kate Taylor, Elizabeth Skarie, Jerry Greenfield, Ben Cohen, and everyone who volunteered on my campaign, putting up lawn signs, handing out fliers, setting up events, and hosting us: Your dedication was an inspiration. I am also grateful to Bob Alexander, webmaster for prosecutegeorgewbush.com and my own Web site (PeoplevBush.com); Katherine Vose for her photography; and Larry Velvel for his help.

To publisher Margo Baldwin; my wonderful editor Joni Praded; Bill Bokermann and Patricia Stone in production; and others in the amazing team at Chelsea Green: It was a joy working with you.

I'll end by thanking four remarkable and courageous men who have been fighting the good fight for decades and inspired me as I wrote my book.

Reverend Phil Wheaton, historian and liberation theologist, was just completing a book on the prophetic rise and fall of empires when he offered to me a rather profound observation shortly after Barack Obama was elected president: "Obama thinks he can trump empire." We are now watching to see if the best of candidate Obama's intentions will survive his presidency. Meanwhile, Phil and his wife, Sue, keep fighting for justice and accountability regardless of the odds.

Reverend William Wipfler, a leader in human rights, called me out of the blue one day and we soon rediscovered a mutual and deeply felt need for accountability on the question of torture. Like Phil Wheaton, Bill had assisted my husband and me years ago as we ventured off to the Amazon for our book, *Thy Will be Done: The Conquest of the Amazon*. Once again, Bill has pitched in to help my book project.

Lou Wolf, whose dedication over the years to exposing the evil side of "covert action" and who for years courageously published a magazine by that name, became a supporter of my campaign and book. Through him, and the Rock Creek Press, which he supports, I learned of the extraordinary work of Washington-based activists fighting for accountability–and of the Department of Homeland Security's unconstitutional meddling and suppression of dissent through the "fusion centers" described in this book. Lou, like my friend Robin, actually served time for peacefully protesting against the U.S. School of the Americas (renamed the Western Hemisphere Institute for Security Cooperation), which provides training in torture techniques to military officers from armies around the world.

And last, but of course not least, is my dearest friend and husband of over thirty years, Gerard Colby. A fearless biographer of some of the most powerful dynasties in America, and later a union president representing freelance writers in The National Writers Union, Local 1981 of the UAW, Jerry instilled in me more than anyone else a love of democracy, a love of country, and a determination that true democracy be expanded to all Americans, beyond the limits currently imposed in what author Michael Parenti calls a "democracy for the few." This book would not have happened without Jerry's advice, support, and love.

Resources for the Accountability Movement

The accountability movement is growing and ever-changing, and this list no doubt omits worthy resources and organizations. If you or your organization has been overlooked, please contact me at Dennett.book@gmail.com. There's more on my Web site, **PeoplevBush.com.**

Bloggers and Web sites

Progressive news sites abound. Among the best: **AlterNet** (alternet. org); **BuzzFlash** (buzzflash.com); **The Huffington Post** (huffingtonpost. com); **The Information Clearinghouse** (informationclearinghouse.info); **TomPaine.com**; and **Toward Freedom** (towardfreedom.com). All are excellent resources on accountability, as are **The Nation** (www.thenation.com) and **In These Times** (www.inthesetimes.com), which have numerous links to other Web sites and blogs. Keep your eyes on **Daily Kos** (dailykos.com). They've got some big plans for accountability.

Brad Friedman (**The Brad Blog** at bradblog.com) writes a feisty blog that won a 2010 Project Censored award for excellence in investigative journalism. The Brad Blog has carefully followed the case of Sibel Edmonds, an FBI whistleblower. After seven years of forced silence, she is now telling all (including some of the machinations behind the war in Iraq).

Glenn Greenwald (**Salon** at salon.com) gave up his practice as a constitutional lawyer to blog about warrantless wiretapping, then ranged into such subjects as state secrets, torture, and the folly of trying detainees in military commissions. He is fearless in speaking truth to power, and is read by the White House.

Jane Hamsher (**Firedoglake** at firedoglake.com), founder and publisher of Firedoglake, is breathtakingly independent in her critiques of corporate and government malfeasance. A former film producer, her live reporting on the Scooter Libby trial, alternating with fellow blogger Marcy Wheeler, brought Firedoglake instant recognition from fellow journalists as a must-read, especially on issues of accountability. Notes Salon blogger Glenn Greenwald, "She doesn't care in the slightest which powerful people dislike her." Firedoglake's Accountability Now PAC is raising millions for progressive candidates and causes.

Scott Horton (**Harper's Magazine** at harpers.org) is a New York lawyer who blogs incisively on human rights and international law. In December, 2008, he wrote "Justice After Bush: Prosecuting an Outlaw Administration." These days, he critiques the Obama administration's stances on Guantánamo, renditions, and state secrets.

Josh Marshall (**Talking Points Memo** at talkingpointsmemo.com), a former writer for *The New York Times,* is a true muckraker who made blogger history when his TalkingPointsMemo broke the story of the politicization (and firing) of U.S. attorneys under the Bush administration.

Jonathan Turley (jonathanturley.org) is a prominent lawyer who has represented whistleblowers, military personnel, and suspected spies. He blogs about constitutional and national security issues and is a frequent guest on MSNBC, where he has critiqued the Obama administration's adoption of Bush policies, including drone strikes in Afghanistan.

Marcy Wheeler (**Emptywheel** at emptywheel.firedoglake.com) wrote a an exposé on the Valerie Plame affair (*Anatomy of Deceit: How the Bush Administration Used the Media to Sell the Iraq War and Out a Spy*) and with Firedoglake.com's Jane Hamsher made blogger history by live-blogging the Scooter Libby trial. Here's Wheeler at her outspoken best when she appeared on MSNBC in July, 2009: "After investigating Bill Clinton for a blow job for five years, we shouldn't investigate the huge, grossly illegal things that were done under the past administration . . . ?"

International Organizations

Amnesty International USA (amnestyusa.org; 212-807-8400) has more than 2.2 million members, supporters, and subscribers in over 150 countries and territories. It has a Ten Against Torture Campaign, in which famous Americans have all written to President Obama, asking him to ensure an end to torture. You can pick the letter that most moves you and send it to the president while adding your own comments.

Human Rights Watch (hrw.org; 212-290-4700) has been front and center in denouncing the detainee policies of the Bush and Obama administrations. Human Rights Watch warns that Obama "should prosecute detainees in federal courts, whose record of trying terrorism cases is solid—and where admission of coerced and hearsay evidence is inadmissable."

Lawyers and Physicians

The American Civil Liberties Union (aclu.org; 212-549-2500; has state chapters also) has forced the U.S. government to surrender 100,000 documents about Bush-era torture policies. It has set up its own "Accountability for Torture" Web page, with a chronology of and links to released torture documents. It has persistently called for the prosecution of high-level government officials.

The Center for Justice and Accountability (cja.org; 415-544-0444) is currently pursuing civil and criminal cases in Bosnia, Chile, China, Indonesia, and Guatemala, among others. The center filed a criminal case in Madrid in November, 2008, against former Salvadoran military officials for their role in killing six Jesuit priests.

The Center for Constitutional Rights (ccrjustice.org; 212-614-6464) advances "the creative use of law as a positive force for social change." CCR was the first law firm to represent detainees at Guantánamo. If you are an activist, CCR's staff is always willing to help. If you are a journalist, CCR will explain even the most complex legal issues of our time.

The Government Accountability Project (whistleblower.org; 202-457-0034) helps whistleblowers and empowers activists focused on national security programs, nuclear safety, and food and drug safety. GAP's Jesselyn Radack, former Justice Department lawyer, now helps whistleblowers expose overseas fraud among military contractors in Iraq.

Lawyers Against the War (lawyersagainstthewar.org; 604-738-0338), with members in thirteen countries, is headquartered in Canada. LAW tried to have Bush arrested for war crimes (2004) and barred from Canada (2009). Though unsuccessful, the group continues to press for the enforcement of local and international laws. LAW is affiliated with Lawyers Against the War in the United Kingdom, Lawyers for Peace in the Netherlands, and the Transnational Foundation for Peace and Future Research, based in Sweden.

The National Lawyers Guild (nlg.org; 212-679-5100) alerted us to "Fusion Centers" linking local police departments to military outposts in order to spy on antiwar activists. In October, 2009, NLG president Marjorie Cohn invited forty-five prominent lawyers and civic leaders to send a letter to Attorney General Eric Holder urging him to appoint a special prosecutor to investigate "all those who ordered, approved, justified, abetted, or carried out the torture and abuse." Signers included the International Association of Democratic Lawyers and the American Association of Jurists.

Physicians for Human Rights (physiciansforhumanrights.org; 617-301-4200) sends doctors and investigators into some of the world's most dangerous places. The group received international attention for their exposé of the George W. Bush administration's cover-up of mass killings of Afghans: the Dasht-i-Leili Massacre.

The Robert Jackson Steering Committee (See After Downing Street; afterdowningstreet.org) is comprised mostly of lawyers and journalists mindful of the lessons of the Nuremberg trials and the need to hold all war criminals accountable. The committee, which is keeping abreast of legal developments under the Obama administration, has called on Attorney General Eric Holder to appoint an independent special prosecutor to investigate "the most serious alleged crimes" of former President George W. Bush, former Vice President Richard B. Cheney, the Bush lawyers who justified torture, and others. It is preparing its own legal brief to assist.

Media

Radio

Air America (airamerica.com). A progressive syndicated radio alternative to the Rush Limbaughs of the world, Air America has reported widely on accountability and has included, among its guests, Vincent Bugliosi.

The Thom Hartmann Program (thomhartmann.com). Billed as the number-one progressive talk-show host in the nation, Thom Hartmann has been an unsparing critic of the George W. Bush administration as well as the increasingly rightward drift of the Republican party. He is a strong advocate of prosecuting Bush, Cheney, and Rumsfeld (among others) for war crimes.

The Mike Malloy Show (mikemalloy.com). Once part of Air America, now with his own syndicated show, Mike Malloy has done more to alert the country to Bugliosi's book than anyone. Says Bob Alexander of ProsecuteGeorgeW. Bush.com: "He gave us a huge amounts of airtime . . . and told his audience to go to the Web site and contribute whatever they could" to help buy the book and distribute it to attorney general and district attorney offices around the country.

Pacifica Radio (pacifica.org). Listener-supported Pacifica Radio gave the TV show Democracy Now! its start and has been cutting edge on issues of accountability. Check its Web site for affiliates near you.

Television

Democracy Now! with hosts Amy Goodman and Juan Gonzalez (democracynow.org). I watch *Democracy Now* to find out what's *really* going on. It's an education—featuring top journalists and experts in their fields. Reporters working for mainstream media are frequent guests and seem only too happy give more than the usual sound bite analysis.

GRITtv with Laura Flanders (lauraflanders. com). Flanders is refreshingly sassy, down to earth, and fearless. She frequently hosts a roundtable to focus on a particular issue.

The Rachel Maddow Show (rachelmaddow.com). Crisp, incisive, and disarmingly self-confident, MSNBC's Rachel Maddow reports the news professionally–but with plenty of wry humor about the workings of big government and big business. She has a huge following and she's watched avidly on the Hill. George H.W. Bush attacked her and MSNBC's Keith Olbermann as being "sick puppies" for their relentless exposés of his son's administration.

Peace, Pro-Prosecution, and Veterans' Organizations

After Downing Street (afterdowningstreet.org) is a nonpartisan coalition of hundreds of organizations. It aims to "expose the lies that create and sustain wars" and "to hold accountable those responsible." Cofounder John Bonifaz represented soldiers, their parents, and congressional representatives in a federal lawsuit challenging George W. Bush's authority to wage war against Iraq. Cofounder David Swanson, an indefatigable activist, recently authored *Daybreak:Undoing the Imperial Presidency and Forming a More Perfect Union.* After Downing Street's "Prosecution" section is must reading.

Code Pink (codepinkalert.org; 301-827-4320). These activists, mostly women, are always finding new ways to confound the powerful, and they seem to have a lot of serious fun doing it. You'll find Code Pink activists sitting in on Congressional hearings and waving their protest banners, making their way in to speeches by cabinet officials, and telling President Obama directly: "We don't need these wars." Check for "Code Pink Alerts"; there may be something happening in your area.

Iraq Veterans Against the War (ivaw.org; 646-723-0989). Representing vets and active-duty members of the U.S. military, with over 1,500 members in 61 chapters, this group strives to mobilize the military community to withdraw its support for the war and end the occupation in Iraq. In one section on its Web page, it provides ten reasons why its members are against the war in Iraq, including: 1) the Iraq war is based on lies; 2) the Iraq war violates international law; and 3) corporate profiteering is driving the war.

Military Families Speak Out (mfso.org; 617-983-0710). With thirty chapters, MFSO is made up of family members who have soldiers serving in Iraq and Afghanistan. They actively oppose both wars. Their Web site updates the casualties from both. They feature defectors, such as Matthew Hoh, a vet and senior representative of the U.S. State Department in Afghanistan who became the first U.S. official to resign over the Afghan war. This group links with **Gold Star Families Speak Out**, founded by Cindy Sheehan, who protested outside Bush's ranch over the death of her son, Casey, in Iraq.

School of the Americas Watch (soaw.org; 202-234-3440). Every November, thousands of citizens make a pilgrimage to Fort Benning, Georgia, where they join SOAW founder Father Roy Bourgeois in trying to close down the "School of Assassins." Since 1946, the school has trained Latin American dictators and soldiers on how to torture, assassinate, and pull off military coups. Most recently, SOA Watch revealed that the leaders of the 2009 coup in Honduras were graduates of the school. While SOAW's focus is on Latin America, it seeks an end to torture everywhere.

United for Peace and Justice (unitedforpeace.org; 212-868-5545). An umbrella organization for 1,400 national groups, UPJ's members have engaged in numerous protests against the war in Iraq and now has a "Working Group on Accountability and Prosecution." Its Web site states that "it is imperative that we prevent future wars and that we reestablish the rule of law. . . . We cannot proceed as a movement within a democracy unless we restore and expand that democracy." Its member groups are listed by state.

U.S. Labor Against the War (uslaboragainstwar.org; 202-521-5265). Originally formed by labor leaders to oppose the war in Iraq, this group has joined with others in torture-accountability protests and is now focusing on the war in Afghanistan.

Veterans for Peace (veteransforpeace.org; 314-725-6005). Vets of all ages—including from World War II and the Korean War—can be found at anti-war demonstrations and accountability protests. They will tell you that their experience in war was horrific, that they were naïve going in, and that they were profoundly disillusioned when they left active duty. In October, 2009, they joined hundreds of demonstrators outside the White House calling for the withdrawal of U.S. troops from Afghanistan. See the group's *War Crimes Times*, which carries news omitted from the mainstream media but reported by many of the groups on this resource list. There is an e-version on their Web site.

Women's International League for Peace and Freedom (wilpf.org; 617-266-0999). WILPF is the oldest international women's peace organization in the world with thirty-seven sections. It boasts two Nobel Peace Prize winners. In five years it will be celebrating its one-hundredth anniversary. WILPF members today are active protesting wars in Iraq, Afghanistan, and Pakistan. WILPF's Robin Lloyd of Vermont played a major role in my campaign to bring President George W. Bush to justice.

World Can't Wait (worldcantwait.net; 866-973-4463). Begun in 2005 to "stop the disastrous course led by the George W. Bush administration," WCW has since set up War Criminals Watch "to ensure that prosecutions of high officials of the Bush administration" occur. It opposes the Obama administration's escalation of troops in Afghanistan and "the global war of terror." See also **FireJohnYoo.org.**

Political Organizations

Democrats.com (democrats.com). This is primarily an action-oriented Web site, a cyber meeting place for "aggressive progressives" inside and outside of the Democratic Party who turn to it for news, analysis, and suggested strategies for action. Founded in 2000 by Democratic Party political consultants Bob Fertik and David Lytel, Democrats.com declares that it is loyal to the Democratic Party but is not controlled by the party in any way. In fact, its posts are often fiercely critical of Democrats.

New Broom Coalition (newbroomcoalition.net). Here's a group that is taking political accountability seriously, and on two levels: first, "by identifying and supporting candidates dedicated to transparency and accountability and serving the interests of the general public," and second, by challenging "those public officials who have *failed* in the performance of their public trust, holding them accountable for their failures." One of its prime movers is Laurie Dobson, who as a state senate candidate from Maine in 2007 put a Bush-indictment resolution before the board of selectmen at the Bushes' hometown of Kennebunk. She now leads a group called EndUSWars.org

Progressive Democrats of America (pdamerica.org). A member of the After Downing Street coalition, this group was founded in 2004 with the express purpose of transforming the Democratic Party into one that represents the people of Main Street instead of the leaders of Wall Street. It works inside the Democratic Party and outside in movements for peace and justice. PDA activists did an impressive job in mobilizing voters to achieve Democratic Party victories in 2006 and 2008 (including the election of Barack Obama). During the past year, it has sent out regular updates on a PDA-Accountability listserve advising activists about pressing issues that need attention.

Vermont Progressive Party (progressiveparty.org). The Vermont Progressive Party has elected a total of thirty-one city councilors and three Burlington mayors and since 1991 has put thirteen progressives into the state house. Like their independent ally in the U.S. Senate, Bernie Sanders, Progressives reject corporate funding and champion single-payer health care. They supported my campaign for Vermont attorney general. Vermont progressives will be happy to talk to anyone who is interested in building their own progressive parties in their different states.

Religious Organizations

The Catholic Worker Movement (catholicworker.org). Founded during the Great Depression by visionary leader Dorothy Day, the Catholic Worker Movement has 185 communities around the country. Members started **Witness Against Torture** (www.witnesstorture.org) in 2005 after twenty-five individuals traveled to Guantánamo to try and visit detainees. When they returned, they began a broad outreach to other interfaith, human rights, and activist organizations to shut down Guantánamo.

National Religious Campaign Against Torture (nrcat.org). Over 250 religious groups have joined NRCAT, including Roman Catholic, evangelical Christian, mainline Protestant, Orthodox Christians, Unitarian, Quaker, Orthodox Christian, Jewish, Muslim, Baha'i, Buddhist, Hindu, and Sikh communities. NRCAT calls torture a moral issue that degrades everyone involved—"policy-makers, perpetrators and victims." At stake, it says, is the "soul of our nation." It calls for a congressional Commission of Inquiry.

The 9-11 Truth Movement (911truth.org). There are now seven separate 9/11 truth groups that represent architects, engineers, firefighters, military and government officials, scholars, medical-health professionals, and pilots. All insist on a new "truly independent" congressional investigation. Go to this Web site to see what 9/11 truth organizations exist in your area.

ENDNOTES

1. Since the Progressives first ran candidates for the Burlington City Council in the early 1980s, they have elected thirty-one councilors and three mayors (Bernie Sanders: 1981–1989; Peter Clavelle: 1989–1993, 1995–2006; Bob Kiss, 2006–2009). Beginning in the early 1990s, the party began to run Progressives for the state legislature, first from the most populous, Burlington-based Chittenden County, and gradually from more rural parts of the state. From 1991 to 2009, thirteen progressives have served in the Vermont legislature.
2. "Vermont Candidate Plans Bush Prosecution," Associated Press, September 18, 2008.
3. The full text of our various responses can be found in the Appendix or on my Web site, PeoplevBush.com.
4. "The Final Days," *Time*, August 3, 2009.
5. See Gerard Colby and Charlotte Dennett, *Thy Will Be Done. The Conquest of the Amazon: Nelson Rockefeller and Evangelism in the Age of Oil* (New York: HarperCollins, 1994).
6. The loss of civilians during the U.S.-led wars in Vietnam and Iraq I (Desert Storm) also rank high in the U.S. hall of shame, though these would be considered part of the inevitable "collateral damage" that accompanies war.
7. Bugliosi, I discovered by looking at his index, had devoted four pages of one continuous footnote on whether the Gulf of Tonkin incident (where three North Vietnamese torpedo boats fired on the USS Maddox in August, 1964) was staged to get us into the Vietnam War. Bugliosi concludes that "no credible evidence has surfaced in almost 45 years that the Gulf of Tonkin incident was provoked or staged" and cites newly declassified transcripts between President Lyndon Johnson and his advisors to prove his point. See his footnote number 101, pp. 285–289. In the same footnote, he also touches on Franklin Roosevelt's response to Pearl Harbor, again dismissing the claim that the president allowed it to happen to get us into World War II. However, he turns both events and both "staged theory" arguments to his advantage when he delivers his ultimate conclusion: "If, in fact, Johnson and Roosevelt did do what many Bush supporters and conservatives say they did, then they should have been prosecuted for murder, too. And if they had, the punkish college cheerleader from Crawford, Texas, may have thought twice about lying to the nation to take us to war in Iraq."
8. Bugliosi, *The Prosecution of George W. Bush*, p. 5.
9. Ibid, p. 6.
10. Casualties on both sides from the 1980–1988 Iran-Iraq war are conservatively estimated at 500,000 dead. The U.S.'s 1991 Desert Storm war in Iraq produced another death toll: 200,000 Iraqis and 148 Americans dead. The second U.S. war against Iraq, from March, 2003 to October, 2009, has resulted in at least 200,000 Iraqi dead (a conservative estimate) and over 4,000 American deaths.

11. It took us eighteen years to research and write our tome, *Thy Will Be Done*.

12. For anyone interested in third-party politics, here is a classic example of how Democratic leaders would rather split the Progressive vote and guarantee another term for a Republican governor than stay out of the governor's race and cede that territory to a third-party candidate. Anthony Pollina had built a base in Vermont and stood a good chance of defeating Republican governor Jim Douglas as a Progressive. But it seems the Democrats could not bear the thought of yielding to a Progressive, and so threw an unprepared and half-hearted candidate into the race, the Speaker of the House. Anthony figured his only option at that point was to raise enough money from a wide base of contributors—including Democrats who favored him—in order to mount a really serious campaign. "I will always be a Progressive at heart, you know that," he said. In the end, he came in second, defeating the Democrat.

13. Jerry's horrifying tale of how his book had been suppressed, or "privished," became the lead essay in the anthology edited by Kristina, *Into the Buzzsaw: Leading Journalists Expose the Myth of a Free Press* (Amherst, NY: Prometheus, 2002). The book won a number of awards, including a National Press Club award for press criticism, giving her the impetus to do another book critical of the press: *Feet to the Fire: The Media after 9/11, Top Journalists Speak Out* (Amherst, NY: Prometheus, 2005).

14. There was something else that set Bugliosi's book apart, something that I knew would intrigue her. For the first time in his career, he had a very difficult time getting his book published, the likelihood of its being a best seller being trumped by fear. It had been ignored by the mainstream publishers, just as Kristina's story on TWA flight 800 had been suppressed. The more skeptical she became of the official truth— that the plane's center-wing fuel tank had exploded because of faulty wiring—the more nervous her producers became. Finally, they simply fired her. She was stunned. This wasn't supposed to happen to her. She was used to getting her way, jokingly calling herself a "Haitian princess" for having been raised in Haiti by a white, well-off "ruling family." Suddenly, she discovered what it was like to be censored for getting too close to the truth.

15. Federal prosecution could also be conducted by any of the ninety-three U.S. attorneys in the ninety-three federal districts in the U.S.

16. See Bugliosi, "Hearing on Limits of Executive Power," www.youtube.com/watch?v=GDAFozFn4kU.

17. The Office of Strategic Services was America's first civilian spy agency, created during World War II. My father was, like so many OSS spies, recruited out of academia. He operated out of Lebanon under State Department cover from 1943– 1947. I was born in Lebanon in January, 1947. Six weeks later, my father, who had become head of counterintelligence in the Middle East for the Central Intelligence Group, died in a mysterious plane crash following a top-secret visit to Saudi Arabia.

18. *The Minnesota Independent*, September 3, 2008, and September 20, 2008, which contains a list of journalists arrested and their affiliations.

19. The resolution read in whole: "Shall the Selectboard instruct the Town Attorney to draft indictments against President Bush and Vice President Cheney for crimes against our Constitution, and publish said indictments for consideration by

other municipalities? And shall it be the law of the Town of Brattleboro that the Brattleboro Police, pursuant to the above-mentioned indictments, arrest and detain George Bush and Richard Cheney in Brattleboro if they are not duly impeached, and extradite them to other authorities that may reasonably contend to prosecute them?" See *Scoop Independent News*, March 5, 2008, and the *Rutland Herald*, March 5, 2008.

20. Since our conversation, Vermont once again became a civil-rights trailblazer. In early April, Vermont became the first state whose legislature passed same-sex marriage, overriding Republican Governor Jim Douglas's veto. Other states that have same-sex marriage achieved it through court decisions, not the vote of an entire legislature.

21. We would discover, from conversations with friends, that many Vermonters do the same thing when they return to their home state: They literally burst into cheers.

22. I would later do some research on Coolidge's statement. Historical accounts focus only on the "brave Vermont" part of President Coolidge's tribute to his home state, which he visited for the first time after the state had been hit by a devastating flood in 1927. Coolidge was reportedly moved by Vermonters' ability to get back on their feet. But why, at this very time, did he refer to Vermont as a kind of last holdout for liberty? I have yet to find the answer, other than his generalized belief in Vermonters' love of democracy.

23. Bugliosi, *Prosecution*, p. 54–56.

24. Ibid., p. 65.

25. Ibid., p. 260.

26. Ibid., p. 261.

27. Ibid., p. 65.

28. Technically, Bush didn't dodge the draft, although he dodged combat, and he failed to complete his active-duty military obligation.

29. Bugliosi, *Prosecution*, p. 38.

30. As a trial lawyer, Bugliosi prides himself in his immense preparation. He believes that this is one thing that separates him from other prosecutors. He always gets deeply engaged in the investigation and preparation of a case. It's how he got tapped to be lead prosecutor in the Manson case that made him famous.

31. In his closing arguments in the trial, Bugliosi began by stating quite simply that "while the evidence at this trial shows that Charles Manson was the leader of the conspiracy to commit these murders, there is no evidence that he actually personally killed any of the seven victims in this case. However, the joint responsibility rule of conspiracy makes him guilty of all seven murders."

32. Bugliosi devotes four pages in a footnote to why Saddam Hussein did not want to attack the United States. See pp. 259–263.

33. Vermont is one of four states (the others being New York, Virginia, and California) that offers the Law Office Study Program.

34. *State v. Fournier*, 68 Vt. 262, was decided in 1868.

35. See, for instance, "Truthfulness vs. Bearing False Witness (Lying)" (www.journal33. org/lovenbr/truth.htm), which says "The original commandment, 'Do not bear false witness against your neighbor' (Exodus 20:16, Deuteronomy 5:20) focuses on a specific aspect of lying and is directly applicable to the testimony a person might

give in court. Other scripture passages focus on the general (and all-encompassing) principle, 'Do Not Lie' (e.g., Leviticus 19:11, Colossians 3:9)."

36. Vermont Yankee is showing its age. In the two years since 2007, the plant has suffered one public-relations nightmare after another, beginning with a clandestine photo released to the press of the collapse of one of its two cooling towers in August, 2007. The picture of water gushing out of a giant hole in the side of the cooling tower illustrated the plant's fragile condition. Subsequently, VY workers had to be evacuated twice because of increased radiation levels. According to the Vermont Public Interest Research Group (VPIRG), "VY has 76 documented cracks in its steam dryer. There have been 3 fires in VY's transformer station. . . . VY's storage system for radioactive waste fuel is dangerously overcrowded. Because there is no viable waste storage solution, Entergy will be indefinitely storing its radioactive waste on the banks of the Connecticut River." See "Several Examples That Highlight the Need for VY's Closure" at www.vpirg.org/vy/index.php.

37. Some thirty-five groups and individuals sent a letter to Massachusetts Attorney General Martha Coakley on August 12, 2008, praising her for her "advocacy on behalf of public health and safety and environmental protection in the U.S. Nuclear Regulatory Commission's license renewal proceedings for the Pilgrim (Mass.) and Vermont Yankee plants." Their nine-page letter can be found at the Public Documents Room, Nuclear Regulatory Commission Library, Whiteflint, Maryland.

38. Louis Porter, "Four in Race for Attorney General," *Rutland Herald*, September 21, 2008.

39. The effects doctrine was spelled out in a U.S. Supreme Court case by Justice Oliver Wendell Holmes, who argued "Acts outside a [state's] jurisdiction, but intended to produce and producing detrimental effects within it, justify a state in punishing the cause of the harm as if he had been present at the effect, if the state should succeed in getting him within its power." See *Strassheim v. Daily*, 221 U.S. 280 (1910). See also Bugliosi, pp. 309–310.

40. *Outrage: The Five Reasons Why O.J. Simpson Got Away with Murder* (New York: Norton, 1996); *The Betrayal of America: How the Supreme Court Undermined the Constitution and Chose Our President* (New York: Nation Books, 2001); *Reclaiming History: The Assassination of John F. Kennedy* (New York: Norton, 2007).

41. In September, 2008, the Vermont Public Interest Research Group (VPIRG) filed a complaint with Attorney General Sorrell asking him to investigate ads put out by Entergy claiming that Vermont Yankee was "clean, safe, and reliable." The group accused Entergy of deceptive advertising, which falls under the AG's duty to investigate fraud. "Safe?" the group asked. "There have been numerous mishaps at Vermont Yankee over the past four years—a transformer fire in 2004, a collapse of one of the cooling towers in 2007, and leaks in another cooling tower this year, just to name a few. And given the radioactivity and other dangers inherent in nuclear-power generation, it's a stretch to call it safe." The *Brattleboro Reformer,* in an editorial, was doubtful that Sorrell would agree. "Despite VPIRG's objections, the ad campaign will probably not be shut down by Sorrell. The main points of the ads are debatable, but it would be a bit of a stretch to call the ads fraudulent. While

Sorrell said his office will take VPIRG's complaint seriously, he believes that the right answers will come out in political debate." *Brattleboro Reformer*, September 4, 2008. To my mind, this was just one more example of the attorney general's failure to "vigorously pursue" the health and safety concerns of Vermonters when it came to this dangerous nuclear power plant in their midst.

42. See Bugliosi, p. 308. "If Bush committed an act that constituted murder under both state and federal law, there would be concurrent jurisdiction to prosecute him, and, in the absence of a federal prosecution, the supremacy clause would not preclude any state court prosecution. The clause would only be applicable if both state and federal authorities wanted to prosecute him at the same time, in which case federal law would prevail . . . though the state could prosecute him after the federal prosecution concluded under the principle of dual sovereignty, which recognizes that the federal government as well as the individual states are separate sovereigns. As the court said in *United States v. Davis*, 'Under the well-established principle, a federal prosecution does not bar . . . a subsequent state prosecution of the same person for the same acts.' " Bugliosi goes on to anticipate what would happen if Bush, as a federal officer, tried to challenge his prosecution in a state court by seeking a writ of habeas corpus. "The writ would be denied unless he could prove that as president, he had a 'duty to do' the act (i.e., take this nation to war) and that his conduct was 'necessary and proper' [his citations omitted]. . . . If the facts are as I believe them to be, this he could not possibly do, and the federal court would not issue the writ."

43. It would take Alexander and other Bugliosi supporters another five months to raise the money, but they succeeded, and the book is now in the hands of every DA in every county where a soldier has died.

44. My Web site is www.PeoplevBush.com.

45. Ralph Lopez, *Truth in the Age of Bushism* (Boston: Sterling Press, 2008).

46. Here's how Kristina responded to one detractor, who asked her to fervently remember that Bush was keeping us safe from future 9/11s. "I often tell my son, a U.S. Marine, how proud I am that he is serving our country and willing to die for it. I also tell him how fervently I hope that he never finds himself in the position of seeing his buddies or innocent civilians die in a war based on lies. If you have a child in the military, I hope the same for him or her. Meanwhile, the United States is not more safe. The Bush administration not only did not protect Americans from 9/11 even though the president was warned, the administration has done more to create terrorism and hatred against America and Americans than virtually any other administration in modern history. There was no al Qaeda in Iraq before the U.S. invasion. Now, the entire world is more dangerous for American citizens, and here at home our civil rights and privacy have been seriously curbed. . . . "

47. Only months after my campaign did I hear that a small group of impeachment activists had met with Symington in her office before the vote, and that they had come away believing that she had been under a lot of pressure to vote the resolution down and that that pressure had come from Senator Leahy. When I subsequently interviewed Symington about any pressure from Leahy, she strongly denied it.

48. The fact that surviving relatives of lost soldiers in Iraq seldom spoke up came as

no surprise to me. Covering the Iran hostage crisis in 1979, I had found only three "hostage families" related to the fifty-three Americans held hostage who were willing to talk to reporters about their ordeal while awaiting their loved ones' release. The State Department had set up an organization called the Family Liaison Action Groups (FLAG), whose job it was to keep the affected families from talking to the press, or from talking to each other outside of official channels. (See my article "Suffering in Silence," *The Nation*, December 13, 1980.) I subsequently learned, as you will read in Chapter Six on the 9/11 widows from New Jersey (the so-called Jersey Girls), that they, too, were subjected to pressure from "liaison" contacts who tried to keep survivors in line with the official explanation of 9/11.

49. "Cindy Sheehan Makes It on the Ballot," The Huffington Post, August 8, 2008.

50. Author's interview with Cindy Sheehan, April 10, 2009.

51. "Pelosi Defeats Sheehan to Win 12th Term," *San Francisco Chronicle*, November 5, 2008.

52. I subsequently confirmed this with both Cindy Sheehan and Cynthia Papermaster.

53. The landmark civil case is *Nixon v. Fitzgerald*, 457 U.S. 731 (1982). The Supreme Court, in a 5–4 decision, ruled that the president is entitled to absolute immunity from liability for civil damages based on his official acts. The court made it clear that the president is not immune from *criminal* charges stemming from his official (or unofficial) acts while in office. As Chief Justice Burger stated in a concurring opinion, "It strains the meaning of the words used to say this places a President above the law.' The dissents are wide of the mark to the extent that they imply that the Court today recognizes sweeping immunity for a President for all acts. The Court does no such thing. The immunity is limited to civil damage claims." *United States v. Nixon*, 418 U. S. 683 (1974).

54. Interview with Vincent Bugliosi, January, 2009. Bugliosi explained that he subsequently learned from Congressman Walter Jones (a conservative Republican appalled by Bush's behavior) that he planned to introduce a bill into Congress, with Fein's help, that would make it a crime to take the nation to war under false pretenses. "I told him that was a bad idea," Bugliosi explained. "If you do that, you in effect are stipulating that there was no law already on the books to go after Bush. We have to prosecute Bush, Cheney, and Rice for murder, and here you are in effect saying we can't because there was no law at the time prohibiting what he did. But there was. It's the murder statute on the books in every state of the union and, federally, under Section 1111 (a) of Title 18 of the U.S. Code." Jones came back and said, "We could make the law retroactive." Bugliosi said "You can't do that under the ex post facto clause of the U.S. Constitution. You can't make conduct a crime which, at the time it was committed, was not a crime."

55. Debbie Hagan, *Against the Tide: How One Law School Defied the Odds* (Andover, MA: Doukathsan Press, 2008) and Lawrence Velvel, *Thine Alabaster Cities Gleam: A Slightly Fictionalized Memoir of a Career in the Last Half of the Twentieth Century* (Andover, MA: Doukathsan Press, 2007). As he wrote in the introduction of his memoir, "The version of the American Dream illustrated by Abraham Lincoln is the one that the protagonists of my story absorbed as children. Yet as they got

older . . . they learned that . . . this version was largely fictive, largely fantasy." What Lincoln referred to as the "race of life" did not reward the talented and hardworking, he wrote, nor those who tried to help people, but the greedy, the self-absorbed, the "thoroughly dishonest and the fraudulent." Small wonder, he added, that "federal judges refused to do their duty, the Congressmen refused to do theirs, that universities uncaringly failed to educate, that businesses lied and cheated, that law firms did the same."

56. "The Torture Team," *The New York Times*, December 18, 2009.

57. "How to Make Terrorists Talk," *Time*, June 8, 2009.

58. ABC News, December 16, 2008. See abcnews.go.com/Politics/story?id=6464697&page=1 and The Huffington Post, December 16, 2008.

59. "Holder Assures GOP on Prosecution," *The Washington Times*, January 28, 2009.

60. *Talking Points Memo*, The Center on Law and Security, NYU School of Law, January 28, 2009.

61. Bush's Justice Department was wracked with controversy and for good reason: It was here, and particularly in the Office of Legal Counsel, where highly conservative lawyers created one of the worst constitutional crises in the nation's history, rewriting the nation's laws to suit the executive's ambitions at the expense of the Bill of Rights. Gradually, word would get out about their actions, causing Attorney General John Ashcroft, the drafter of the Patriot Act, to retire after Bush's first term. His replacement, White House Counsel Alberto Gonzales, was forced to resign in 2007, leaving Attorney General Mukasey to try to mend the tattered reputation of the DOJ as best he could. All of this is explained in greater detail in Chapter Six.

62. Jason Leopold, Consortium News, December 6, 2008.

63. *Reigning in the Imperial Presidency* [hereinafter The Conyers Report] is available by contacting the House Judiciary Committee or downloading the voluminous report from the Judiciary Committee's Web site.

64. Jason Leopold (*The Public Record*), Consortium News, January 7, 2009. Fascinatingly, the mainstream press by and large ignored Conyers' call for a blue-ribbon commission, and it was only alternative media like Daily Kos, TPMMuckraker, and Consortium News that widely covered his proposed commission and the *Imperial Presidency* report.

65. Jason Leopold, "Mukasey's Nixon Defense of Bush," Consortium News, December 8, 2008.

66. The Republicans on the committee had actually wanted to make the Iran-Contra report public, believing that it would exonerate President Ronald Reagan from growing accusations that he had encouraged the secret sale of arms to Iran in order to obtain revenues to finance the CIA's secret support of Contra rebels against the Nicaraguan government. Leahy would later explain that his motive for releasing the document was to show that the draft report was full of holes and therefore not ready for release.

67. "Iran-Contra Hearings: Senator Leahy Says He Leaked Report of Panel," *The New York Times*, July 29, 1987.

68. Yoo and Bybee had already become household words, at least among the

intelligentsia, with the publication of Jane Mayer's book, *The Dark* Side, in July, 2008. Mayer detailed their legal defense of torture, especially their "torture memo" of August, 2002, which made it easier for CIA operatives to torture detainees based on new definitions of what constituted torture. See Mayer, *The Dark Side* (New York: Doubleday, 2008), pp. 151–154.

69. *Democracy Now,* interview with Michael Ratner, February 5, 2009.

70. *Democracy Now*, Interview with Matthew Alexander and Scott Horton, December 3, 2008.

71. Robert Parry, "Jail All of Bush's Lawyers," Consortium News, February 3, 2009.

72. The key torture memos, including this one, can be found in the "Accountability" section of the ACLU Web site. See "Send Evidence of Torture to the DOJ, Demand Accountability Now," www.aclu.org/accountability/action.html.

73. I would subsequently hear from several people that they had gladly signed Leahy's petition because they wanted something to be done but were then turned off when they read that he had highlighted his call for a truth commission in his first campaign fund-raising letter for his reelection race of 2010. One of my most credible sources in Washington, D.C., suggested to me from the outset that Leahy's truth commission was never going to go anywhere and was likely designed to keep his name in lights. I found that hard to believe, although his true intentions for his truth commission— how deep and how high up would it go and what was his idea of accountability?— continued to perplex me, as will be shown in this and later chapters.

74. John Nichols, *The Genius of Impeachment: The Founders' Cure for Royalism* (New York: The New Press, 2006), pp. 165–166.

75. The resolution, as submitted and resoundingly passed in DeWalt's town of Newfane, read:

Whereas George W. Bush has:

1. Misled the nation about Iraq's weapons of mass destruction;

2. Misled the nation about ties between Iraq and Al Quaeda;

3. Used these falsehoods to lead our nation into war unsupported by international law;

4. Not told the truth about American policy with respect to the use of torture; and

5. Has directed the government to engage in domestic spying, in direct contravention of U.S. law.

Therefore, the voters of the town of Newfane ask that our representative to the U.S. House of Representatives file articles of impeachment to remove him from office.

For more, see "Vermont Towns Vote to Impeach," www.thenation.com/blogs/thebeat/66746.

76. Adrienne Kinne would later reveal on ABC News that as part of her job as U.S. Army Reserves Arab linguist assigned to a special military program at the NSA's Back Hall at Fort Gordon between November 2001 and 2003 she eavesdropped on phone calls from "everyday, average, ordinary Americans who happened to be in the Middle East." She described the conversations as "personal, private things with Americans who are not in any way, shape, or form associated with anything to do with terrorism." See "Inside Account of U.S. Eavesdropping," ABCnews.com, October 9, 2009. Previously, on May 15, 2008, Kinne told *Democracy Now* (www.democracynow.

org) in an exclusive interview that she had eavesdropped on humanitarian-aid organizations, journalists, and non-governmental organizations (NGOs).

77. Cindy Sheehan, "Vermont: Land of Hope," Opednews.com, March 6, 2007.

78. Dan DeWalt, "Changes Begin in Vermont," The Huffington Post, April 30, 2007.

79. Dan DeWalt, "Support John Nirenberg's March in My Name," Opednews.com, December 3, 2007. Nirenberg's Web site, MarchinMyName.org, has details about why he decided to walk and anecdotes about the people he met along the way. "I was born in the midst of the Nuremberg Trials," he writes. "I grew up conscious of that place as both the beginning of the hate and violence that destroyed all of Europe and the trials that confirmed a powerful moral sense of what is acceptable and unacceptable even in the depths of war." Among his observations: "First, Washington is under a thick miasma of fear and intimidation that emanates from the White House, but is perpetuated and enforced by robotic, obstructionist, staunchly ideological, extremist, Republican party members uninterested in real-people problems or the Constitutional issues raised by the Bush/Cheney administration. But the Democrats have been the enablers, fearful of standing up for what they know is right but shrink from facing. Second, the public sees what is going on and knows that impeachable acts have been committed (and new ones, such as the executive treaty with Iraq bypassing the Senate, are being committed)—even without much mainstream mention of the issues or impeachment."

80. See endnote 19 for the wording of the resolution.

   USA Today and many other newspapers reproduced a statement from town officials posted on their Web site amid all the hullabaloo about the petition:

   "On January 25 the Town Clerk's office received a petition from Brattleboro resident Kurt Daims. Per Town Charter, a petition containing signatures from 5% of Brattleboro voters can be placed on the ballot for a Town-wide vote. Mr. Daims' petition did contain the required number of signatures. At a meeting on January 25, the Brattleboro Selectboard voted 3-2 to place the petition on the ballot. Reasons given by Board members voting in the affirmative centered on the belief that if a petition contained the required signatures, the voters should have the opportunity to vote on the matter. Reasons given by Board members voting on the dissent centered on the belief that articles outside the scope and authority of the Town should not go before the voters of the Town. The Brattleboro Town Attorney has stated that the petition has no legal standing, as the Town Attorney has no authority to write an indictment and the Town Police Department has no authority to attempt an arrest of the President of the United States.

   "The Town will vote on the article on March 4."

   See "Vt. Town Hammered over Petition to Arrest, Prosecute Bush and Cheney," *USA Today*, January 30, 2008.

81. These and other memos can be viewed on the Web site of the ACLU at www.aclu. org.

82. Glenn Greenwald, "The Newly Released Secret Memos of the Bush administration," Salon.com, March 3, 2009.

83. Here's an excerpt of my testimony, which I included in an article I wrote for the

Vermont Bar Journal in the summer of 2005:

> Government secrecy removes accountability, and prevents elected
> leaders from making wise decisions on behalf of their constituents.
> It deters the executive branch from carrying out its law-mandated
> duties in an accountable, professional manner. It reduces us all to
> being helpless bystanders, unable to intervene if we detect mistakes in
> policy or intelligence gathering.

Little did I know that I would taking the issue of accountability to a whole new level three years later.

84. See my essay "War on Terror and the Great Game for Oil: How the Media Missed the Context," in *Into the Buzzsaw: Leading Journalists Expose the Myth of a Free Press* (Ed: Kristina Borjesson) (Amherst, NY: Prometheus, 2002), paperback edition, p. 85.

85. William Raspberry, *The Washington Post*, cited in *Into the Buzzsaw*, p. 85. My essay includes several other critiques from Terry McDermott of the *Los Angeles Times* and Gail Sheehy, who interviewed 9/11 widows for her book *Middletown, America*.

86. Letter from the four September 11 advocates (Jersey Girls) to Senator Leahy, March, 2009.

87. In June, 1949—almost two years after my father's plane crash in Ethiopia—a B-29 bomber with three civilians on board crashed shortly after takeoff from South Florida to test secret navigational equipment. Everyone was killed. The surviving families tried in vain to get the official accident report, and in 1953 the U.S. Supreme Court sided with the government, ruling that the accident report had to remain classified based on national security, citing the "state secrets" privilege. Since that decision, the privilege has been used to justify a whole host of abuses, from refusing to turn over documents pursuant to FOIA requests to allowing detainees to remain imprisoned without due process. The ordeal of the families is described in the book *Claim of Privilege: A Mysterious Plane Crash, a Landmark Supreme Court Case, and the Rise of State Secrets*. Ironically, when the aggrieved families finally got the accident report, they learned there were no secrets to hide—but rather, simply outright negligence.

88. Edmonds, a language specialist fluent in Turkish, Persian (Farsi), and Azerbaijani, had joined the FBI shortly after 9/11 thinking it was her patriotic duty to use her language skills in service of the country. But after she reported on FBI incompetence to superiors, she was fired. And when she offered to testify in a 9/11 class-action suit brought by 700 families against Saudi banks, charitable organizations, and companies (since dismissed), her deposition was barred on the basis of state secrets. For more information, see www.independent.co.uk/.../i-saw-papers-that-show-us-knew-alqaida-would-attack-cities-with-aeroplanes-558612.html.

89. It became clear to them that there was a concerted effort to ridicule the "complainers" and divide the families and isolate them from one another. "We always had to go through a 'liaison,'" Lori muttered bitterly. Liaison? That rang a chord with me. Back in December, 1980, I had written an article for *The Nation* titled "Suffering in Silence" about the so-called hostage families—families of diplomats and members of the armed services seized by Iranian militants and held hostage in the American embassy in Tehran for 444 days—and how they were being treated

by the State Department. Back then, the government had created a "Family Liaison Action Group" (FLAG), purportedly a "patriotic self-help group" to help families overcome their feelings of isolation. In fact, it played just the opposite role, muzzling dissent among family members who began to ask too many questions and criticize the government about its dealings with the Iranian hostage takers. FLAG had one overarching purpose: to make sure that families all spoke with one voice.

90. Author's interview with Martha Hennessy, July 30, 2009.

91. In an interview of Michael Ratner by Naomi Wolf posted on Alternet on March 26, 2009, she asked Ratner if the DOJ memos written by John Yoo provided evidence of treasonous behavior. Answered Ratner: "I do think that a plan to control the military, use it in the United States contrary to law and the Constitution and employ it to levy a war or takeover that eliminates the democratic institutions of the country constitutes treason, even if done under the president of the United States."

92. Jonathan Mahler, "After the Imperial Presidency," *The New York Times Magazine*, November 7, 2008.

93. Ibid.

94. Reported *Time*: "Democrats had targeted Jeffords as a possible party switcher practically from the day he came to Congress 26 years ago. [Senator Tom] Daschle, a former Air Force intelligence officer, knew that spymasters don't have a chance of bagging a high-value defector unless he is eager to defect. Even then, he has to be slowly and carefully cultivated. By last month, Jeffords seemed ready to come over. His disenchantment with the Republican Party had been building for months." For Jeffords, it was a matter of principle. "I became a Republican," Jeffords told the press in Vermont the following day "not because I was born into the party but because of the kind of fundamental principles Republicans stood for—moderation, tolerance, fiscal responsibility. Our party was the party of Lincoln," he said, but now that it was under the control of ultraconservatives, "it has become a struggle for our leaders to deal with me and for me to deal with them." Douglas Waller, "How Jeffords Got Away," *Time*, May 27, 2001.

95. Jay Nordlinger, "The Nastiest Democrat," *National Review*, July 9, 2001.

96. The letters were sent from New Jersey and postmarked October 9. The Daschle letter was opened by an aide on October 15; the unopened Leahy letter was discovered in an impounded mail bag on November 16.

Seven years later, in September, 2008, the Senate Judiciary Committee held hearings on the FBI's investigation of the anthrax attacks following the death "by suicide" of the government's sole suspect, Dr. Bruce Ivans. Senator Leahy told FBI Director Robert Mueller flat out that he did not believe Ivans was the sole person responsible for the anthrax attacks, which had killed five and sickened seventeen people. "If he is the one who sent the letter, I do not believe in any way, shape or manner that he is the only person involved in this attack on Congress and the American people. I do not believe that at all," Leahy said, adding, "I believe there are others involved, either as accessories before or accessories after the fact. I believe that there are others out there, I believe there are others who could be charged with murder. I just want you to know how I feel about it, as one of the people who was aimed at in the attack." *USA Today,* September 17, 2008.

97. The June 8, 2004, hearings were prompted by a revelation the day before that a March, 2003, legal memorandum had been drawn up by civilian and military lawyers for Defense Secretary Rumsfeld, reportedly arguing that when the nation's security was at stake the president wasn't bound by laws or treaties outlawing torture. As reported by the MacNeil/Lehrer Report of June 8, "the 2003 memo was based in part on two earlier memos prepared in 2002 by Justice Department lawyers."

98. Senator Patrick Leahy, "Oversight of the USA Patriot Act," statement for the U.S. Senate Committee on the Judiciary, April 5, 2005.

99. "Cheney Dismisses Critic with Obscenity," *The Washington Post,* June 25, 2004.

100. Chris Suellentrop, "Did Al Gonzales Say the President Can Authorize Torture?" Slate, January 6, 2005.

101. Interview with Lawrence Velvel, July 20, 2009.

102. Lawrence Velvel, *Thine Alabaster Cities Gleam.*

103. As Pyle noted, *New York Times* columnist Anthony Lewis was the first to utter the "mafia" indictment after he read some of the declassified OLC memos.

104. *Youngstown Sheet and Tube Co. v. Sawyer,* 343 U.S. 579 (1952), pp. 646, 653.

105. As for the OLC lawyers themselves, they apparently felt they were untouchable. Why shouldn't the creators of "golden shield" memos, which sought to immunize government officials from criminal prosecution, fall under the shield as well? As Jane Mayer points out, OLC memos have the weight of law, and when an OLC lawyer "issues an opinion on a policy matter, it typically requires the intervention of the attorney general or the president to reverse it" (Mayer, *The Dark Side,* p. 231). As long as Bush and his subservient attorneys general were in power, they had nothing to fear.

106. A "star chamber" is "any judicial or quasi-judicial action, trial, or hearing which so grossly violates standards of 'due process' that a party appearing in the proceedings (hearing or trial) is denied a fair hearing. The term comes from a large room with a ceiling decorated with stars in which secret hearings of the privy council and judges met to determine punishment for disobedience of the proclamations of King Henry VIII of Great Britain (1509–1547)" (http://legal-dictionary.thefreedictionary.com/).

107. Scott Horton, interviewed on *Democracy Now,* January 28, 2009.

108. Chris Pyle, *Getting Away with Torture* (Washington, D.C.: Potomac Books, 2009), p. 166.

109. For an in-depth analysis in the role of Congress on the issue of accountability during and after the Bush years, see David Swanson, *Daybreak: Undoing the Imperial Presidency and Forming a More Perfect Union* (New York: Seven Stories Press, 2009).

110. According to a 1998 report put out by the South African Center for the Study of Violence and Reconciliation, most of the several hundred surveyed victims of human rights abuses said that they did not feel the truth commission accomplished reconciliation between black and white communities, and that what was needed for reconciliation was justice, not an alternative to justice.

111. Interview with Bruce Marshall, September 10, 2009.

112. Peter Freyne, "The Rutland Massacre," *Seven Days*, April 12, 2006.

113. *Boumediene v. Bush*, 553 U.S. (2008).

114. See gtmoblog.blogspot.com.

115. Candace Gorman, The Huffington Post, January 11, 2007. Her regular blog is gtmoblog.blogspot.com.

116. Candace Gorman, July 25, 2009, gtmoblog.blogspot.com.

117. In 2008, Ratner published *The Trial of Donald Rumsfeld,* a "prosecution by book" of the former defense secretary. Since Congress, in all its investigative zeal, had steered clear of the top people who authorized the torture, and since the French and Germans had failed to arrest Rumsfeld for a case brought under universal jurisdiction by the CCR, he saw the book as the only way to make public the evidence of Rumsfeld's war crimes, of which he had plenty, including a document signed by the secretary of defense authorizing torture in contravention of the Geneva Conventions.

118. Michael Ratner and Ellen Ray, *Guantánamo: What the World Should Know* (White River Junction, VT: Chelsea Green, 2004), p. 12.

119. Ibid., pp. 18–19.

120. See the biography of John Brennan on WhoRunsGov.com, a Web site of *The Washington Post.*

121. Mark Ambinder, "The Rubicon of Indefinite Detention," *The Atlantic*, May 22, 2009. Adds Ambinder, "According to administration officials, Obama finds this outside pressure healthy and useful."

122. Glenn Greenwald, "There Are No Excuses for Ongoing Concealment of Torture Memos," Salon.com, April 6, 2009.

123. Ibid.

124. "Interrogation Memos Detail Harsh Methods of Interrogation," *The New York Times*, April 16, 2009.

125. The released August, 2002, memo by the OLC's Jay Bybee gave the green light to waterboarding al-Qaeda suspect Abu Zubaydah. This memo and the other three memos, written in 2005, found that waterboarding did not cause extreme mental or physical harm and therefore was not torture.

126. Mike Madden, "Obama Feels the Love of the CIA," Salon.com, April 21, 2009. Apart from the morale issue, Obama was a student of history. Perhaps he had learned that no president wants the CIA to turn against him. This was a lesson learned at great cost by two of his predecessors: John F. Kennedy and Richard Nixon. For a new analysis of the Kennedy assassination and Watergate, based on new information, see Russ Baker, *Family of Secrets* (New York: Bloomsbury, 2008), chapters 4–11.

127. Michael Ratner, "Granting Immunity Makes Obama Complicit" Michaelratner.com/blog, April 17, 2009.

128. As if to back up Horton's claim, the Senate Intelligence Committee produced a report on April 21 that revealed that military and intelligence officials had begun the torture program in December, 2001, well before the 2002 legal memoranda from the OLC. See "Senate Report: Torture Planning Preceded Prisoners' Capture, Legal Approval," *Democracy Now,* April 22, 2009,

129. Interview with Code Pink founder Medea Benjamin, July 19, 2009.

130. "Obama Won't Bar Inquiry, or Penalty, on Interrogations," April 22, 2009.

131. "Any Indictment of Interrogation Policy Makers Would Face Several Hurdles," *The New York Times,* April 22, 2009.

132. "Torture Report Could Be Trouble for Bush Lawyers," *Newsweek,* February 14, 2009. The OPR report was due to be released imminently. (By the time of this writing in mid-November, 2009, it still had not been released.)

133. "Obama Resisting Push for Interrogation Panel," *The New York Times,* April 24, 2009.

134. "Madoff Receives Maximum Sentence, 150 Years, for Big Ponzi Scheme," *The New York Times,* June 30, 2009.

135. Patrick Leahy on Face the Nation, April 26, 2009.

136. "Top U.S. Lawyer Warns of Deaths at Guantánamo," *The [London] Observer,* February 8, 2009.

137. Catholic News Service, April 28, 2009.

138. Author's interview with Martha Hennessy, July 31, 2009.

139. Author's interview with Debra Sweet, July 19, 2009.

140. *The Washington Post,* May 6, 2009.

141. The sad fate of both books is described in Jerry's chapter "The Price of Liberty," in *Into the Buzzsaw: Leading Journalists Expose the Myth of a Free Press.*

142. I first discovered what a powerful negative force sovereign immunity has become from suing the Office of Child Support in Vermont for gross negligence. This was a case in which this large government bureaucracy withheld over $3,000 in child support monies from my client, didn't tell her about it until she bitterly complained for months about nonreceipt of funds, prevented her from getting access to her records, failed to inform her of her ex's court appearances, lied to her—the list goes on and on. But after going all the way up to the Vermont Supreme Court—and, interestingly, facing off with the attorney general's office, which by law defends all cases against state agencies—I lost to the doctrine of sovereign immunity, as well as to some curious legal reasoning by justices on the Vermont Supreme Court who wrote that "Vermont's statutory scheme was not intended to benefit individual children and custodial parents, but was intended to benefit Vermont society as a whole." In other words, "Vermont law does not create a specific duty owed by OCS to any particular groups of persons" (*Powers v. OCS,* 173 Vt. 190, 2002).

143. I'm appealing an "attorney-client privilege defense" by the attorney general's office.

144. For more on this, read my article "The True Cost of Vermont Yankee," in the Barre-Montpelier *Times Argus,* March 1, 2009.

145. *Dictionary of British History,* 2004.

146. For more on this case, see the interview with Glenn Greenwald, "Obama Administration Claims 'Sovereign Immunity' in Attempt to Dismiss Lawsuit Against NSA" on *Democracy Now,* April 16, 2009.

147. Ibid.

148. Glenn Greenwald, "An Emerging Progressive Consensus on Obama's Executive Power and Secrecy Abuses," Salon.com, April 13, 2009.

149. The exact quote from Thomas Paine is this: "But where, say some, is the king of America? I'll tell you, friend, he reigns above, and doth not make havoc of mankind like the Royal Brute of Great Britain. . . . So far as we approve of monarchy, that in America the law is king."

150. Interview with Glenn Greenwald, July 27, 2009.

151. The actual machinations between competing powers to get control of Middle Eastern oil are well documented in such books as Daniel Yergin, *The Prize: The Epic Quest for Oil, Money & Power* (New York: Simon & Schuster, 1991); Anthony Cave Brown, *Oil, God, and Gold: The Story of Aramco and the Saudi Kings* (Boston: Houghton Mifflin, 1990); and Michael Klare, *Blood and Oil* (New York: Metropolitan Books, 2004).

152. Quoted in Dennett, "The War on Terror and the Great Game for Oil," *Into the Buzzsaw*, p. 75.

153. Daniel Yergin, *The Prize: The Epic Quest for Oil, Money & Power*, p. 183.

154. It's not a coincidence that the first strategic target for American soldiers invading Iraq was to seize control of Iraq's oil installations. Nor was it a coincidence, more recently, that upon withdrawal of American troops from the major cities of Iraq, that the Iraq government would open negotiations to major western oil companies to exploit its oil.

155. The Great Game for Oil began well over a century ago, just as oil was viewed as a cheaper and more effective replacement for coal as the world's major energy source. The Great Game is and has always been a deadly game of fierce competition among nations with imperial ambitions. In the still-relevant words of the U.S. ambassador to Turkey during World War II: "I have never seen such astounding intrigues and devilish ruses to get the oil." Why the intrigues? Because oil, ever since 1908, has been the fuel of choice for the world's militaries. By the 1930s the Great Game for oil would be a major factor in World War II. Says a government document from the period, "World War II is largely a war by and for oil. Petroleum is one of the most important weapons of modern military conflict. More than half of our military shipments to the war zones are petroleum. . . . But this war is not only a war by oil; it is also a struggle for oil. In the search for raw materials the have-not nations of the Axis were principally concerned with petroleum, and much of the strategy of all the campaigns so far has been determined by the need for oil."

156. Fleischer quoted in "The World: After Hussein, Controlling Iraq's Oil Wouldn't Be Simple," *The New York Times*, November 3, 2002.

157. "The Iraq War Was About Oil," *The [UK] Guardian*, June 4, 2003. According to this article, Wolfowitz's comments were made during an address to delegates at the Asian security summit in Singapore.

158. For a more in-depth analysis of Iraq's oil and the "pipeline politics" that went into the neocons' plans to seize it, see Dennett, "The War on Terror," *Into the Buzzsaw*, pp. 79–82.

159. "Israel's Pipe Dream: Getting Oil from Iraq," *St. Petersburg Times*, August 15, 2004. According to this report, Chalabi "began to slide from U.S. favor when it became apparent his Iraqi National Congress provided faulty intelligence on Iraq's alleged

weapons of mass destruction. A rival, Iyad Allawi, became Iraq's new interim prime minister and an arrest warrant issued last week [early August, 2004] accuses Chalabi of counterfeiting Iraqi currency."

160. "Iraq-to-Haifa Oil Pipeline Could Spur Economic Rebirth," *Jerusalem Times*, April 18, 2003.

161. Netanyahu's comments and other news commentary on the Iraq to Haifa pipeline can be found at portland.indymedia.org/en/2003/06/266769.shtml.

162. "Energy Security Challenges for Israel Following the Gaza War," *Journal of Energy Security*, February 10, 2009.

163. *Israel News*, June 14, 2009.

164. Ron Suskind, *The Price of Loyalty: George W. Bush, the White House and the Education of Paul O'Neill* (New York: Simon & Schuster, 2004), pp. 174–175.

165. To see the maps of the Iraqi oilfields, go to judicialwatch.org/Iraqi-oil-maps.shtml.

166. John Foster, "Afghanistan and the New Great Game," *Toronto Star*, August 12, 2009.

167. Mayer, p. 61.

168. Ratner, *The Trial of Donald Rumsfeld*, p. 15.

169. Chris Pyle, *Getting Away with Torture*, p. 9.

170. Quoted by Richard Clarke in *Against All Enemies: Inside America's War on Terror* (New York: Free Press, 2004), p. 24.

171. See Conyers' *Reigning in the Imperial Presidency*, p. 349, footnote 11, for the legislative history and text of this draft war resolution. According to Tom Daschle, the Senate majority leader, the Bush administration also sought war powers to be used inside the United States, "potentially," Daschle would later comment, "against American citizens. I could see no justification for Congress to accede to this extraordinary request for additional authority. I refused." In hindsight, according to the Conyers report, "it appears the Administration may also have been seeking this additional phrase to cite as congressional authorization for conducting warrantless surveillance inside the United States, without regard to the legal requirements of FISA" (The Foreign Intelligence Surveillance Act). And who were the targets of such anticipated *warrantless* surveillance? Not just suspected terrorists, but Americans protesting against the war in Iraq.

172. *United States v. Hamdi*, 542 U.S. 507, 568–9, 2004 (Scalia, J. dissenting).

173. Ratner and Ray, *Guantánamo*, p. 9. As Ratner points out, not all the people seized were on the battlefield. "Many were from Pakistan and the surrounding areas; many were in civilian clothes; many were taken in midnight raids that had nothing to do with the Taliban or with al Qaeda. And most of them were picked up not by US forces but by the Northern Alliance, a loose coalition in a small corner of Afghanistan whom the Taliban had been fighting to oust."

174. Frontline, "Cheney's Law" (PBS television broadcast), transcript available at www.pbs.org/wgbh/pages/frontline/cheney/etc/script.html.

175. Mayer, p. 81.

176. Ibid., p. 82.

177. Pyle, p. 16.

178. 10 U.S.C. Section 821 simply states that "jurisdiction of courts martial is not

exclusive" and that "provisions of this chapter conferring jurisdiction on courts martial do not deprive military commissions . . . of concurrent jurisdiction. . . . "

179. Conyers report, p. 79.

180. This order caught many powerful people by surprise: Secretary of State Colin Powell, National Security Adviser Condoleezza Rice, military lawyers, and Michael Chertoff, head of the Justice Department Criminal Division. Even Attorney General John Ashcroft had been left out of the loop when his subordinate, John Yoo, had written his secret legal memo of November 6, which effectively gave power over the military commissions to the Department of Defense instead of the Department of Justice (Mayer, p. 82).

181. Mayer, p. 89.

182. Gellman and Becker, "Angler—The Cheney Vice Presidency," *The Washington Post*, June 24, 2007.

183. William Safire, "Seizing Dictatorial Power," *The New York Times*, Nov. 15, 2001.

184. Pyle, *Getting Away with Torture*, p. 15.

185. Mayer, p. 105.

186. Mayer, p. 135.

187. According to Ray McGovern, an intelligence analyst under seven presidents, Dick Cheney effectively told CIA director George Tenet what he needed from Egyptian interrogators, and Tenet obliged. McGovern characterized their relationship this way: "Dick Cheney was the acting president. Dick Cheney told George Tenet what to do, and George Tenet said, 'Yes, sir. How high would you like me to jump? . . . You want ties between Iraq and al-Qaeda? I can do that. . . . We have a very friendly Egyptian intelligence service, which is now working on this fellow [Ibn al-Shaykh] al-Libi, who ran a training camp for al-Qaeda. And we think he knows about Saddam Hussein training al-Qaeda in chemical and biological weapons, and we've told the Egyptians that. We couldn't really get very much out of him, but I'll bet the Egyptians can." "Who's Afraid of the CIA?", Realnews.com, May 19, 2009.

188. Pyle, p. 17.

189. Ibid.

190. "Al-Libi, Whose False Confession under Torture Tied Iraq to Al-Qaeda, Found Dead in a Libyan Jail," The Huffington Post, May 11, 2009.

191. Pyle, p. 18.

192. Ibid., pp. 19–20.

193. See Conyers report on the Geneva Conventions, footnotes 422, 399.

194. Pyle, p. 24.

195. Ibid.

196. Memorandum from White House Counsel Alberto Gonzales to President Bush, "Application of the Geneva Convention on Prisoners of War to the Conflict with Al-Qaeda and the Taliban," January 25, 2002.

197. Memorandum from William Howard Taft to Alberto Gonzales, "Comments on Your Paper on the Geneva Conventions," February 2, 2002.

198. *The New York Times* had a slightly different take on the role of Bush's lawyers when it erupted into a national controversy in April, 2003:

The [Justice] Department's Office of Professional Responsibility . . . is believed to have obtained archived email messages from the time the memorandums were being drafted. If it turned out that the lawyers initially concluded that aspects of the proposed program would be illegal, then reversed that conclusion at the request of policy makers, then prosecutors could make a case that the officials knowingly broke the law. ("Any Indictment of Interrogation Policy Makers Would Face Several Hurdles," *The New York Times,* April 23, 2009)

199. Michael Haas, *George W. Bush, War Criminal?* (New York: Praeger, 2008), p. 4.
200. Memorandum from President Bush, "Humane Treatment of al Qaeda and Taliban Detainees," February 7, 2002, cited in footnote 448, Conyers report.
201. Quoted in Mayer, p. 143.
202. Pyle, p. 86.
203. Article 21 of the Third Geneva Conventions outlaws "close confinement."
204. Pyle, p. 87.
205. Torture, they wrote, required "the intent" to inflict suffering "equivalent in intensity to the pain accompanying serious physical injury, such as organ failure, impairment of bodily function, or even death." Mental suffering would have to be "of significant duration, e.g., lasting for months or years," resulting in "significant psychological harm."
206. Pyle, p. 88.
207. Ibid., p. 89.
208. Ibid., p. 90.
209. Mayer, p. 160.
210. Ron Suskind, *The Way of the World* (New York: HarperCollins, 2008), p. 361.
211. Ibid., p. 364.
212. Suskind interviewed on *Democracy Now,* August 13, 2008.
213. Suskind, p. 378.
214. Mayer, pp. 271–281.
215. Ibid., p. 135.
216. Mayer, p. 143.
217. Author's interview with Debra Sweet, July, 2009.
218. My Web site, www. peoplevbush.com, provides links to the photos.
219. Ratner and Ray, *Guantánamo,* p. 7.
220. Glenn Greenwald, Salon.com, April 20, 2009.
221. Jonathan Turley, May 14, 2009.
222. Reported by the BBC on May 14, 2009. For a transcript, see news.bbc.co.uk/2/hi/8048774.stm.
223. Glenn Greenwald, Salon.com, May 19, 2009.
224. Human-rights lawyers were irritated, for instance, with Obama's repeating Bush's claims that only a "few bad apples" were responsible for the torture—when, in fact, recently released memos had indicated that the authorization for the torture went to the highest levels and the implementation of the torture was pervasive. Yet on May 13, Obama told the press that "the publication of these photos would not add any

additional benefit to our understanding of what was carried out in the past by *a small number of individuals*" (emphasis added). See "Obama Moves to Prevent Release of Torture Photos," *Los Angeles Times,* May 14, 2009.

225. This vet also described his fellow vets' frustration in seeking accountability from members of Congress. "We have followed every peaceful avenue," he said. "We have petitioned Congress. We met with John Conyers as vets, begging him to implement the Constitution. There's never been a more thorough case for impeachment. But once we realized that Congress won't impeach, we'll seek prosecution." He said he loved what Vincent Bugliosi did by writing his book. "He's a serious man. He said 'I don't have time for frivolous pursuits. If I didn't think I had a rock-solid case, I wouldn't pursue it.'"

226. Rachel Maddow Show, NBC, May 20, 2009.

227. Debra Sweet, "Who Will Step out Boldly?" www.worldcantwait.net/, May 24, 2009.

228. Code Pink Alert, www.codepink.org, April 17, 2009.

229. Author's interview with Medea Benjamin, July, 2009.

230. *The New York Times,* July 12, 2008; multichannelnews.com.

231. See, for example, the hostility between Dick Cheney and Donald Rumsfeld on the one hand, and that of Nelson Rockefeller, which exploded when they convinced Ford to drop Rockefeller as his running mate. Our book also described the origin of Southern conservative hatred of the Eastern establishment, reflected in the recent right-wing, evangelical drift of the Republican Party. John D. Rockefeller, Sr.'s "ruthlessness in the new oil business," we wrote, "had earned him the fear of small businessmen across the nation. The rebates he forced on railroads, accounting for at least some of the higher freight charges the railroads imposed as compensation on everything from grain to furniture, had stirred the ire of populist farmers for over half a century. From these farmers had come the greatest political challenge to the new eastern wealth Rockefeller represented, a giant rural movement [fed by] Fundamentalist preachers of the literal Bible." By the 1960s, the movement embraced not only small farmers and businesses, but also independent oilmen who tried—and all too often failed—to compete with the oil majors in securing major fields. Their movement was led by Senator Barry Goldwater of Arizona, Richard Nixon and Ronald Reagan of California—and George H. W. Bush of Texas (Colby and Dennett, *Thy Will Be Done,* pp. 765–767).

232. Colby and Dennett, *Thy Will Be Done,* p. 335. See also our chart on p. 338 showing how Rockefeller forces influenced Kennedy's foreign-policy and national-security strategies.

233. For more on the Trilateral Commission, see Samuel P. Huntington et al., *The Crisis of Democracy: Report on the Governability of Democracies to the Trilateral Commission* (New York: New York University Press, 1975); Holly Sklar, *Trilateralism: The Trilateral Commission and Elite Planning for World Management* (Cambridge: South End Press, 1980); and Stephen Gill, *American Hegemony and the Trilateral Commission* (Cambridge: Cambridge University Press, 1990).

234. Henry Kissinger quoted on MSNBC, January 6, 2009.

235. "The Project on National Security Reform Praises the Selection of Guiding Coalition Members . . . Blair and Jones . . . to Serve in Obama Administration," January 9, 2009.

236. Pilger finished his piece by pointing out that "Lawrence Summers, Obama's principal economic adviser, is throwing $3 trillion at the same banks that paid him more than $8 million last year, including $135,000 for one speech. Change you can believe in."

237. Chris Pyle, *Getting Away with Torture*, pp. 247–248.

238. "Garzón Investigation Reveals Abuse Suffered by Detainees," Wsws.org, May 9, 2009.

239. "Spanish Judge Orders New Guantánamo Probe," Associated Press, April 29, 2009.

240. "Spanish Judge Opens Guantánamo Investigation," *The Christian Science Monitor*, April 30, 2009.

241. Ibid.

242. Jeremy Scahill, "Little Known Military Thug Squad Still Brutalizing Prisoners at Gitmo under Obama," AlterNet.org, May 15, 2009.

243. John Burns, "Britain's Iraq Inquiry Opens With a Vow to Be Rigorous," *The New York Times*, July 30, 2009.

244. Philippe Sands, "The Iraq Inquiry Must Be Transparent," *The Observer*, June 21, 2009.

245. Mark Danner, "The Red Cross Torture Report: What It Means," *The New York Review of Books*, April 30, 2009.

246. Christopher Pyle, on *Democracy Now*, July 29, 2009.

247. For more, go to their Web site at nrcat.org.

248. For more, go to soaw.org.

249. "Military Coup by SOA Graduates in Honduras Shines Spotlight on Controversial U.S. Military Training School," SOA Watch, Soa.org, July 6, 2009.

250. For the full story of how John Walker Lindh got involved with the then-American-backed Taliban in fighting a civil war against the Russian-backed Northern Alliance in northern Afghanistan, see Amy Goodman's exclusive interview with his parents on *Democracy Now*, July 31, 2009.

251. For excerpts of her book, see Radack's Web site, patriotictruthteller.net.

252. Diane Wilson's book, *An Unreasonable Woman* (White River Junction, VT: Chelsea Green, 2005), is an extraordinary tale of the difference one woman can make in a struggle for justice.

253. See Swanson's book, *Daybreak: Undoing the Imperial Presidency and Forming a More Perfect Union* (New York, NY: Seven Stories Press, 2009), p. 277, for more information on the origins of After Downing Street.

254. David Swanson, "Why Do We Torture Detainees," Afterdowningstreet.com, April 28, 2009.

255. Author's interview with attorney Ben Davis, August, 7, 2009.

256. Lawrence Velvel, "To Whom It May Concern," letter provided to the author and Vincent Bugliosi, September 22, 2008.

257. Cindy's book is titled *Myth America: 10 Greatest Myths of the Robber Class and the Case for Revolution*.

258. "Anti-War Activist Cindy Sheehan Brings Bush Protest to North Dallas," *The Dallas Morning News*, June 9, 2009.

259. Two books are essential reading for understanding the background to our current war in Afghanistan: Ahmed Rashid's *Taliban: Militant Islam, Oil and Fundamentalism in Central Asia* (New Haven: Yale University Press, 2000) and Paul Fitzgerald and

Elizabeth Gould, *Invisible History: Afghanistan's Untold Story* (Berkeley: City Lights, 2009).

260. See afghanistan.phrblog.org.

261. *Newsweek*, July 11, 2009.

262. Salon.com, July 16, 2009.

263. Author's interview with Glenn Greenwald, July, 2009.

264. *Standing Up to the Madness* is the title of Amy Goodman's new book, coauthored with her brother, David Goodman.

265. With regard to Watergate, there is a growing body of evidence that Nixon, for all his abuses of power, was actually overthrown by a silent coup of even more powerful and abusive people who wanted control of the presidency. See Russ Baker, *Family of Secrets*.

266. For Garry Davis's historic struggle, see his Web site, www.worldgovernment.org.

267. Quoted in *Time*, August 10, 2009.

268. Ibid.

Katherine Vose

Author and attorney Charlotte Dennett has been practicing law since 1997 with an emphasis on personal-injury litigation and suing the government under the Freedom of Information Act. She's also been a reporter in the Middle East and is the coauthor with her husband, Gerard Colby, of *Thy Will Be Done. The Conquest of the Amazon: Nelson Rockefeller* and *Evangelism in the Age of Oil.* She and her husband live in Cambridge, Vermont.

INDEX

Abu Ghraib, 136–37, 212
accountability movement, 2, 116, 131, 145, 150, 193, 195, 203, 204, 236–37. *See also* Bush, George W., proposed impeachment of; murder, prosecution of Bush for; *specific organizations and specific individuals*
   equality under the law, 159–60
   lawyer-activists in, 129
   Leahy meeting (*See* Leahy, Patrick)
   Obama's election, effect of, 153
   "100 Days" campaign, 115, 138, 151–53
   special prosecutor, petition for, 146–47
   torture memos, release of, 142
   truth commissions, response to, 100
   2008 election, effect of, 228
activists, Bush-era investigation of, 215–17, 219
Addington, David, 130, 167–70, 172, 176, 209
Afghanistan, 232
   Obama's position on, 86, 195–96, 198, 201
   oil/gas pipelines through, 167
   prisoners, treatment of, 130–31, 140, 161, 171–78, 212, 232–34 (*See also* torture)
   U.S. invasion of, 171
   war crimes, mass graves indicating, 232–34
aggressive war, crime of, 229–30
Alexander, Bob, 65–66
Alexander, Matthew, 96–97
Allen, Ramona, 194
al-Libi, Ibn al-Shaykh, 174, 183–84
al-Qaeda, 140, 176–78, 222
al-Qurani, Mohammed, 208
American Civil Liberties Union (ACLU), 154–55, 189, 193, 210–13, 216, 245
   FOIA requests, 131, 141
   Jawad detention, challenge to, 189
   special prosecutor, support for, 133, 146–47
   torture memos, position on, 141, 144
anticipatory self-defense, 182

Arar, Maher, 124–25, 141
Arbiter, Lauri, 41
Arredondo, Carlos and Mélida, 77–78
Ashcroft, John, 121–22, 173, 184, 221–22
Atkins, Lindol, 37–38
Atta, Mohamed, 183
Attorney General, Vermont, 2–3, 24–25, 60. *See also* Sorrell, William
Attorney General, Vermont, Dennett
   campaign for, 1–10, 18
   ads, 71–73, 81
   announcement, 1, 4, 42–43, 55–56
   Bugliosi's support for (*See* Bugliosi, Vincent)
   Bush murder prosecution as campaign plank, 3–9, 19, 25–26, 28–29, 42, 64–65, 70–71, 82
   campaign team, 65–70
   debates, 63–64, 70–71, 79
   donations, 11, 66, 71, 77, 82
   election results, 79–83
   husband, support of, 26–28, 42, 74
   loss of election, 9–10
   media coverage, 6–7, 56, 65–66, 75–78, 80, 83
   other candidates, 63 (*See also* Sorrell, William)
   platform, 60–62, 70–71
   security concerns, 40, 73–74
   Web site, 65–66
attorney general appointment, history of, 157–58

Bagram Airbase, 140, 212
Benjamin, Medea, 146, 195–97, 225
Betrayal of America, The, 6
bin Laden, Osama, 171, 174
Bond, Christopher, 90–91
Bonifaz, John C., 227, 247
Borjesson, Kristina, 29–30, 38, 43, 46, 55–56, 68–69, 71

Boumediene v. Bush, 137–39

Bourgeois, Roy, 219–20

Bovard, James, 155–56

Bradbury, Steven G., 143

Brattleboro, Vermont, 33, 44, 81, 104

Brennan, John, 141, 142, 143

British Iraq War investigation, 209–10

Brzezinski, Zbigniew, 200

Bugliosi, Vincent, 1–6, 9, 16–40, 96–98, 182, 185, 230–31. *See also Prosecution of George W. Bush for Murder, The*
  bolero music release, 62–63
  call to action of, 17
  Dennett campaign, support for, 8, 11, 57, 65, 69, 73–77, 80, 82–83
  Dennett candidacy announcement, at, 42–43, 55–56
  Dennett's introduction to, 29–34, 38–40
  House Judiciary Committee, testimony before, 34–37, 72
  impeachment, opinion on, 26
  on torture *vs.* murder prosecutions, 97

Bush, George W., 178–79. *See also* Bush, George W., proposed impeachment of; Iraq War; Office of Legal Counsel (OLC)
  extraordinary powers claimed for, 5, 167–80
  legal advice to, 91–92, 95–99, 122, 138–34 (*See also* Addington, David; Gonzales, Alberto; Office of Legal Counsel (OLC))
  military commissions created by, 172–74
  pardons, possibility of, 12–14
  prosecution of (*See* murder, prosecution of Bush for; war crimes, prosecution of Bush administration officials for)
  sovereign immunity, effect of, 156
  torture authorized by, 12, 86, 91–92, 184–85, 192 (*See also* torture memos)
  war, cavalier attitude toward, 47–48, 72

Bush, George W., proposed impeachment of, 32, 67–68, 228
  Congress, opinions in, 34, 78–79, 105–6
  Vermont, support in (*See* Vermont)

Bybee, Jay, 95, 96, 186, 195, 209, 226
  Iraq War, legal justification for, 95, 181, 185

judge, proposed impeachment as, 132
  torture memos written by, 98–99, 115, 130, 140, 143, 179–80

Center for Constitutional Rights (CCR), 95–96, 139–40, 188, 193, 208, 216, 245. *See also* "100 Days" campaign; Ratner, Michael

Cheney, Richard B. (Dick), 123, 133, 226
  Iraq War promoted by, 165, 166–68
  legal advice to, 91–92, 95–99 (*See also* Addington, David)
  Libby commutation, 13–15
  military commissions, support for, 172–73
  9/11 used by, 167–69
  Obama criticized by, 191, 192
  sovereign immunity, effect of, 156
  torture authorized by, 12, 86, 89–90, 95–96, 183–85, 192, 207 (*See also* torture memos)

Chilcot, John, 209–10

Church Committee, 119–20, 129

CIA, 108, 110, 218–19. *See also* extraordinary renditions
  Afghanistan mass graves, 232–34
  amnesty, Obama grant of, 144–45, 146
  Inspector General report, 209, 210
  special prosecutor investigation, 15, 204, 209, 213, 235
  torture by, 15–16, 89, 92, 131, 143–45, 174, 180, 186–87, 189, 202
  weapons of mass destruction, 181–83

civil liberties, suppression of, 121, 168, 215–17, 219. *See also* domestic spying

Clinton, Hillary, 200, 201

Code Pink, 145–47, 195–97, 225–26, 248

Colby, Gerard (Jerry), 19, 26–28, 40, 42, 74, 80, 155, 197

conspiracy to commit murder, 9, 51, 53–54

Conyers, John, 34, 36, 93–94, 134, 228

Crawford, Susan, 90

Daims, Kurt, 44, 81, 82, 104, 107, 116

Dalasio, Mathew, 152

Davis, Ben, 231

Davis, Garry, 237
D.C. Anti-War Network (DAWN), 215
debates, attorney general campaign, 63–64,
    70–71, 79
De la Vega, Elizabeth, 160
democracy, erosion of, 6, 202. *See also* civil
    liberties, suppression of
Democratic Party, 79, 86, 103, 105–7,
    148–50, 227–28
demonstrations, antiwar/antitorture, 41,
    117, 151–52, 186–88, 191, 195, 215–20,
    225–27. *See also* Code Pink; "100 Days"
    campaign
Dennett, Charlotte, 17–18, 110. *See also*
    Attorney General, Vermont, Dennett
    campaign for
De Pue, John, 222
DeWalt, Dan, 100–104, 106, 116–19
domestic spying, 122, 129, 158–59, 189,
    215–17, 219
Dostum, Abdul Rashid, 232–33
Dratel, Joshua, 58, 131–32
dual sovereignty, principle of, 64

effects doctrine, 9, 70
Elder, Pat, 215
Emanuel, Rahm, 145, 146, 190
*End of America, The: Letter of Warning to a
    Young Patriot*, 58
enemy combatants, 140
Entergy, 61, 157
equality under the law, 159–60. *See also*
    sovereign immunity
Executive Branch, power of, 126, 167–80
extraordinary renditions, 124–25, 141,
    212–13

Fager, Chuck, 227
false pretenses, Iraq War started under, 5–7,
    58, 101
    Bush prosecution based on, 20–21, 23,
        49, 50, 52–54
    House Judiciary Committee, Bugliosi
        testimony before, 35
    official white paper, lies in, 72
Farmer, John, 108

fascism, 57–59
FBI interrogations, 174, 222–24
Fein, Bruce, 82–83
Feingold, Russ, 134, 148, 216
FOIA. *See* Freedom of Information Act
    (FOIA)
Foreign Intelligence Surveillance Act, 122
Fredrickson, Caroline, 154–55
Freedom of Information Act (FOIA), 123,
    141, 196–97, 212–17
Freyne, Peter, 136
fusion centers, 215–17, 219

Garzón, Baltasar, 206–7, 209
Geneva Conventions, 140, 175–78, 222
German, Mike, 216
globalization, 200
Goldsmith, Jack, 167–68, 177, 190
Gonzales, Alberto, 118–19, 123–26, 130, 134,
    225–26
    Geneva Conventions memo, 140, 176–78
    investigation of, 209
    joint war resolution drafted by, 169
Goodman, Amy, 235–36
Gorman, Candace, 137–38
government surveillance. *See* domestic
    spying
Gradenwitz, Dominique, 57, 59
Greenspan, Alan, 166
Greenwald, Glenn, 105, 141–42, 145, 146,
    158–60, 188, 190, 235, 243, 244
Guantánamo, 138. *See also* "100 Days
    Campaign"; torture
    closing of, 87, 110–11, 115–16, 137,
        151–53, 192–93
    detainee trials, 90, 131, 140–41
    indefinite detention at, 193, 195
    legal justification memos, 178
    prisoner treatment at, 117, 136, 151–52,
        186–87, 208

Habbush al-Taknti, Tahir Jalil, 182–83
Hamdan v. Rumsfeld, 172
Harman, Susan, 71
Haynes, William J., II, 134, 209
Hennessy, Martha, 104, 115, 152

Herbert, Bob, 11
Holder, Eric, 87, 95–96, 146, 147, 190
    CIA, investigation of crimes by, 15, 204,
        209, 213, 235
    criminal prosecutions, position on,
        89–93, 98, 104, 214, 217
    Jawad detention, position on, 189
    Spanish judiciary actions and, 117, 207–9
    special prosecutor, appointment of, 204
    state secrets, position on, 189
    torture memos, release of, 141–43, 145,
        150
Horton, Scott, 133, 142–43, 145, 209, 244
Hussein, Saddam, 21–23, 164–66
    alleged involvement in 9/11 attack, 49,
        95, 161, 174, 183
    as threat to U.S., 23, 35, 48–49, 52–54, 72,
        180–82, 214

impeachment. *See* Bush, George W.,
    proposed impeachment of
innocent agent doctrine, 51–52
International Criminal Court, 9, 70
Iraq War, 167–80. *See also* false pretenses,
    Iraq War started under; murder,
    prosecution of Bush for
    British investigation of, 209–10
    Bush's lawyers, role of, 161–62, 168–81,
        185
    neoconservative support for, 164–66
    9/11 victims' response to, 113
    Obama's position, 86, 195–96, 198, 201–2
    oil as motivator for, 161–67
    preemptive strategy, 53, 58, 114, 169
    pretexts for, 162, 180–81, 183–85, 210,
        230 (*See also* Hussein, Saddam)
    prisoners, treatment of, 136–37, 212 (*See
        also* torture)
Irwin, William, 156–57
Isikoff, Michael, 190, 223
Israel, 164–66

Jawad, Mohammed, 138, 189
Jeffords, James, 120, 121
Jeppesen, ACLU suit against, 212–13
Jersey Girls, The, 108–14, 118, 126, 164

Jewel v. NSA, 158
Johnsen, Dawn, 142–43
Jones, James L., 200–201
Joyce, Brian, 76–77
jurisdiction, Vermont. *See* Vermont
Justice Robert H. Jackson conference. *See*
    Planning the Prosecution of High Level
    American War Criminals conference
Justice Robert Jackson Committee, 117, 132

Kennedy, John F., 199
Kerin, Karen, 63–64
Kinne, Adrienne, 102
Kissinger, Henry, 199–201, 211
Kleinberg, Mindy, 108–14, 126, 164
Koh, Harold, 142–43, 180
Krugman, Paul, 184–85
Kucinich, Dennis, 134, 228

Latoff, Blair, 6, 8
Leahy, Patrick, 16, 91, 94–95, 116, 119–25.
    See also truth commission
    activists' meeting with, 100–101, 104–7,
        114–19
    Attorneys general and, 117–18, 121,
        123–26
    FOIA supported by, 123
    Justice Department attorneys, opinion
        on, 134
    Patriot Act opposed by, 121
    Vermont impeachment effort, response
        to, 135
Libby, I. Lewis (Scooter), 13–15
Lindh, John Walker, 174–75, 222–25
Lloyd, Robin, 19, 46, 69–70, 219
Lopez, Ralph, 67–73, 81, 100, 232

malice, express and implied, 52
Marshall, John, 159, 244
Massachusetts School of Law, 83–84. *See also*
    Planning the Prosecution of High Level
    American War Criminals conference
Mayer, Jane, 183–84
media, coverage by
    activists investigated by government,
        216–17

attorney general campaign (*See* Attorney General, Vermont, Dennett campaign for)

demonstrations, 187, 227

Iraq and Afghanistan wars, 78–79, 181, 185

military commissions, 193

Obama administration, 152–53, 188–89, 194–95

torture, 185, 188

war-crimes prosecutions, 32, 86, 90, 95–96, 127, 146, 147, 154, 233, 235

Middle East, Dennett's attachment to, 17–18, 39

military commissions, 130–31, 133, 172–73, 191, 193

Mohammed, Khalid Sheikh, 89–92, 183, 228

Mukasey, Michael, 92, 94, 154

murder, prosecution of Bush for, 96–98, 160–61, 185, 229–31. *See also* Attorney General, Vermont, Dennett campaign for; *Prosecution of George W. Bush for Murder, The*

analyzing support for, 85–95

co-conspirators, 15

dangers of, 73–74

at federal level, 31–32, 64

Gonzales's Geneva Conventions memo and, 177

House Judiciary Committee, Bugliosi testimony before, 34–37

jurisdiction, 8–9, 24–25, 53–54, 77

Leahy meeting, discussion at, 117

legal framework, 23–24, 46, 50–54

torture prosecution compared, 97

Muslims, targeting of, 122

National Religious Campaign Against Torture, 220, 252

national security, as defense to Bush-era prosecutions, 140

National Security Agency, 158

neoconservatives, 164–66

Nichols, John, 101, 102

9/11 Advocates for Truth. *See* Jersey Girls, The

9/11 attack, 95, 167–69. *See also* Hussein, Saddam; Iraq War; torture; War on Terror

9/11 Commission hearings and report, 107, 111–14, 118, 164, 219

Nirenberg, John, 104, 119

Nonpartisan Commission of Inquiry. *See* truth commission

Nordlinger, Jay, 120–21

Northeast Impeachment Coalition, 66–68, 228

Nuremberg trials, 57–58, 132–33, 229–30

Obama, Barack, 137, 188–96, 220

blogosphere commentary on, 188–89

CIA and, 141–46, 210

criminal prosecutions, position on, 88, 92–94, 96, 107, 189–90

election victory of, 80–81

elites and, 198–200

first 100 days of presidency, 115, 138, 151–53, 189

foreign policy of, 199–203

Guantánamo, closing of (*See* Guantánamo, closing of)

Guantánamo conditions and, 151–52

human-rights activists hosted by, 190

military commissions position, 191, 193

national security speech, 190–95

Office of Legal Counsel and, 137, 142–43, 148–49

state secrets, protection of, 87, 111

torture and (*See* torture)

truth commission position, 148, 193

wars, position on, 86, 195–96, 198, 201–2, 231–32

Office of Legal Counsel (OLC), 130

accountability movement response to, 145–47, 150

civil liberties, advice on, 168

Congressional response to, 148–49

military commissions, justification for, 172–75

military lawyers, review of opinions by, 134

Obama and, 137, 142–43, 148–49

Office of Professional Responsibility investigation, 95, 147–48, 154–55, 176–77
  torture memos authored by, 91–92, 95–99, 115, 128–34, 136, 140–45, 154–55, 179–80, 222
  wars, legal framework for, 161, 168–81, 185
oil interests, 161–67, 198–201, 230
"100 Days" campaign, 115, 138, 151–53

Papermaster, Cynthia, 226
pardons, possible Bush, 12–14
Parry, Robert, 98–99
Pelosi, Nancy, 12, 67, 78–79, 104, 105–6
Perry, Pete, 215
Physicians for Human Rights, 233–35, 246
Pilger, John, 201–2
Plame, Valerie, 14, 93
Planning the Prosecution of High Level American War Criminals conference, 33, 38–42, 57–58, 77–78, 84–85, 127–33
Powell, Colin, 173, 176
preemptive invasion, 53, 58, 114, 169
Progressive Party, 1, 26, 28–29, 42, 45, 77, 251–52. *See also* Attorney General, Vermont, Dennett campaign for
Prosecution of George W. Bush for Murder, The, 3, 18–25, 180, 214. *See also* murder, prosecution of Bush for
  emotional underpinnings of argument, 46–50, 52, 73
  mainstream media, suppression by, 32
  reader response to, 19, 32–33
  state attorneys general, jurisdiction of, 24–25
Pyle, Christopher, 129–31, 133, 161, 168, 173, 179, 202, 217

Radack, Jesselyn, 221–25
Randolph massacre, 135–36
Ratner, Michael, 95–97, 138–41, 144–45, 188
renditions. *See* extraordinary renditions
Republican National Committee (RNC), 6, 8
Republican National Convention, 41
Republican Party, 103, 118, 148, 228

retribution, 148–49
Rice, Condoleezza, 184, 207
Rockefellers, power of, 197–200
Ross, Chuck, 118–19, 135
Rótolo, Laura, 133, 156, 211–13
Rumsfeld, Donald, 84, 165, 212
Rutland resolution, 45–46, 75, 103, 135–36

Sands, Philippe, 84–85, 132, 134, 205–6, 210
Scahill, Jeremy, 208
Scalia, Antonin, 170
Schneider v. Kissinger, 211
School of the Americas, 218–20
self-defense, as Bush defense for Iraq War, 182
separation of powers, Bush's contempt for, 5
September 11 attack. *See* 9/11 attack
Serpa, Susan, 66–68, 100, 160, 228
Sheehan, Cindy, 51–52, 78–79, 82, 101–3, 231–32
Shenon, Philip, 113–14
Sirkin, Susannah, 234–35
Sorrell, William, 8, 70, 75–77, 81, 157, 207
  debate, attack on Dennett at, 64–65
  election victory, 80
  Labor Council endorsement, 37–38
  record, 25–26, 60–61
South Africa truth commission, 134–35
sovereign immunity, 155–61, 189, 212–13
Spanish judiciary, prosecution of Bush administration officials by, 15, 117, 206–9
special prosecutor, 96, 108, 193
  American Civil Liberties Union support for, 133, 144, 146–47
  Bugliosi, Dennett's planned appointment of, 3–5, 39, 72
  CIA investigation by, 15, 204, 209, 213, 235
  citizen support for, 15, 86–87, 92, 106
  Congress, consideration by, 133–34
state secrets privilege, 87, 110, 111, 158–59, 189
Sullivan, Andrew, 189–90
Swanson, David, 147, 227–30
Sweet, Debra, 153, 186, 194–95, 226–27
Symington, Gaye, 46, 75, 103, 136

Taft, William Howard, IV, 173, 176
Taguba, Antonio M., 136–37
Taliban, 140, 176–78, 222
Taylor, Jeff, 74–75, 103, 135–36
Thomas, Helen, 49
Thy Will Be Done. The Conquest of the Amazon: Nelson Rockefeller and Evangelism in the Age of Oil, 19, 197
Todd, Chuck, 235
torture, 86, 117, 202, 220–21. *See also* war crimes, prosecution of Bush administration officials for
  ACLU suits concerning, 189, 212–13
  Bush administration's reasons for, 161, 173–74, 183–85, 228–29
  Bush lawyers' advice on, 122 (*See also* torture memos)
  Bush's approval of (*See* Bush, George W.)
  Cheney's approval of (*See* Cheney, Richard B. (Dick))
  ex post facto legal justification for, 133, 177
  Gonzales's confirmation hearings and, 124–25
  Lindh interrogation, 174–75, 222–24
  military commissions and, 130–31, 133, 172
  Obama, banned by, 87, 115, 137, 192
  Obama administration, during, 208, 220
  Obama administration, photos withheld by, 186–87, 189, 192–93
  Pelosi, position of, 105–6
  prohibitions against, 175–78 (*See also* Geneva Conventions)
  protests against (*See* demonstrations, antiwar/antitorture)
  Senate Judiciary Committee hearings on, 122
  U.S. antitorture statute, definition of torture in, 178–80
torture memos
  Obama, released by, 141–45, 150, 192, 206, 214
  Office of Legal Counsel, written by (*See* Office of Legal Counsel (OLC))
Trilateral Commission, 199–201

truth commission, 16, 94, 99, 100, 105–7, 126, 134–35, 149
  hearing on, 108
  9/11 widows, questioned by, 108–9, 111–12, 114, 118
  Obama's position on, 148, 193
  Republican opposition to, 118
Turley, Jonathan, 159, 189, 244

Uniform Code of Military Justice, 171–75
United Nations Convention Against Torture, 86, 89, 96, 132, 179
United States Army Intelligence School, 129
United States Congress, 126, 193. *See also* United States Senate
  activists investigated by government, action on, 216–17
  House Judiciary Committee, 34–37, 72, 93–94, 134
  impeachment, positions on, 34, 78–79, 105–6
  military tribunals, power to create, 172
  prosecution of Bush, positions on, 86, 90–91, 93–95, 133–34, 148
  Republicans, Obama appointments opposed by, 142–43
  truth commission, proposal for (*See* truth commission)
  war, positions on, 227–28
  wars, authorization for, 76–77, 168–71, 181
United States Constitution, 50, 67, 170–71, 181, 191, 194. *See also* "100 Days" campaign
United States Department of Defense, 134, 138, 140
United States Department of Homeland Security, 215–17
United States Department of Justice. *See also* Office of Legal Counsel (OLC); special prosecutor
  Attorneys general (*See* Ashcroft, John; Gonzales, Alberto; Holder, Eric; Mukasey, Michael)
  Bush administration, prosecution of, 193, 206–8

Jewel v. NSA, position in, 158
judges' reluctance to second-guess
   opinions of, 108
Office of Professional Responsibility
   OLC investigation (*See* Office of Legal
   Counsel (OLC))
Office of Professional Responsibility
   Radack investigation, 221, 224
politicization of, 125
Republicans, Obama appointments
   opposed by, 142–43
sovereign immunity and Bush-era spying
   programs, 189
United States House of Representatives. *See*
   United States Congress
United States Senate. *See also* United States
   Congress
   Armed Services Committee report on
      detainee treatment, 86, 90
   Holder nomination, 90–91
   Intelligence Committee, 148
   Judiciary Committee, 94–95, 116, 120–
      26, 134
United States v. George W. Bush et al., The, 160
universal jurisdiction doctrine, 207, 208
USA Patriot Act, 121, 122

Van Auken, Lorie, 108–14, 126, 164
Velasco, Eloy, 206, 209
Velvel, Lawrence, 42, 57–58, 83–84, 117,
   127–28, 132, 203, 231
Vermont
   conspiracy, statutory definition of, 53–54
   impeachment of Bush, support for,
      45–46, 75, 101–4, 135–36
   jurisdiction to prosecute Bush, 8–9,
      24–25, 53–54, 77
   politics of, 1, 10, 44–45 (*See also*
      Progressive Party)
Vermont State Labor Council, AFL-CIO,
   37–38
Vermont Yankee nuclear power plant,
   60–62, 70–71, 156–57
vicarious liability doctrine, 51

Wall Street Journal blog, 6–8
war crimes, prosecution of Bush
   administration officials for, 7, 84, 107, 186,
   228. *See also* accountability movement;
   murder, prosecution of Bush for;
   Planning the Prosecution of High Level
   American War Criminals conference;
   Spanish judiciary, prosecution of Bush
   administration officials by
   Afghanistan, mass graves in, 232–34
   analysis of support for, 85–95
   Bugliosi's opinion on, 97
   defenses to, 140, 182 (*See also* sovereign
      immunity)
   International Criminal Court, 9, 70
   Obama administration, position of, 88–
      94, 96, 98, 104, 107, 189–90, 214, 217
   special prosecutor for (*See* special
      prosecutor)
   torture, evidence of, 89–90, 145 (*See also*
      torture)
War Crimes Act, 175–78
war on terror, 167–80, 194, 201
   American activists, investigations of,
      215–17, 219
   Bush, extraordinary powers claimed for,
      167–68
   oil and, 161–67
Warren, Vince, 208
waterboarding, 86, 97, 99, 143, 180, 184, 192
   of Khalid Sheikh Mohammed, 90, 183
   legalization of, 133
   of Zubaydah, 179–80
WCAX television station, 76–77, 80
weapons of mass destruction, 52, 72, 164,
   181–84, 210
Web sites, 65–66, 226–27
Western Hemisphere Institute for Security
   Cooperation, 218–20
whistleblowers, 62, 70, 221–25
Whitehouse, Sheldon, 99, 133, 135
Wilson, Diane, 225–26
Wilson, Joseph, 14, 49, 93
Wilson, Woodrow, 20–21
Witness Against Torture, 151–52

Wolf, Lou, 218–19

Wolf, Naomi, 58–59

Wolfowitz, Paul, 164, 165

World Can't Wait, 153, 186–88, 194–95, 226–27, 250

World War I, 20–21

Yoo, John, 95, 96, 132, 209, 226–27. *See also* Office of Legal Counsel (OLC), torture memos authored by
  Geneva Conventions, opinion on, 176–78

Iraq War, justification for, 169–81

military commissions, justification for, 172–75

torture memos written by, 98–99, 115, 130, 140, 179–80

Zelikow, Philip, 113–14

Zubaydah, Abu, 178–80, 184, 228

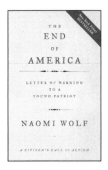

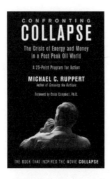
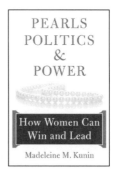

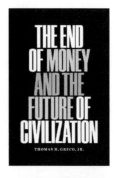